# Ecological Security

Climate change is increasingly recognized as a security issue. Yet this recognition belies contestation over what security means and whose security is viewed as threatened. Different accounts – here defined as discourses – of security range from those focused on national sovereignty to those emphasizing the vulnerability of human populations. This book examines the ethical assumptions and implications of these 'climate security' discourses, ultimately making a case for moving beyond the protection of human institutions and collectives. Drawing on insights from political ecology, feminism and critical theory, Matt McDonald suggests the need to focus on the resilience of ecosystems themselves when approaching the climate–security relationship, orienting towards the most vulnerable across time, space and species. The book outlines the ethical assumptions and contours of ecological security before exploring how it might find purchase in contemporary political contexts. A shift in this direction could not be more urgent, given the current climate crisis.

MATT MCDONALD is Reader in International Relations in the School of Political Science & International Studies, University of Queensland, Australia. He is the author of *Security, the Environment and Emancipation* (2012) and co-author (with Anthony Burke and Katrina Lee-Koo) of *Ethics and Global Security* (2014).

T0384517

# Ecological Security

## Climate Change and the Construction of Security

MATT MCDONALD
*University of Queensland*

CAMBRIDGE
UNIVERSITY PRESS

Shaftesbury Road, Cambridge CB2 8EA, United Kingdom

One Liberty Plaza, 20th Floor, New York, NY 10006, USA

477 Williamstown Road, Port Melbourne, VIC 3207, Australia

314–321, 3rd Floor, Plot 3, Splendor Forum, Jasola District Centre, New Delhi – 110025, India

103 Penang Road, #05–06/07, Visioncrest Commercial, Singapore 238467

Cambridge University Press is part of Cambridge University Press & Assessment, a department of the University of Cambridge.

We share the University's mission to contribute to society through the pursuit of education, learning and research at the highest international levels of excellence.

www.cambridge.org
Information on this title: www.cambridge.org/9781009010801

DOI: 10.1017/9781009024495

First published 2021
First paperback edition 2023

*A catalogue record for this publication is available from the British Library*

ISBN    978-1-316-51961-5    Hardback
ISBN    978-1-009-01080-1    Paperback

# Contents

# Acknowledgements

This book has been a long time coming. I first developed plans to write this book in around 2012, when my focus on mapping competing discourses of climate security in global politics encouraged me to explore the contours of a 'defensible' climate security discourse. What followed was an extended gestation and reading period, one necessary given the wide range of scholarship that this project ultimately necessitated engaging with.

Given the length of time involved, and my willingness to try to secure feedback from a wide range of people and sources, it's inevitable that this brief note of thanks will involve the omission of some people who helped shape my ideas for this book. But for their feedback on draft chapters of the book, I'm particularly grateful to Simon Dalby, Rita Floyd, Seb Kaempf, Andrew Phillips, Megan Price and Jon Symons. I'm also really grateful for feedback on earlier versions of chapters or an outline of the broader project from Chris Browning, Tony Burke, Olaf Corry, Robyn Eckersley, Jairus Grove, Lene Hansen, Kate Lee-Koo, Lucile Maertens, Audra Mitchell, Vincent Pouliot, Delf Rothe and Brent Steele. I'd also like to thank the manuscript reviewers, John Haslam and the Cambridge UP team for their hard work, suggestions and guidance, and Katja Cooper for her excellent work on the index.

I presented a version of this project – in initial years in aspirational terms – at various conferences and at departmental seminars at Glasgow, St Andrews, Warwick, Birmingham (UK), Hamburg (Germany), Sciences Po Paris (France), UQ and ANU (Australia). The paper published in *International Theory* in 2018 best captures the focus of these presentations, and for that and the book itself, I'm grateful for feedback received from audience members and reviewers, and the editorial team at IT.

Other colleagues in the School of Political Science and International Studies at the University of Queensland, where I've worked throughout the long gestation of this book, also provided really important feedback in a range of ways and sites. I'm particularly grateful to Nicole George and Chris Reus-Smit for the opportunity to present this work in its earliest stages in a 'Giving Form Colloquium' seminar to colleagues prior to taking my ideas on the road. The quality of feedback I received then and the quality of researchers around that table remind me how fortunate I am to work in that school. I'm also grateful to the broader institution, in particular for the two distinct periods of study leave that enabled me dedicated periods for reading (2015) and writing (2018) the book. I'm acutely aware these aren't opportunities available to all or even many colleagues in the academy, and I've been in a privileged position to research and write the book.

Of course, none of these institutions or people should be held in any way accountable for the content of the following pages, and any effigies burnt for the subsequent claims made should be of me only (with every effort made to minimise any greenhouse gas emissions produced through the effigy construction and burning process, of course).

At a personal level, Helen and my sons, Liam and Frank, have reminded me of a wonderful world of walking, travel, sport, board games and so on outside the academic world and, more importantly, beyond the clustercuss that is global climate change and its associated politics. They also embody values in their relationship to the ecological space and world they occupy that I could do worse than simply trying to capture in the following pages. Being part of a loving family that together embraces cycling, vegetarianism, climate protests and volunteer local ecosystem management is a constant source of energy and a reminder that we can all do something about the (admittedly massive) climate challenge we face. When on the subject of family, it would be remiss of me to also not recognise that they have turned a blind eye to the increase in craft beer consumption accompanying the latter drafting stages and attempts to work through revisions. And I might as well note that Harry the greyhound has been a constant (if oblivious) companion through the writing process.

I could ultimately dedicate this book to the many number of mentioned and forgotten colleagues who have supported this project, or to the family members who have given me the love and support that has inspired and given me energy every day. But as I was finalising the manuscript, bushfires were raging in my home country of Australia. We saw broken families who had lost childhood homes, whole communities gutted and people in major cities choking on smoke haze while the Australian government tried to defend an utterly abject climate policy. It's understandable that the focus of media attention and commentary was on these elements of the fires and, in particular, the people killed fighting the fires or trapped in their path. But we also lost millions of hectares of forests, millions of ecosystems of varying size and billions of animals. These other (once living) beings were unable to escape, to follow instructions from authorities in the face of emergency, and were rendered acutely vulnerable by climate policies (and inaction) they have been unable to substantively address. We cannot continue to allow ourselves to contribute so directly – and so thoughtlessly – to their vulnerability and, ultimately, harm. And we cannot continue to allow ourselves the hubris of thinking of ourselves as separate from the natural world that seems to many to be increasingly turning on us. This Anthropocene reality is, as the name suggests, a reality of our own making. And it requires new ways of thinking about ourselves, the ecosystems in which we live and our ethical responsibilities to others, both human and non-human.

That's what this book's about, really. And so this book is dedicated to living beings unable to consciously act to address the climate crisis but rendered acutely vulnerable by the decisions we make and the actions we undertake.

# Acronyms and Abbreviations

| | |
|---|---|
| ASEAN | Association of Southeast Asian Nations |
| CBDR | Common But Differentiated Responsibility |
| $CO_2$ | Carbon Dioxide |
| COP | Conference of the Parties (to the UNFCCC) |
| EU | European Union |
| GDP | Gross Domestic Product |
| IGO | Intergovernmental Organization |
| IPCC | Intergovernmental Panel on Climate Change |
| IR | International Relations |
| IUGS | International Union of Geological Sciences |
| NATO | North Atlantic Treaty Organization |
| NGO | Non-governmental Organization |
| OSCE | Organization for Security and Cooperation in Europe |
| R2P | Responsibility to Protect |
| UN | United Nations |
| UNCED | United Nations Conference on Environment and Development (1992) |
| UNDP | United Nations Development Programme |
| UNEP | United Nations Environment Programme |
| UNFCCC | United Nations Framework Convention on Climate Change |
| UNGA | United Nations General Assembly |
| UNSC | United Nations Security Council |
| UK | United Kingdom |
| US | United States of America |
| WHO | World Health Organization |
| WMD | Weapons of Mass Destruction |
| WWF | World Wild Fund for Nature |

# Introduction

Climate change is increasingly identified as a first-order security issue. It has been debated in the United Nations Security Council, has found its way into states' national security strategies and has been linked to large-scale conflict in Darfur and Syria. While policy practitioners and policy-oriented think tanks have clearly promoted this relationship between security and climate change, academic scholarship has also increasingly embraced the idea that climate change constitutes a threat to security. In a recent survey of scholars of international relations, albeit conducted prior to the onset of the coronavirus pandemic, climate change was three times more likely to be identified as the most pressing threat to global security than the next most significant threat (McDonald 2017; see also Harrington and Shearing 2017:18).

Of course, only a small and ever-dwindling number of sceptics would deny that climate change is a significant *problem*. The increasing concentration of greenhouse gas in the atmosphere since the pre-industrial era has driven an increase in the earth's average temperatures, already at over 1 degree Celsius. While the scale of change and its effects have been different and experienced differently across the world, manifestations of this change include rising sea levels, changing rainfall patterns, desertification, an increase in vector-borne disease and an increase in the frequency and intensity of natural disasters, among other effects. These manifestations have, in turn, driven biodiversity loss, an increase in disease, economic privation, population displacement and the loss of arable land, again among many other implications. While these effects are clearly significant, business-as-usual emissions scenarios pointing to a likely increase of 3–4 degrees by the end of the century would be truly catastrophic, rendering large parts of the currently populated earth uninhabitable and killing off a sizeable percentage of the earth's living beings (Christoff ed. 2013; Burke 2019).

But does the current scale of this problem, or even the spectre of catastrophic future climate scenarios (see also Steffan et al. 2018), suggest that it makes sense to view and approach climate change as a *security* issue? Climate change could be viewed through the lens of science, technology, justice, health, economics, development or international cooperation, for example. In practical terms, these different choices about how to conceive and approach the issue might encourage a central role for different agents or actors (from companies to NGOs to epistemic communities to international organizations), or even different branches within national governments (from treasury to departments of trade, international development, health, environment or foreign policy, for example).

Beyond this reality, which speaks to the genuinely multifaceted and holistic nature of the challenge posed by climate change, climate change ultimately sits uneasily with existing accounts and practices of security in international relations (IR). Dominant accounts of security in IR focus on the role of the military instruments of the state in protecting the integrity of the nation state from intentional external military threat. Yet climate change challenges this focus in multiple ways. Climate change is a problem caused not just by outsiders but also by our own actions, and actions that produce greenhouse gas emissions are not (at least not usually) *intended* to cause harm. It is also a problem that transcends borders in effect, and even significant unilateral action by a state to address the problem itself may have minimal effects depending on the emissions profile of that state and its relative contribution to the problem of climate change. Finally, while we associate security agency with the military, redressing climate change clearly extends far beyond the capacity of these traditional agents of security to all those sectors of government and society that contribute to greenhouse gas emissions every day. In short, while it is certainly *possible* to view climate change through the lens of national security (as will be noted), the problem itself – increasing temperatures caused by everyday actions of a range of agents throughout the world – appears to challenge dominant accounts of the nature of threats, the nature of security agents and the means through which security is preserved or advanced.

In this sense, (increasingly prominent) attempts to draw a link between climate change and security raise a series of fundamental questions about how security is understood and what implications would follow from conceiving and approaching climate change as a security issue. First, what does security mean? Is it viewed, for example, as protection from the threat of armed violence (in which climate change fits if creating conditions in which conflict is more likely) or the advancement of individual welfare and well-being (in which case climate change constitutes a clear and imminent danger)? Related to this, whose security is to be protected from climate change? Are we talking here about nation states, vulnerable human populations or even future generations and other living beings? And finally, what are the practical implications of approaching climate change as a security issue? Does it, as some critics argue (e.g., Deudney 1990; Buxton and Hayes 2015; Marzec 2015), raise the spectre of the militarization of the environment, promoting a central role for states' armed forces in the face of an issue beyond their capacity to fundamentally address? Or does it serve to mobilize concern and priority for an issue like climate change by tying it to the 'high politics' of security?

A range of academic accounts have attempted to answer these questions in definitive terms. Some fix a meaning of security, tied to a particular referent object, and explore how climate change serves to constitute a threat to that referent object. For these analysts, the answer to the question of whether climate change constitutes a threat to security can essentially be resolved as a tick box exercise. Here, the analyst establishes criteria for when a problem becomes a threat to the nation state or the international community (see, e.g., Busby 2007, 2008; CNA 2007; Smith and Vivekananda 2007; Matthew et al. eds. 2010).

The inclination towards fixing a universal and definitive definition of security can be discerned in a genuine range of approaches to the politics of approaching an issue like climate change as a security threat. For early advocates, the need to recognize environmental change broadly (or climate change specifically) as a security threat followed from their view of security as 'high politics'. In the particular context of the post–Cold War 'threat vacuum' (Dumaine and Mintzer 2015:8), a range of analysts pointed to the need to include climate change in an extended definition of security in order to ensure it received the political attention, priority and funding necessitated by the challenge itself (see Hartmann 2009). For others, the 'securitization' (Wæver 1995) of climate change was to be avoided. For them, the political implications of conceiving and approaching climate change as a security issue include militarizing the problem (Deudney 1990); according a central role for states and their militaries in responding to it (Buxton and Hayes 2015; Marzec 2015); and/or taking the issue outside the normal realm of (appropriate) deliberation and treating it with secrecy, urgency and exceptional responses (e.g., Wæver 1995). While these theorists and analysts clearly come to very different conclusions about the politics of security and the desirability of defining climate change as a security threat, these alternate accounts suggest a specific, universal logic of security with inevitable sets of political implications.

In this book, by contrast, I argue that it is not possible to answer questions about what security means, whose security matters and what security does in abstract and universal terms. The meaning given to security – and its associated connection with climate change – is political and socially constructed. Different political communities will answer the question of what security means (or should mean) in different ways, making different sets of choices about whose security matters and why. These meanings are themselves the product of processes of contestation and negotiation between different actors within those communities.

This book also suggests that the way climate change and security are linked serves to determine the political effects of what might be termed 'securitization'. In some instances, fears of the dangers of militarization or illiberal, exceptional measures may indeed be borne out by the way in which climate change is conceived and approached, particularly if through the lens of a narrow conception of national security. But this does not capture the universal essence of the meaning or politics of security. In other instances, representing climate change as a security issue may serve to drive increasing attention and responses to the problem consistent with redressing it (see Hayes and Knox-Hayes 2014). The extent to which regressive or progressive action follows from representations of climate change as a security threat will be determined significantly by the way in which that linkage is made.

Ultimately, and following the above, the relationship between climate change and security can be understood in terms of *climate security discourses*: frameworks of meaning that determine whose security is prioritized, from what threats, by what agents and by what means. These discourses can be categorized according to their choice of referent object – the answer to the question 'security for whom?'. Here and in other work (McDonald 2013a), I make a distinction between four discourses, focusing respectively on the nation state, international society, people and ecosystems themselves. These discourses – of national, international, human and ecological security – can serve to provide the framework through which climate change is conceived and approached in different ways and have experienced varying degrees of success in influencing the way in which political communities approach the issue of climate change.

Crucially, these discourses entail different sets of ethical assumptions and have different ethical and practical implications. If security is viewed through the lens of the nation state (and, in particular, its preservation from external military threat), we would expect responses to climate change that prioritize adaptive responses to instability triggered by climate change, for example (see Busby 2007, 2008). The concern here might be dealing with populations displaced by manifestations of climate change (rising sea levels or natural disasters, for example), who in turn challenge the sovereignty and territorial integrity of the state in such a way as to necessitate emergency border control measures or even military intervention. If, by contrast, climate change is viewed through the lens of human security, we would expect responses to climate change focused on mitigation efforts and even the redistribution of economic resources towards those populations in the world most vulnerable to manifestations of climate change. In these alternate discourses, we may variously view those displaced by manifestations of climate change as those primarily in need of our protection or as threats to our (national) security.

In short, discourses matter for the sets of practices that follow. And while some practices are oriented towards addressing the problem itself in a manner consistent with the needs of vulnerable beings, some are oriented towards insulating the nation state from external threat in a manner that does nothing to redress the problem and even treats its victims (e.g. those displaced by rising sea levels or natural disasters) as a source of threat.

In previous work I have attempted to map these discourses of climate security – to point to their core assumptions and implications (McDonald 2013a). In this book, I draw on this research but go further. Specifically, this book follows directly from recognition of the existence of different climate security discourses and their varied ethical assumptions and practical implications. If this is the case – if some discourses of climate security are, to put it bluntly, better than others – then we need to explore what an ethically defensible climate security discourse looks like. And we need to examine the possibility for such a discourse to find purchase and come to inform the way political communities understand and approach climate security. That is precisely what this book attempts to do.

What follows, then, is a defence of a particular discourse of climate security that builds on three central foundation points. The first of these is that the linkage between climate change and security is difficult to contest regardless of how we conceive of the referent object of security or the particular nature of a security threat. In this sense, we need to engage with the climate–security relationship rather than simply advocate 'escaping' a security framing.

The second foundational claim is that through examining the relationship between climate change and security, especially the way this linkage is made by key political actors and via processes of contestation and negotiation, we can, in fact, discern a range of different accounts or discourses of climate security. And third, again following from the above, these discourses are underpinned by different sets of ethical commitments and have different political and practical implications. Some of these commitments and implications are more defensible than others in terms of the ethical foundations upon which they are built and the policies and practices they encourage.

## Towards Ecological Security

Having laid these foundations, the remainder of the book will develop and defend an ecological security discourse of climate security. In this discourse, the referent objects of climate security are ecosystems themselves and, in particular, their resilience in the face of climate change. This focus on ecosystems – communities of interacting organisms in a given space – is a response to three key considerations.

First, the emphasis on ecosystems follows from recognition that other discourses of climate security (whether national, international or human) stop short of recognizing key harms arising from climate change for a range of beings. This applies even to a human security discourse, for example, arguably reflecting the broader limits of cosmopolitan ethics in an ecological context (see Eckersley 1992). While a human security discourse orients our attention and concern to the vulnerability of impoverished populations in the developing world to manifestations of climate change, for example, it does not extend moral consideration to the (even more acute) vulnerabilities of other living beings and future generations. Other living beings and future generations are not only harmed by the everyday actions of human populations in the context of climate change but also are less able to communicate their needs or exercise direct agency in impacting decisions and practices that affect their current and/or future life prospects. A focus on ecosystems as the referent object of security, in particular in the context of their long-term resilience, is viewed here as the best means for ensuring adequate consideration for vulnerable beings. While raising complex and challenging ethical and practical questions, such a discourse – if providing the lens through which the relationship between climate change and security is viewed – is most likely to encourage a set of practices associated with addressing the problem of climate change itself.

Second, and following recognition of the limits of existing climate security discourses, the emphasis on ecosystems here follows recognition of the need for an ethical framework with the potential to adequately account for harms experienced in the context of climate change. In the process of endorsing the focus on ecosystems, this book draws on a holistic approach to ethics (see Pojman 2005; Nolt 2011), one that emphasizes the complex interrelationships between species (see Eckersley 1992; Wienhues 2020). While informed by ecological thought, this focus on interrelationships also attempts to move away from traditional anthropocentric–ecocentric binaries in ecological thought in a manner broadly consistent with so-called 'second wave' or pluralist green political theorists (see Plumwood 2002; Eckersley 2005:365; McShane 2014:85). The goal here is to escape a tendency to view environmental issues through the lens of *either* human survival or environmental integrity, and rather emphasize the connectivity and interrelationships between human communities and the so-called natural world (see also Burke et al. 2016; Harrington and Shearing 2017). This in turn suggests the impossibility of defending a distinction between 'humanity' and 'nature' in the context of climate change.

This emphasis on interrelationships relates to a third key rationale for the focus on ecosystems here: the arrival of the Anthropocene. Existing accounts of climate security not only neglect the vulnerabilities of key actors, and with it encourage practical responses to climate change effects inconsistent with redressing the problem itself, but also serve to differentiate human populations, institutions and collectives from the (environmental) conditions of their own existence. While this distinction – central to modern thought (Soper 1995) – has always been difficult to justify when considering environmental change, it is particularly untenable in the context of the geological era of the Anthropocene. The Anthropocene, a term attributed to Paul Crutzen in 2000, refers to the contemporary geological age, one in which

> human activities are now so pervasive and profound in their consequences that they affect the Earth at a global scale in complex, interactive and accelerating ways; humans now have the capacity to alter the Earth System in ways that threaten the very processes and components, both biotic and abiotic, upon which humans depend. (Steffan et al. 2004:1)

The arrival of the 'Anthropocene', and in particular the politics of the 'Anthropocene framing', is far from universally endorsed. Some have expressed concern, for example, that this conceptualization of humanity's role on the earth and in the contemporary ecological crisis risks serving as a 'writ of empowerment' that enables already powerful actors to implement 'an ecological state of emergency' (Luke 2013; see also Lövbrand et al. 2015; Chandler 2018; Grove 2019; Wakefield et al. 2020). But the broader recognition of the scale of humanity's impact on the functioning of Earth systems, in which humanity's contribution to climate change is the archetypal example, does point to a context in which the separation between humanity and nature cannot feasibly be sustained. In an era in which humanity is so implicated in the functioning of ecological systems, we need new means of conceptualizing the human condition, along with the way we think about both politics and security (see Clark 2014; Harrington and Shearing 2017). The onset of the coronavirus pandemic further serves to underscore this point (see Heyd 2020). O'Callaghan-Gordo and Anto (2020:1), for example, memorably characterize the coronavirus as the 'disease of the anthropocene', noting the role of ecological destruction in 'altering the patterns and mechanisms of interaction between species and facilitating the transmission of infectious diseases across species and to humans' (see also Heyd 2020; Lidskog et al. 2020).

The scale of the climate crisis and the arrival of the geological era of the Anthropocene, in combination with the limited and anthropocentric nature of dominant ideas about security (Harrington and Shearing

2017:25–6), have encouraged a range of attempts to reconceptualize security with an ecological focus. A number bear parallels to the ecological security discourse endorsed here. Drawing on their earlier work on post-human international relations (Cudworth and Hobden 2011), Cudworth and Hobden (2017) have made a case for 'posthuman security', understood broadly as an approach to security that challenges the primacy attached to human populations (see also Eroukhmanoff and Harker eds. 2017). Audra Mitchell (2014) has explored the related notion of a 'worldly' approach to security, which similarly challenges the anthropocentrism of contemporary accounts of security while going further to also engage material foundations of the Earth system and the role of non-living entities. Judith Hardt (2017) directly endorses the notion of Anthropocene security in the context of climate change, in which the arrival of the Anthropocene era is used to challenge existing accounts of the relationship between the environment and security. Harrington and Shearing (2017) also explore security in the context of the Anthropocene, making a case for an 'ethics of care' in our engagement with other living beings and the development of a 'global consciousness' to promote such an ethics.

This book, and in particular its conceptualization of ecological security, bears many similarities with such (parallel) attempts to challenge or reconfigure security. But the specific attempt here to outline the contours of this discourse (in terms of foundational ethical principles, referent object, agents, means and the nature of threats), alongside the exploration of conditions of possibility for its embrace and realization, constitute a key point of difference with such projects. And while the use of the single case study of climate change limits the scope of analysis, it focuses our attention on an archetypal threat to ecosystems while enabling specificity about the nature of threats, agents, means and possibility.

As noted, in conceptualizing a focus on ecosystems as the referent object of security in this discourse, the emphasis is not on the conservation or preservation of these ecosystems but their resilience. Resilience here is defined as the capacity of ecosystems to function to sustain life over time and space, to retain 'organization structure following perturbation' (Barnett 2001:110) and to 'absorb change while retaining essential function' (Adger et al. 2011:696). This focus on resilience can be distinguished from earlier attempts to conceptualize ecological security. For Denis Pirages (2005), for example, ecological security rested on dynamic and interrelated equilibriums among human populations and between human populations and the natural world. Implying notions of balance and with it a broader goal of conservation, such an approach seems inconsistent with the reality of the Anthropocene, the scale of environmental change and the reality – in the specific context of climate change – that some degree of change is 'locked in' (see, e.g., Schlosberg 2013; Dalby 2015a). Viewed in this context, the goal is not attempting to preserve what we have or even return to a previous environmental context. Rather, it is to ensure that ecosystems can continue to function in the face of current and future change. This accounts for the embrace of the concept of 'resilience' in this book and its conceptualization of ecological security.

While the concept of resilience had important origins in ecological thought and allows us to conceptualize a goal in the context of ongoing change, it is also clearly a concept with both critics and apparent dangers in the means of its application. Indeed resilience has proven to be a controversial concept in recent international relations scholarship and bears similarity to the concept of 'security' as a site of contestation in itself. For some critics, the danger here is that the notion of resilience is inherently conservative and has neoliberal underpinnings (see Grove 2013; Chandler 2014; Evans and Reid 2014; Cavelty et al. 2015; Oels 2015; Kareiva and Fuller 2016). In particular, the focus on entities themselves (whether ecosystems, human communities or institutions) in coping with external sources of harm, perturbation or change risks taking our attention away from the sources and nature of that change itself. In the context of climate change, the specific concern is that we focus more on helping communities manage harmful manifestations of climate change and less on actually addressing the problem at its source (see Schlosberg 2013).

In this book, I defend a particular interpretation of this concept (drawing on ecological thought) and suggest that it allows us to come to terms with goals for ecosystem sustainability in the face of ongoing change. I recognize the dangers of some interpretations and applications of 'resilience' while rejecting the inevitability of such implications. In this I follow a range of critical scholars of resilience. Boas and Rothe (2015), for example, suggest that we can discern different conceptualizations or discourses of resilience in both thought and practice. More directly, Corry (2014) and Bourbeau (2015, 2018) suggest that resilience does not bring with it a singular set of effects or practices: ultimately, different accounts and, indeed, discourses of resilience matter significantly for the types of practices that follow.

In short, the case made for ecological security in this book is one that conceives of it as a necessary correction to ethically limited accounts of harm in the context of climate change, particularly in the context of the Anthropocene; enables an emphasis on vulnerable beings across time, space and species; and is attentive to ongoing dynamics of change. This discourse of climate security is one that is grounded on a more defensible set of ethical principles and encourages sets of practices oriented towards addressing the problem of climate change itself.

Yet, while ethically defensible, it does not follow that such a discourse enjoys favour among powerful actors or is consistent with the traditional concerns of powerful institutions, whether states, intergovernmental organizations or broader forces of global politics like capitalism. Indeed, while expressing normative sympathy for a focus on ecosystems in the context of security, Jon Barnett (2001:121) simultaneously dismissed this discourse as a political non-starter, a 'bystander on the sidelines of the substantive contest' over how we might conceive and approach security in the face of environmental change. Barnett in subsequent work has endorsed a focus on 'human security' (Barnett and Adger 2007; Barnett et al. 2010), even serving as a lead author on the human security chapter of the 2014 IPCC report.

In this book I recognize the need to engage with the political possibility for a particular discourse of security to become the lens through which climate change is viewed. (On climate change more broadly, see Eckersley 2004; Barry and Eckersley eds. 2005.) Yet, in this book, this engagement does not lead to the rejection of ecological security. I suggest here that if we are ultimately convinced by the ethical claims and practices associated with a particular approach, there is a compelling case to explore the extent to which such an approach might serve to provide the lens through which particular political communities come to view security. The key challenge in this context, one taken up in the book, is the challenge of advancing and realizing ecological security through engaging both existing institutions in progressive ways and outlining a role for new forms and sites of practice and agency (see Lövbrand et al. 2015; Burke et al. 2016). Here I identify immanent possibilities for the advancement of ecological security, evident not least in already endorsed international principles such as the precautionary principle and the notion of common but differentiated responsibility. I also draw on the political sociology of Pierre Bourdieu in both conceptualizing political impediments to the articulation and embrace of this discourse and identifying possibilities for advancing its claims in existing social and political contexts.

## Structure of the Book

The book proceeds with three key ambitions in mind, drawing on Andrew Linklater's (1998) suggestion that the project of critical theory entails sociological, normative and praxeological concerns. The first, broadly consistent with Linklater's conception of the sociological task of critical theory, makes a case for how we might understand the relationship between climate change and security in particular political and social contexts. Here I argue that we should conceive the climate–security relationship in terms of *discourses* of climate security that provide the lens through which political communities approach this relationship. The second, the normative task, makes a case for a particular discourse of climate security, namely ecological security. Here I suggest why this discourse is more ethically defensible and why it will serve to drive more progressive sets of practices. The third, the praxeological, engages with the question of how such a discourse might come to provide the lens through which political communities come to conceive and approach the relationship between climate change and security. This account captures the central goals of the book in outlining how we should view the relationship between climate change and security (in terms of competing discourses); why a particular discourse of climate security (ecological security) is needed; and how it might come to be embraced and enacted in practice.

More directly, the book is divided into three sections.

In the first section, which consists of Chapters 1 and 2, I provide a foundation for the elaboration and defence of an ecological security discourse regarding the relationship between climate change and security. Chapter 1 outlines the theoretical framework. Drawing on constructivist and critical theoretical engagement with security and its construction, I outline how the book conceives security. Here, I approach security as a site of negotiation and contestation, one in which competing discourses of security are built upon particular sets of ethical assumptions and have important political implications. In the process I argue that engaging with the concept of security to conceive and approach an issue such as climate change is not only possible but also necessary.

In Chapter 2, I examine existing accounts – in theory and practice – of the relationship between climate change and security. Here, I particularly note and draw out competing discourses of climate security, discourses that (crucially) encourage different sets of practices in response to the threat of climate change. This serves as necessary foundation for the subsequent defence of ecological security and together ensures that the initial two chapters of the book provide a basis for how we might conceive and approach security and its relationship to climate change.

The second section of the book outlines the contours of an ecological security discourse. Chapter 3 notes the normative and philosophical foundations of the discourse, one drawing on holistic accounts of ecological thought and second-generation green theory scholarship: an account that emphasizes interrelationships and attempts to escape an anthropocentric–ecocentric binary. This chapter also outlines the important context of the Anthropocene in making a case for the articulation of an ecological security discourse; directly defines the ecological security discourse and its contours; and specifies the interpretation of key constituent elements such as ecosystems, resilience and vulnerability.

Chapter 4 builds on the above foundation, more directly outlining a particular interpretation of what an ecological security discourse looks like in practice. While the preceding chapter outlines the referent object of security in an ecological security discourse and the nature of threats to it, this chapter explores the means and agents of security. It engages with the question of appropriate means for advancing ecological security, one raising difficult ethical and practical questions about the relative role of a wide range of practices (from mitigation action to geoengineering). It then explores the similarly complex questions of responsibility and agency, making a case for a genuine array of actors (from intergovernmental organizations to states, non-state actors and community groups) as potentially significant agents in the provision of climate security, with responsibility determined by capacity. I emphasize the importance of precaution as a foundational principle in conceiving appropriate means of practicing ecological security.

The chapter concludes by noting the importance of reflexivity, humility and dialogue in ensuring that the ethical thrust of ecological security is realized effectively in practice.

The third section of the book – Chapter 5, the final substantive chapter – explores the challenge of advancing and realizing ecological security. If Chapters 1–4 outline what ecological security is, why it is needed and what it entails, Chapter 5 focuses on the difficult question of how we might get there. What prospects are there, in short, for this discourse genuinely informing the way political communities come to conceive and approach the relationship between climate change and security? Here, after building a case for precisely engaging with this question rather than 'giving up' on ecological security, I employ immanent critique (Linklater 1998) as a means of identifying existing possibilities within the prevailing order, including in the endorsement of core principles such as precaution and common but differentiated responsibility. I also acknowledge a role for imagining alternative (and new) institutional arrangements and practices. In both contexts, I draw on the political sociology of Pierre Bourdieu to identify political possibilities for the articulation and embrace of the ecological security discourse in particular political and social contexts.

We don't *need* a security frame to articulate or pursue a progressive vision of climate politics. Clearly this is the case. But two points serve to underscore the importance of engaging with what a progressive linkage between security and climate change might look like. First, key institutions in world politics increasingly identify – and engage with – climate change as a fundamental and existential security challenge. This linkage has been made in the UN Security Council and by the majority of states outlining their own security priorities and strategies. In this context, we need to recognize there are different ways of conceiving this relationship, explore the implications of those different discourses in practice and build a case for a progressive approach to the climate–security relationship.

Second, security is politically significant. While we should avoid simplistic and reductionist assumptions that security always means priority, funding or, indeed, exceptional practices, we should also recognize that key institutions of global politics – from states to international organizations – consistently identify their central reason for being as the provision of security. This is central to the social contract and to the legitimacy of states in particular – still the most important actors in the international system. In that context, it is crucial to systematically outline what the effective provision of security amounts to and entails, one engaging with its long-term effects and consequences. This is especially so in the context of the collapse (of even the facade) of a distinction between humanity and nature in the Anthropocene and in the face of the fundamental and existential threat posed by climate change.

# 1 | *The Construction of Security*

Making sense of the relationship between climate change and security necessitates a clear conception of what we mean by the latter. How exactly is security to be defined and understood? One approach, of course, is for the analyst to outline their own definition of security, then set about assessing the extent to which – against that standard or criteria – climate change threatens it. While not an uncommon strategy, such an approach is not consistent with recognizing that there are multiple different ways of conceiving of security, both theoretically and (more importantly) in practice. In short, different analysts, practitioners and political communities themselves understand security – and, by extension, the relationship between security and climate change – in different ways. Recognizing this reality encourages us to examine the process through which security is constructed and the extent to which alternative accounts might come to capture the way the relationship between security and climate change is addressed.

As noted, in this book I make a case – on ethical and practical grounds – for the embrace of an ecological security discourse oriented towards the resilience of ecosystems when approaching the particular issue of climate change. This chapter serves to provide theoretical foundation for this argument. In simple terms it outlines how security is understood, making three important points that draw upon insights from critical theoretical approaches to security: security is constructed, security is political, security is ethical.

First, security is *constructed* in the sense that it is ultimately given meaning in particular empirical contexts through dynamic processes – over time and by different political communities in different ways. Second, security is *political* in the sense that the promise of providing security is fundamental to the legitimacy of key actors in the international system. It is also political in the sense that the way in which security is conceived and approached has important implications in practice, although this will vary according to the issue and especially

16

the way security more broadly is understood. And finally, security is *ethical* in the sense that different security discourses are built upon ethical choices, and the practices they encourage have ethical implications. Recognizing these three elements of security encourages us to explore how security is given meaning in different political settings (constructed), examine the implications of particular security discourses for political practice (politics) and assess the ethical defensibility of alternative meanings and practices of security (ethics).

This chapter is divided into four sections. First, it engages with debates about the meaning of security in international relations, arguing that the specific meaning of security can only be discerned in particular contexts. Here I make a case for locating particular meanings of security in discourses – frameworks of meaning with specific conceptions of whose security matters, from what threats, by which agents it is to be provided and through what means. This provides a foundation for the examination of climate security discourses in Chapter 2.

Second, and building on this insight, the chapter suggests the importance of approaching security as a social construction. I point here to the imperative of recognizing the changing meaning of security across time and space, arguing that we should approach security as a site of negotiation and contestation. I also outline the methodology of discourse analysis, used here to explore and illuminate how different meanings are given to security – and in particular climate security – in different times and sites. This section concludes by distinguishing the approach to the construction of security taken here with the most prominent alternative approach to this question – the securitization framework of the Copenhagen School. I argue that while useful in pointing to the composition of threat, the securitization framework is narrower in focusing exclusively on this dimension of security's construction, while also working with limiting claims about the meaning and politics of security.

The third and fourth sections outline the way this book approaches the politics and ethics of security, respectively. The discussion of the politics of security makes the case that security is 'political' at two core levels. First, the promise of providing security is central to the political legitimacy of key actors in world politics, principally states. This makes the stakes over the way security is understood and addressed particularly high and helps us make sense of the contestation that defines debates about the meaning and practice of security in particular political

communities. Second, security is political in the sense that representations of security – our core values in need of protection – and threat are
potentially politically consequential, serving to define political communities themselves and encouraging the dedication of significant attention
and resources to ensure their protection.

The fourth – and final – section of the chapter explores what it
means to conceive of security as 'ethical'. Like the discussion of security politics, the conception of security ethics explored here suggests that
security is ethical at two levels. First, discourses of security are necessarily underpinned by ethical commitments. This is apparent in choices
made about whose security matters and which sets of values do – or
should – inform the way we approach the pursuit of security. Second,
and following this, security is ethical in the sense that the practices
aimed at advancing or realizing security have ethical implications.
However, and parting ways with a range of scholarship in the broad
tradition of critical security studies, in this book the ethical implications of viewing and approaching an issue as a security issue relate not
simply to an issue's securitization. Rather, it is determined by the way
in which security itself is understood: the discourse of security. Central
here is the question of *whose* security is under consideration.

In sum, the chapter provides a framework for examining the relationship between climate change and security. The understanding of
security as constructed, political and ethical outlined in this chapter
provides us with a compelling rationale for examining this issue
through the lens of security discourses; for examining how security is
understood and pursued in different contexts regarding climate
change; and for mapping the implications of these climate security
discourses in practice. Ultimately, this serves in turn to make a case
for focusing on ecosystems and their resilience when considering the
relationship between security and climate change.

## What Is Security?

Scholars in international relations would tend to agree that security is
important. Some view it as a foundational concept in the field, one that
ultimately explains why the key actors (indeed the only significant
actors) in world politics – states – behave the way they do. For these
theorists, the actions of states are driven by a concern with ensuring their
survival, read security (see, e.g., Walt 1991). While this representation

risks decoupling formal institutions from actual human populations, others have noted that at the heart of this (realist) vision of security is the social contract. In this schema, the state ultimately exists to provide for individual protection in an anarchic state of nature (see Williams 1998). For others still, security constitutes a 'master narrative' (Neocleous 2008) that allows states to justify their own existence and, more specifically, the limits to individual autonomy. Critics here would note that the primacy of states and the state system – built on the promise of providing security – endures despite the litany of contemporary problems (from environmental change to refugees, poverty, inequality, conflict and disease) that the current international order has failed to address adequately (see Dillon and Reid 2009).

While disparate positions, what unifies the above accounts is a sense that security *matters*. But agreement that security is important does not translate into agreement as to how we might make sense of the concept itself. At a fundamental level, and even while broadly orienting their accounts of security around the centrality of the state, the above suggest views of security ranging from a relatively straightforward analytical category (i.e., security equates to state survival) to a Foucauldian 'political technology' that positions security less as 'a noun that names something, but a principle of formation that does things' (Dillon 1996:16) – namely, tying individuals to the state (see also Burke 2001:xxxiii–xxxxv). The latter vision of the politics of security, often drawing on post-structural thought and linked to the notion of the exception, will be explored in more detail later in this chapter. It is important to note here, however, that there are fundamental category distinctions about security in different intellectual traditions, some of which resist any attempt to give more specific meaning to it.

To the extent that it is possible to discern any general agreement about the meaning of security among those acknowledging the possibility of defining the concept, it would be at the (broad) level of 'freedom from danger or harm', for example, or the 'preservation of a group's core values' (see Wolfers 1952; Baldwin 1997). Yet in both cases, fundamental questions remain about the constituent elements of security itself and (importantly) the practical implications to follow from different answers to key questions. Whose security are we referring to? What constitutes a threat to security? Who are the key agents for providing security? And what are the key means of realizing it?

While the latter two questions come closer to conceptualizing the process through which security is to be achieved, all four are constituent elements of particular *discourses* of security.

A discourse of security is a lens through which meaning is given to the composition of a group and its core values; the nature of threats to those values; the agents capable or indeed responsible for providing security; and the means through which it might be provided. This builds on a broader conception of discourse, following Maarten Hajer (1995:44), as 'a specific ensemble of ideas, concepts and categorizations that are produced, reproduced and transformed in a particular set of practices and through which meaning is given to physical and social realities'. This approach draws on Foucault's (1977) conception of discourse, but Hajer suggests that not all discourses *constitute* reality in the way Foucault implies. Rather, Hajer (1995) argues that discourses compete with each other to define how communities can or should understand particular issues and approach them, and only when a discourse becomes dominant or hegemonic through this process of contestation would we expect it to take on the qualities Foucault suggests – the appearance of permanency, objectivity and reality that conditions how all engage that 'reality'.

Ultimately, it may be possible to give security some abstract content: to define it in terms of the preservation of a group's core values, for example. But it is in the (necessary) attempt to give meaning to the scope and definition of the group, the nature of those values, the means through which they are to be protected or advanced and the agents responsible for doing so that we necessarily move to something that can only have specific meaning – and associated implications – in particular contexts. In some contexts, one particular discourse may *appear* so dominant as to capture something about the fundamental essence or meaning across time and/or space. This suggests that it has shifted, again in Hajer's terms, from *a* discourse to a dominant or hegemonic discourse.

Such an answer to the question 'what is security' – one which ultimately suggests that meanings are given to the concept in particular contexts – will clearly not satisfy everyone. For some, this approach involves giving up too much by way of clarity or specificity of analysis (e.g. Walt 1991). In this account, clear analytical limits are required to provide intellectual boundaries and ultimately tell us what we are examining (see Busby 2018). For others, and at the other end of the theoretical spectrum, opening up the possibility that security is given meaning in different ways by different political communities potentially cedes too much ground to perverse or morally indefensible definitions of security (e.g., Booth 1991, 2007). What, in simple terms, if these communities are just wrong? But if we are trying to understand how the meaning of security changes over time, how ideas about a community's values and the means of their protection come to prominence, and crucially if we are trying to understand what security actually does in practice, we need to engage its meaning in context and explore the processes of its construction.

## Security as Constructed

Security is socially constructed in the sense that it is given meaning in particular ways by particular political communities at particular times. This meaning is produced through dynamic processes of negotiation and contestation within those communities over how that community and its values requiring protection should be defined; what threats to those values are; who is capable or responsible for realizing security; and through what means.

This approach to security is clearly one that situates its meaning in particular contexts, though, of course, we can also see broad shifts over time in the meaning attached to security at the international level. And the way in which states understand and approach security is not the product exclusively of dynamics within the state, but is also influenced by world events or dynamics and the meanings given to these processes by domestic and international actors.

The idea that the meaning of security in broad terms has shifted over time is central to a range of genealogical accounts of security. In the field of international relations, theorists such as Helga Haftendorn (1991), Emma Rothschild (1995), Costas Constantinou (2000) and Ole Wæver (2002) have all – in different ways – traced the changing meaning attached to security over time. In Rothschild's (1995) case, exploring the changing meaning of security involved locating these meanings in broad philosophical traditions, and against the backdrop of shifting international political dynamics. The latter is a particular feature of Buzan and Hansen's (2009) survey of the discipline of security studies within international relations scholarship. In their account (2009:50–65), shifting meanings of security post World War II

were a product of five driving forces: great power politics, technological change, events, internal dynamics of academic debates and
the institutionalization of security studies as a (sub)discipline. Here,
the first three forces refer to dynamics in world politics that serve
to influence and condition the way academics made sense of the
concept of security, while the next two referred to factors within the
academy itself.

This complex and mutually constitutive relationship between substantive political developments and debates within the academy has
been a core feature of a range of accounts of the meaning and scope of
security in international relations thought (see Smith 1999). Few would
argue, for example, that the dominance of a narrow and traditional
conception of security tied to the nation state and the threat and use of
force in the 1960s–80s was not significantly influenced by Cold War
considerations in the Western world generally and the US specifically.
Similarly, movements in the academy in the 1980s and 1990s to
interrogate the meaning of security and advance a case for alternative
approaches to it significantly reflected the waning and end of Cold War
tensions and the apparent possibility for advancing international
responses to pressing transnational problems (Buzan and Hansen
2009). In both cases, the association of a dominant meaning of security
in international relations thought with the concerns facing Western,
and in particular American, scholars reflects the dominance of these
scholars within the international relations academy as a whole, a point
made consistently by scholars drawing on postcolonial thought (see,
e.g., Barkawi and Laffey 2006). This provides another powerful
rationale for approaching security as contextual, given meaning and
content across a *range* of contexts: approaching it in such a way helps
us avoid the tendency to assume that a Western or American vision of
security captures something timeless, essential and universal about the
concept itself.

The above accounts of the evolution of security's meaning, in
practice and within the discipline of international relations, all focus
ultimately on identifying a dominant account of security. Clearly,
recognition that the meaning of security has changed over time takes
us beyond accounts that fix a *particular* meaning to security. And some
(for example, Buzan and Hansen 2009) do explore the conditions and
even processes of contestation through which particular ideas about
security have come to prominence. Yet all these accounts do tend to

downplay or ignore the existence (simultaneously) of multiple discourses of security in any context and tend toward being incurious
about the dynamics and logics of security beyond particular (usually
Western) contexts. In short, while capturing something about the
changing meaning of security over time, these accounts risk eliding
the way meaning is given to security in different sites.

As a conceptual framework, approaching security as a social construction means examining the meaning given to the constituent elements of security discourses – referent, threats, agent and means – in
particular contexts. Identifying this 'meaning' entails recognizing and
exploring the dynamics of contestation and negotiation associated
with attempts to render a particular discourse of security dominant
and resonant with key constituencies. And it also entails, more directly,
examining the language and practices of actors that serve to articulate
or give content to a particular security discourse. These points will be
elaborated below.

## Negotiation, Contestation and Resonance

Security is a site of contestation. Given the political significance of
claims associated with security, not least its status as the central reason
for being for key actors in the international system, it should hardly be
surprising that different actors in a given setting compete to define
what security is, how it is threatened and how it should be realized.
This is especially the case if we develop an account of security tied to
the values of a particular political community (see Wolfers 1952).
Here, different actors contest not simply whether extended deterrence
or an expansion of intelligence gathering capabilities, for example, are
required as tools for achieving security. Indeed, more fundamentally,
different actors hold and advance radically different views about the
composition of that community itself and its core values.

In a range of states, these dynamics of contestation were particularly
evident in the context of the so-called war on terror, for example. At an
immediate level, states grappled with the question of whether and how
significantly they should pursue domestic counter-terror legislation,
surveillance capacity and even international military action to minimize the possibility of a future terrorist attack. For advocates, the risk
associated with terrorism, especially since 2001 attacks in the United
States, necessitated the radical extension of state power and international

military action to address the threat of terrorism at its source. For
critics, the risk of terrorism was overstated; the extension of state
power and surveillance constituted a threat to multiculturalism,
liberal values and vulnerable (suspect) communities in these countries;
and the pursuit of military action simultaneously increased the likelihood of future terrorist attacks in that state while threatening the lives
of already vulnerable populations in target states (see Jackson et al.,
eds. 2009).

These debates and dilemmas are familiar to us but are often characterized in terms of a debate or trade-off between security and
liberty, for example. Yet in a fundamental sense, these interventions –
by advocates and critics on the question of counterterrorism – could
be viewed as arguments for competing discourses of security. While
advocates make a case for the emphasis on national security and the
central role of the state in achieving it, critics challenge this in a range
of ways. Some suggest that our emphasis should be on the security
of a broader vision of multicultural and inclusive society committed
to liberal values, one threatened by elements of the counter-terror
agenda. Others suggest the need to focus attention on those vulnerable populations in the Middle East and Afghanistan, for example,
who would be killed or displaced by the military prosecution of the
'war on terror'. And both sets of critics suggest that those measures
pursued in response to the terror threat are unlikely to genuinely
advance security at best, or constitute a direct threat to it at worst
(see, e.g., Aradau 2008; Horgan and Boyle 2008; Jackson et al. eds.
2009; Githens-Mazer and Lambert 2010; Horgan and Braddock
2010).

The above is an illustration of the role of security as a site of
contestation and competition, one focused on competing answers to
the question of whose security matters, how it might be protected, by
whom and from what threats. And in the process of attempting to
make a case for a particular set of answers to these questions over
others – one discourse of security over another – actors making this
case attempt to enable the agents and practices they see as advancing
their vision of security by attempting to ensure this vision resonates
with the values of that political community, and by marginalizing
alternative discourses of security and the actors articulating them (see
Mattern 2001; Krebs and Jackson 2007; Krebs and Lobasz 2007;
Thrall 2007; McDonald and Merefield 2010).

To apply these insights again to the example of the 'war on terror' and its prosecution in Western states, we can see such dynamics in evidence in attempts to enable or justify the specific case of military intervention in Iraq in 2003. In the face of significant domestic opposition to participation in the 'coalition of the willing' in Iraq, the Howard Government in Australia sought to make the case (as a range of states did) that Saddam Hussein's WMD program represented a pressing threat to national and international security necessitating a military response. This would be consistent with the expectations of theorists of securitization, who suggest that emergency measures are enabled through the designation of threat. But the government went further, arguing that Australian participation in the 'coalition of the willing' was consistent with Australian identity and Australian values (standing shoulder to shoulder with mates on the battlefield, for example). And it also denigrated political opponents at both the international and domestic level – for being motivated by their resentment of US power or for helping ensure Saddam Hussein could remain in power in Iraq despite his record of human rights abuses (McDonald and Merefield 2010). The former attempt to link intervention to national values can be viewed as an attempt to define the community and its values in need of protection and to best ensure this vision of security resonated with domestic audiences. The latter attempt to marginalize opposition views – consistent with conceptions of 'rhetorical coercion' (Krebs and Jackson 2007) or 'representational force' (Mattern 2001) – can be viewed as attempts to reduce resonance for alternative security discourses and ensure the government's security vision 'won out' over others (McDonald and Merefield 2010). Both dynamics point to the role of security as constructed, and in particular to the competition and contestation between different security discourses.

This approach to security – as a site of negotiation and contestation – clearly draws on constructivist thought. A range of theorists drawing on critical constructivism – concerned with conditions of political possibility and how foreign and security policy comes to be 'sold' to domestic constituents – particularly focused on examples from Western states' experience with the 'war on terror' to point to the efforts political leaders were making to build a case for military intervention in Iraq in particular (see Western 2005; Krebs and Lobasz 2007; Thrall 2007; Schmidt and Williams 2008; Holland 2012). For these theorists, our concern should not simply be with why particular security discourses come to prominence but with how they become possible in terms of being imagined, articulated and effectively sold (see Holland 2013). In doing so, these theorists draw on post-structural thought concerning the power of discourses and discursive representation while attempting to retain a greater role for domestic constituencies as agents or at least audiences in the negotiation of security (see Doty 1993; Weldes 1996; Fierke 1998).

My account of security as a site of negotiation and contestation draws on these insights, but also the political sociology of Pierre Bourdieu. Bourdieu is concerned with the conditions for substantive and effective political action. In his 'structuralist constructivism' (Bourdieu 1990), actors are influenced and constrained by structural contexts on one hand, while retaining the capacity for meaningful agency on the other. The latter is most likely to be effective when actors demonstrate an understanding of the 'fields' of their action; the distribution of capital within those fields; and the capacity to build and wield symbolic power. For Bourdieu (1991:171–202), the political field is defined by contestation between actors seeking to speak and act for the communities they claim to represent, while capital within that field is related to resources to advance particular messages. Symbolic power (Bourdieu 1977), meanwhile, is defined as the capacity of actors to articulate – and secure endorsement for – a compelling vision of the world, a community's role within it and/or particular actions that advance this vision (see McDonald 2016). Like critical constructivism's insights on the construction of security, there is recognition here of the centrality of contestation and the reality of both constraint and possibility facing actors attempting to advance a particular vision of security. Bourdieu's framework is one with particular insights into how such actors might go about enabling their preferred discourse of security.

## Discourses in Action: Language and Practice

The above account of the construction of security clearly necessitates tools that allow us to recognize and situate security discourses when they are invoked. This is particularly the case if our interest is in mapping the (changing) meaning given to the relationship between climate change and security in different contexts. This is not the central concern of the book,[1] which is more concerned with making a case for an ecological security discourse and exploring the circumstances in which it might come to be articulated and embraced. But particularly in advancing the latter concern, a brief discussion of where we might locate security discourses and how dynamics of contestation manifest themselves in practice is required.

In locating and examining the contours of discourses of security, methods of discourse analysis are (predictably) central. While there are a wide range of ways in which discourse analysis is understood and employed, whether in the study of international relations or beyond (see Milliken 1999; Hansen 2006), the approach endorsed here is a broad one entailing an interpretive approach to linguistic representations that attempts to discern and interrogate core meanings evident in speech and text, in the process organizing these representations into broader frameworks of meaning – discourses. In Chapter 2, a systematic examination of existing accounts of the relationship between climate change and security evident in speech informs a typology of climate security discourses focusing on the referent object of security and ranging (as noted) from national to international, human and ecological security. While organizing discourses according to this first principle question of whose security is defined and represented as important, this typology also identifies consistent themes with other constitutive elements of security discourses: threats, agents and means.

Of course, discourses are given meaning through more than the spoken or written word. A range of recent work has pointed convincingly to the powerful role of images, for example, in instantiating particular discourses of politics and, indeed, security. This has been evident in analyses of Danish cartoons depicting the prophet Mohammed (e.g. Hansen 2011) and in images of asylum-seekers on the borders of Europe (e.g. Huysmans 2006a, 2006b; Lenette and Miskovic 2018). In both cases, analysts make the compelling case that images serve to invoke and produce meanings, potentially influencing the way security, threats and responses to these threats are viewed (whether in the form of Islam or asylum-seekers).

---

[1] This is the central concern of my work on environmental change and security generally (McDonald 2012), and on climate change and security specifically (McDonald 2013a).

Practices are also potentially significant means through which discourses of security are evoked and given content. The focus in a number of these contexts is the ways in which apparently mundane, everyday and taken-for-granted sets of practices associated with the conduct of diplomacy or the management of borders, for example, serves to evoke and instantiate a particular idea about security (see Pouliot 2010; Adler and Pouliot 2011; Bigo 2011; Adler-Nissen ed. 2013).[2] But there remains scope to read significant and large-scale practices – protest marches or the deployment of troops – as themselves evoking a particular security discourse. These practices can be constitutive of discourses too in ways we don't necessarily find simple to discern or establish. In the process, they move beyond accounts that suggest security practices *follow* speech, a claim evident in the securitization framework's discussion of the process of securitization and its effects, for example (see Buzan and Wæver 2003; Stengel 2019).

Speech, images and practices can all be identified as illustrative of climate security discourses in action. Images of starving polar bears and dying coral reefs evoke an ecological security discourse focused on the vulnerability of non-human beings, while the construction of barriers to prevent climate-induced displaced persons from crossing borders is a practice evocative of a national security discourse. Ultimately, however, in this book the particular focus will be speech and text – those forms in which the meaning given to the relationship between climate change and security is made most directly and those forms that are of particular significance to the dynamics of contestation between competing accounts of whose security matters, from what threats, by what actors and by what means.

## Beyond Securitization

The preceding account of the construction of security suggests that the meaning of security is produced in particular contexts through processes of negotiation and contestation and that the meaning of security (therefore) changes across time and space. The chapter then made a case for making sense of these disparate accounts of the meaning of

---

[2] The so-called practice turn in international relations draws significantly on Bourdieu, whose framework encourages us to engage in empirically detailed examinations of the conduct and operation of societies at the level of the everyday to gain a fuller understanding of the way societies operate.

security as different *discourses* of security: frameworks of meaning defining whose security is under consideration, from what threats, by what means it should be protected and by which agents. Approaching the relationship between climate change and security in this way ultimately allows us to recognize the multiple ways in which this relationship could be, and has been, understood. And crucially, as will be outlined in the following section, it allows us to explore and interrogate the political and ethical implications that follow from approaching this relationship in particular ways.

The above suggests a focus on multiple sites, dimensions and implications of 'security'. This places significant onus on the researcher in locating security discourses in a wide range of contexts, exploring dynamics of contestation and negotiation and ultimately mapping the implications of security discourses across time and space. A much simpler, more parsimonious and ready-made conceptual framework is of course the Copenhagen School's securitization framework, which provides a basis for examining the discursive construction of threat (see Buzan et al. 1998). Given the concern in this book with the construction of security and its implications, and the growing prominence of securitization in the academic field, it is worth reflecting briefly here on the key points of difference between the approach taken here to the construction of security and the securitization framework.

The securitization framework emerged in the context of debates regarding the meaning and composition of security in international relations, especially between those advocating the broadening of security to include a wide range of threats and those advocating a narrow definition of security (and threats to it) focused on the territorial preservation of the nation state from external military threat (see Walt 1991; Kolodziej 1992). The approach taken by Ole Wæver (1995) and others involved in the development of the securitization framework was to suggest the possibility of escaping this distinction by focusing instead on the question of how security was actually given meaning by political actors. Rather than develop an abstract analytical definition of security, then, the framework suggested the need (as advanced in this book) to conceive of the meaning of security as contingent and constructed. In the process, the suggestion here was that what constituted a threat to security should not be abstractly defined by theorists but should instead be determined by political actors and communities themselves.

In making this claim, Ole Wæver (1995) drew on Austin's theory of language to argue that security should be viewed as a speech act. Here, the naming of an issue as a threat was not simply a descriptive label but was, ultimately, a performative act. When political actors defined an issue as an existential threat, and this position was accepted by a relevant audience, this served to construct that issue as a security threat and ultimately enabled emergency, extraordinary measures to deal with that threat.

Much about the above account has been debated and refined over time, not least in the context of the application of the framework to an ever-growing array of threats and sites. Among key points of debate are the nature of the speech act, the role of the audience in the framework, and the political implications of securitization.

First, while the speech act itself is clearly helpful in drawing attention to the important and potentially performative role of representations, critics have suggested that this emphasis narrows the form of representation while serving to exclude others; lacks recognition of different contexts; and fails to resolve a key tension regarding the extent of the speech act's 'performativity'. In different works, Lene Hansen (2000, 2011) has pointed both to the tendency of the framework to reaffirm the agency of already powerful actors – those capable of speaking and having their voice heard (see also Guillaume 2018) – while also excluding the important role of images in the process of securitization. Others have suggested that assumptions about the form of the speech act and its effects may be applicable in Western, liberal democratic states but are less applicable in other (non-Western) contexts (see Bertrand 2018). This speaks to the broader tendency in accounts of security to focus or draw upon the Western tradition, conceptions and assumptions when making universal claims about the politics of security.

On the interpretation of the speech act and the nature of its performance, Thierry Balzacq (2005) has suggested that there is a tension between conceptions of the speech act as 'illocutionary' or 'perlocutionary'. In both accounts, the speech act is performative. But in the former, which Balzacq sees evident in earlier accounts of securitization, the speech act essentially *constitutes* securitization – by designating a threat through speech, an issue is securitized. In the latter, more prominent in later refinements of the securitization framework, the speech act is a necessary but insufficient step for securitization. It can better be viewed as a 'securitizing move' (see Stritzel 2011), one that ultimately relies upon endorsement by a relevant audience or constituency to constitute securitization (and, in the process, enable emergency measures). In their later attempts to refine the securitization framework, Copenhagen School theorists pointed to the importance of facilitating conditions that served to create the circumstances in which a securitizing move might be more likely to be accepted – a refinement with different sets of implications for making sense of the performative power of the speech act itself (Wæver 2000:252–3).

Second, and following this set of criticisms or tensions regarding the speech act, other critics have pointed to issues concerning the role of audiences in the broader framework. Some of these criticisms build on the preceding points, with critics pointing to confusion about whether an audience is needed at all (depending on the performative power of the speech act) and whether the assumptions about a role for the audience are built upon Western, liberal democratic conceptions of the political space in which securitization occurs (see McDonald 2008; Balzacq ed. 2010; Balzacq et al. eds. 2015). Does securitization really look the same in non-democratic and authoritarian settings (see Bertrand 2018)? This is a particularly significant question if the envisaged effects of securitization (to be noted) are to take issues and responses to them out of the 'political' realm of deliberation and debate. What does the framework look like if nothing like open political deliberation exists in that context and if something approaching exceptionalism is the norm (rather than the exception?)

Others have suggested that even if we focus deliberately and exclusively on a liberal democratic context, it still remains unclear who the audience might be. To return to the example of the case made for military intervention in Iraq in Western states, Paul Roe (2008) has argued that Parliament ultimately constituted a more significant audience for attempts at justifying military intervention in Britain than the broader public. In the process, he notes that this conclusion seems to challenge the implied primacy of the broader public in the securitization framework. And while the audience itself may be less than clear in the framework, so too is the issue of what constitutes 'acceptance' by that audience. Are we talking here about a specific threshold (Parliamentary majorities, opinion polling over 50 per cent) or more ethereal and context-specific understandings of the circumstances in which securitization is ultimately successful (see McDonald and Merefield 2010)? While Wæver (2011) has endorsed the idea of analysts developing, using and applying the framework in their own way to their own empirical research puzzle, the lack of clarity and specificity here may also push against the broader desire to ensure the framework functions as a (parsimonious) conceptual framework.

Third, and the final key tension or criticism to be discussed here, is the issue of the political effects of securitization. Put simply, does securitization really have the set of implications Copenhagen School theorists suggest? To reiterate, its proponents suggest that securitization involves taking issues out of the 'normal' realm of politics and imbuing (and treating) them with a sense of urgency, secrecy and exceptionalism. In the process, securitization enables emergency measures in defence against an existential threat, to the point that at times these measures have been characterized and approached as evidence of securitization itself (Buzan and Wæver 2003). Critics here have identified and challenged the stark divide presented between a broadly liberal vision of politics and a Schmittian vision of the exception that characterizes security (see Williams 2006; McDonald 2008). Others have suggested that it provides too little scope for recognizing and exploring the politics of risk and its management (see Abrahamsen 2002; Bigo 2002) – an insight applied specifically to the issue of climate change (see, e.g., Corry 2012; Methmann and Rothe 2012; Oels 2012). The binary in the securitization framework between (a particular vision of) security and politics is one of the most challenged elements of the framework, not least as it takes attention away from the politics of security itself (McDonald 2008; Kirk 2020).

Related to this, and significantly given the focus of this book, is the question of whether securitization should be viewed as something to be avoided, as Wæver (1995) ultimately argued when introducing the concept. While acknowledging there may be times in which emergency measures are necessary and desirable for addressing a particular issue, Wæver nonetheless suggests that because of the illiberal effects of securitization, and because 'at the heart of the concept (of security) we still find something to do with defence and the state' (1995:47), we should ultimately aim for desecuritization of most issues. In this account, we should expect issues characterized as security threats to be dealt with in particular ways by particular sets of actors (the latter associated largely with the state). This view of a sedimented meaning of security sits uneasily with Wæver's (2002) earlier work outlining the conceptual history and indeed evolution of the concept of security.

More importantly, in this book I challenge the associated argument that the political effects of security and even securitization are determined by the act of designating threat. Instead, I suggest that the political effects of linking climate change and security are determined not by the linkage in and of itself but by the broader discourse of security in which that conceptualization of threat is embedded. This argument, and the account of the politics of security endorsed in the book and underpinning the case made here for ecological security, will be addressed in more detail in the following section.

While a ready-made conceptual framework for exploring the construction of security, and an important corrective to attempts to define security in universal terms at an abstract or universal level, the account of the construction of security in this book therefore requires moving beyond the securitization framework in key ways. In particular, the focus only on the designation and construction of threats amounts to a limited account of security, in which designations of agency, means and, in particular, referent are downplayed or ignored. This is particularly important for the purposes of this book, as the argument I make here for ecological security is one that suggests that the practices and implications that follow from defining and approaching an issue as a security issue are determined by *how* that linkage is made, not by whether it is made. Approaching security as a construction ultimately means focusing on how meaning is given to security not only through the specific designation of threat but also through depictions of which values and what community are in need of protection; how are they to be protected; and who is responsible for this.

## Security as Political

When it comes to the question of how security is defined and whether climate change is conceived and approached through the lens of a particular security discourse, this book suggests that the stakes are high. To be sure, it is entirely possible for researchers to engage in an analytical tick-box exercise that sets out to determine whether and/or how climate change threatens security against an abstract analytical definition of the term itself. Indeed, this characterizes a number of prominent academic interventions on the climate–security relationship (see Busby 2007; Smith and Vivekananda 2007). But aside from the limits of this approach in coming to terms with the construction of

security in particular contexts – the focus of the preceding section –
such an exercise also fails to adequately appreciate the *implications* of
this construction.

This section explores the politics of security in making a case for
ecological security. It outlines how the politics of security is understood and approached here, locating it in the broad tradition of
critical security studies. It then identifies the politics of security at
work at two levels. The first concerns the centrality of the promise of
providing security for key actors in the international system, suggesting in the process that claims about what constitutes a threat, to
whom, through what means it might be addressed and via what
agents are – if possible – even more consequential to the legitimacy
of key actors in the international system than we presently acknowledge. The second concerns the question of what representations of
security *do* politically. When it comes to climate change, for example,
we see radical differences between those who view the climate
change–security linkage as progressive (even necessary) on the one
hand (Busby 2007, 2008; Smith and Vivekananda 2007; Mazo 2010)
and those who view it as dangerous on the other (Buxton and Hayes
2015; Chaturvedi and Doyle 2015; Marzec 2015). Perhaps surpris-
ingly this distinction is particularly evident *within* critical security
studies – the tradition that engages most directly with the performative effects of security representations and the politics of security (see
Browning and McDonald 2013).

The first point to note here is a reiteration of an earlier claim – a
conception of security as political is central to the tradition of critical
security studies. Indeed, in earlier work, Christopher Browning and
I defined this, along with the idea of a necessary and intimate relationship between security and ethics, as one of two core concerns of
scholars working in this tradition. As we noted then (Browning and
McDonald 2013:236),

critical security studies scholarship is interested in the function of representations or discourses of security in defining group identity, enabling particular
policy or legitimating particular actors as security providers. This commitment, albeit evident in different ways and to different degrees, follows the
recognition that security is socially constructed and politically powerful.

As such, the discussion here of the politics of security, in a manner
consistent with the commitments evident in the broad tradition of

critical security studies, follows a discussion of the constructed nature of security and precedes a discussion of the ethics of security.

The promise of providing security is, as noted, central to the political legitimacy of key actors in the international system. This clearly applies to states, whose existence and raison d'etre is founded on the social contract. Here, individuals give up some degree of autonomy to the strong state (the Leviathan, in Hobbes's terms), which is viewed as the best means of providing for individual protection and safety in an anarchic state of nature (see Williams 1998; McSweeney 1999). Viewed in this light, it is not simply that the provision of security is a core function or responsibility of the state; it is the very reason for its existence. In this context, an intimate relationship between politics and security is inescapable. And while contemporary states may emphasize other sets of goals or responsibilities to their citizens, national security strategy documents and key foreign policy statements consistently identify the provision of security as *the* central goal of government. And, of course, another key (international) institution, the United Nations, lists the first purpose of the institution in its Charter as the maintenance of international peace and stability (see Conca 2015).

In the case of states in particular, the centrality of the provision of security to their reason for being means that claims and counterclaims regarding their success in advancing or realizing security are significant. Indeed, more than other issue areas, widespread belief among the citizens of a particular state that the government is failing in its duties to provide security speak directly to questions of legitimacy. If the state fails in the duty to provide security, what exactly is the state for? This is particularly significant in the context of climate change, where traditional agents, instruments and means of security (unilateral action by military forces within states) are clearly less immediately relevant to addressing the problem of climate change itself. I will return to this point in Chapter 2.

The above suggests that the promise of providing security is central to the raison d'être of key institutions in international politics, especially the most powerful of these: states (see Burke 2001). This already implies that representations of state success or failure in the provision of security are politically significant, and establishing the criteria for assessing state success or failure becomes particularly consequential. A range of interventions, again in the broad tradition of critical security studies, attempt to move beyond the general point that claims or representations of security and threat are politically consequential, seeking to outline a particular conception of the work that these representations ultimately do. Two broad trends in the literature are particularly evident here.

In the first, security mobilizes and raises the importance and significance of an issue. The simple argument here, one underpinning much early scholarship on the relationship between environmental change and security more broadly (see Hartmann 2009), is that representing an issue as a security threat serves to take it into the realm of 'high politics'. In the process, that issue would receive political attention and funding that would help prioritize an effective response to it. For early advocates of linking environmental change and security, the argument here was that perhaps through framing environmental issues as security challenges, those issues would receive attention, priority and funding consistent with their significance (see Levy 1995b; Ronnfeldt 1997).

A more nuanced – but related – account of the politics of security is evident in Ken Booth's (1991, 2007) work. For Booth, security does indeed occupy a position of high politics and is indeed central to the reason for being of states in particular. But in his account, the traditional association of security with the nation state and the threat or use of force means that we should not assume defining an issue as a security threat will have progressive implications, and we certainly should not endorse this understanding of security. Rather, Booth (2007:112) made a case for security defined as emancipation, broadly conceived as 'the securing of people from those oppressions that stop them carrying out what they would freely choose to do, compatible with the freedom of others'.

In the process of advancing this understanding of security, informed by Critical Theory (see also Wyn Jones 1999), Booth made two key points regarding the politics of security that take us beyond the simple recognition of security as 'high politics'. The first is that defining an issue as a security issue can have progressive implications *if* security is associated with defensible ethical commitments such as emancipation. The second is that the political importance and significance of security is such that we should not seek to retreat from it or escape it, but rather to engage and reform it. As Booth (1991:317) asks with reference to security, '[I]f we cannot name it, can we ever hope to achieve it?' Both of these points inform my own conception of the politics of security, to be noted.

In an important sense, Ken Booth's account of the politics of security is a response to the alternative tradition within critical security studies that views security as something best avoided. For theorists drawing on post-structural insights and for the Copenhagen School, there is something problematic about security. For some, it is simply the case that we cannot – no matter how hard we try – disentangle the meaning of 'security' from the military, defence and the state (Wæver 1995; Dillon 1996; Burke 2001). These critics might agree with Booth that emancipation would be a more progressive conceptualization of security, even that approaching an issue as a threat to security-as-emancipation might be progressive. But they are ultimately unconvinced that the meaning of security can be so redefined. This is evident in Wæver's (1995) conceptualization of security as ultimately wedded to defence and the state and in Daniel Deudney's (1990) criticism of attempts to link environmental change and security.

For others, it is not simply that security has a core meaning that cannot be shifted, but that there is a *logic* of security that has problematic implications. This is of course evident in the Copenhagen School account of securitization as exceptionalism, as a process that involves taking issues out of 'normal' politics and ensuring they are approached with urgency and secrecy in ways that limits deliberation, debate and decision-making based on a range of voices. It is also evident in a range of post-structural accounts of security, noted earlier, which suggest it is a master narrative of a modern liberal state project or a political technology tying individuals to the nation state (see Dillon 1996; Burke 2001; Dillon and Reid 2009). In these accounts, again evident in a range of criticisms of attempts to link climate change and security, approaching an issue like climate change as a security issue is a means through which already powerful actors can justify their own existence, budgets and political power without addressing the problem itself (Floyd 2010; Buxton and Hayes 2015; Marzec 2015; Oels 2015).

Of course, it should be noted that mobilization and illiberal, exceptionalist practices are not mutually exclusive. This is acknowledged in Wæver's (1995) own case for desecuritization and in Rita Floyd's (2019) account of 'just securitization'. But the particular vision of security the emphasis on one or the other tends to encourage – as something to be embraced and reformed or something to be avoided and contested – do push in very different directions. And when it comes to the question of climate change in particular, the two approaches might encourage us to endorse and embrace the idea of climate change as a first-order security threat or challenge any attempt to view the issue itself through the lens of 'security'.

My response to this apparent binary constitutes a crucial foundational point for the book generally and the defence of ecological security specifically. Centrally, I argue that while we do indeed need to be aware of the potential for pernicious politics arising from the representation of climate change as a security threat, we also need to avoid sweeping claims about the meaning or politics of security. There are two reasons for this. First, and most importantly, the politics of security flows from the *way* in which this linkage is made, and the contours of the discourse invoked. If security is constructed, we need to focus on *how* it is constructed and given meaning or substance rather than simply assume a particular politics follows from invoking security and threat (see Doty 1998–9; McDonald 2012). Second, as identified by Booth (2007), there is a potential conservatism evident in 'giving up' on security. If we believe security is mobilizing and politically significant, it is important not simply to escape it but rather, as Booth argues, to reform and redefine what security means in this vision.

While I part ways with Booth in his account of emancipation as 'real security' (rather than a discourse of it) and the particular case made for emancipation in the context of climate change, this insight clearly informs the way I view the politics of security and the engagement with the concept of security in this book. I would certainly endorse the claim that in recognizing the politics of security, we also need to acknowledge that some discourses have better or worse implications for the way we conceive and address climate change. This raises the question, of course, of how we assess these. This requires attention to the *ethics* of security.

## Security and Ethics

As noted, the idea of an intimate relationship between security and ethics is central to the critical security studies tradition. Indeed this follows the idea that representations of security are politically significant. If this is the case – if definitions of security and threat are politically and practically consequential – then we need to examine and assess choices made to approach security in particular ways and reflect on the defensibility of these choices.

While this is a central claim for critical security studies theorists, of course traditional approaches to security are founded upon a particular conception of ethics. The realist tradition, as noted, is a framework built on ethical considerations associated with the social contract (Williams 1998; Molloy 2018). Yet theorists and analysts working in the Realist tradition relatively rarely engage directly with the question of whether a focus on the nation state as the referent object of security is ethically defensible, for example, especially in the context of the increasing volume and severity of transnational security challenges (see Burke et al. 2016; for an exception, see Ayoob 1997). The emergence of such challenges, including climate change, provides a powerful rationale for re-examining the limits of this ethical vision and potentially making a case for an alternative conceptualization of security.

Ultimately, I suggest that security is ethical in two distinct senses. First, security is necessarily underpinned by ethical assumptions around whose security matters and what values of particular communities are in need of being preserved or advanced, including through what means. Second, and drawing on the previous discussion of the politics of security, security has ethical implications. Simply put, the choices made around the prioritization of whose security matters, from what threats and how security might be protected or advanced necessarily has ethical implications. National security policy and practice, for example, can serve to protect some while endangering the lives of others.

In these senses, it is important to explore and assess alternative conceptions (or discourses) of security in terms of their ethical commitments and implications. In the context of the book, this ultimately serves to provide a foundation for the claim that when considering the challenge of climate change, we need to orient our ethics towards vulnerable human populations, future generations and other living beings via the commitment to ecosystem resilience. This, in turn, will encourage practices consistent with genuinely addressing the challenge of climate change itself. While subsequent chapters will outline the contours of this discourse and its ethical basis in more detail, this section will expand on the idea that security is built on ethical assumptions and has ethical implications.

First, discourses of security are necessarily founded on particular ethical commitments and principles. This is evident not simply at the

broad level of whose security is viewed as important but what particular values of communities are in need of protection. On the former,
ethical choices are clearly made regarding whether we should prioritize
the security of the nation state or whether we have obligations
to outsiders.

One prominent example employed here by theorists of critical security
studies is that of immigration and especially asylum.[3] A focus on the
nation state, its sovereignty and territorial integrity has precisely encouraged some states to conceptualize unauthorized or irregular arrival of
asylum-seekers as a threat to (national) security. Yet an emphasis on
human security and the welfare of vulnerable people (regardless of
nationality) would, by contrast, encourage the view that asylum-seekers
constitute a referent object of security rather than a threat to it (see Doty
1998–9). And while some theorists and practitioners would make a case
that it is appropriate or even obligatory for elected representatives of the
state to focus solely on the welfare of their own citizens (see Gelber and
McDonald 2006), this still constitutes a choice built on a set of ethical
principles and commitments (associated with the social contract). The
endorsement of communitarian over cosmopolitan ethical commitments
here, again evident in the way a number of countries appear to approach
this issue, runs contrary to the terms of international agreements associated with asylum and refugees and is inconsistent with the way other
states can and have approached this issue (for a good overview of these
debates, see Gibney 2004, 2018).

Further, it is not solely the choice of a referent object in broad terms
that is built on a set of ethical commitments and choices, but also the
definition of the values of that particular community in need of preservation or advancement. Even at the level of an international security
discourse, for example, choices need to be made about the nature of the
international society that it is in need of preserving. In a dilemma
familiar to English School theorists of international society (see Bull
1995; Dunne 1998; Bellamy and McDonald 2004), even if settling on
the idea that 'international society' or the 'international community' is
worth protecting, there are ethical choices to be made here about the
content of key norms and values of that society or community. At its
broadest, we might decide that values associated with the minimization
of instability and with it the dangers of interstate conflict necessarily

[3] See, e.g., Huysmans (2006a); Guild (2009); Bigo (2002).

trump concerns with localized abuses of human rights in specific context. Hedley Bull (1995) saw this as a tension between prioritizing order and justice, evident in pluralist and solidarist accounts of international society, respectively. More recently, this issue has been debated significantly in the context of the 'responsibility to protect' (see Bellamy 2014).

At both of the above levels – the choice of referent object and the values attributed to that particular community – ethical choices are evident. But security also has important ethical implications in terms of the practices and politics that follow from choices around whose security matters. This is evident in the earlier example of asylum and national security, where ethical choices transform into practices with significant ethical implications. In Australia, for example, the framing of asylum-seekers as a national security threat ushered in a set of practices that extended to their long-term detention. In these contexts, ongoing suffering and uncertainty created significant implications for mental health and widespread instances of self-harm (see McMaster 2002; McDonald 2011).

The means through which security is advanced also reflects ethical considerations and has potentially significant implications. As theorists engaged in the just war debate have long argued, choices associated with the means through which security is pursued can have consequential effects, for example (Walzer 1977; O'Driscoll 2008, 2018). This clearly applies to the use of force generally, but even to the *way* in which force is used. In his analysis of the use of force by the United States military, Sebastian Kaempf (2018) has argued that the desire to avoid combat casualties (through the use of unmanned aerial vehicles and air power, more broadly) has meant an increasing likelihood of non-combatant, civilian casualties in target states. In this context, choices around the means of achieving security, along with associated choices about which agents should provide it, have important ethical implications.

As this discussion suggests, separating security from ethics is neither possible nor desirable. We need to be aware of choices made about whose security is important and the implications of these choices for the practices that follow. These are not simply abstract analytical choices but are ethical ones, with significant ethical implications. As the above discussion suggests, all constituent elements of a security discourse – referent, agent, means and threat – entail some degree of ethical choice and have important ethical effects.

The centrality of ethical questions to security applies too to the relationship between climate change and security. The focus on preserving national security in the face of climate change is one that limits the ethical universe to the boundaries of the nation state, (perversely) in the face of a genuinely global problem. And as will be noted in subsequent chapters, it encourages sets of practices inconsistent with addressing the problem, even creating or increasing vulnerability for others (future generations and vulnerable outsiders, for example).

This suggests the need to reflect upon and explore the ethical assumptions – what we might call first principles – of security discourses. But beyond deconstruction, this book makes a case for a reconstructive move in suggesting the need not simply to interrogate the ethics of different security discourses but to make a case for a particular security discourse on ethical grounds and explore the conditions in which it might find purchase and resonance. Crucially, this does not mean rejecting the idea that security is socially constructed. As noted, in making the case for defining security as emancipation, Ken Booth (1991, 2007) ultimately advocated emancipation as *real* security, a move eliding (if not rejecting) the reality of security meaning different things to different communities at different times. While his interventions rightly remind us of the need to take ethical questions seriously, in this book I suggest the need to ensure that the case for a particular approach to security is not only grounded in defensible sets of principles and encourages progressive action. Rather, it should be advanced in a manner that engages directly with the conditions of political possibility in different contexts. In that sense, the approach taken here means not only making a case for a progressive approach to (climate) security but also asking how such an approach might come to provide the lens through which particular political communities understand and approach their security. This task draws together the key themes of this chapter as a whole – construction, politics and ethics – and provides a rationale for precisely this focus in the broader book.

## Conclusion

The account of security in this chapter provides a foundation for the substantive case made for ecological security in the book itself. The case for ecological security advanced here is one that follows recognition of security as socially constructed: as brought into being in particular ways by particular political communities at particular times and as given meaning in these contexts through dynamic processes of negotiation and contestation. Once we acknowledge the constructed nature of security, we recognize both the range of ways in which meaning can be given to the nature of the relationship between climate change and security, and the contexts in which particular meanings – discourses – are elaborated and come to genuinely inform the way political communities approach that issue.

While recognizing the constructed nature of (climate) security allows us to acknowledge the *possibility* of understanding and approaching this relationship in different ways, the subsequent discussion of the politics and ethics of security provides a foundation for advancing a particular discourse of security – one oriented towards ecosystem resilience. If security is politically significant, central to the political legitimacy of key actors and has important performative effects in practice, it becomes crucial to engage the question of how meaning *should* be given to security in different contexts. And recognizing the inescapable relationship between security and ethics means not only acknowledging the ethical choices made in articulating a particular understanding of (climate) security but also advancing a discourse of (climate) security with defensible ethical foundations and ethical implications in practice.

In short, recognizing security as constructed, political and ethical provides both a foundation and rationale for exploring the way in which the relationship between climate change and security is given meaning and in particular for advancing a specific understanding of this relationship – a climate security discourse. To reiterate a claim made at the outset of this book, we can certainly explore the issue of climate change through a framework other than security. But as climate change is increasingly represented as a security issue, we need to ask how it is represented, why it is conceived and approached in this way, what effects these representations have in practice and (crucially) whether we can articulate and find purchase for more defensible alternatives. That is the task of the remainder of this book.

# 2 | Climate Security Discourses

One of the central claims of this book is that there are multiple different ways of conceiving and approaching the relationship between climate change and security. These different accounts are based on particular sets of ethical commitments and have different ethical implications in practice. I approach these different accounts here as 'discourses': frameworks of meaning with particular sets of answers to the questions of whose security matters, from what threats, by what means it is to be provided and which actors are responsible for providing it. Conceiving of the relationship between climate change and security in these terms means identifying key contours of different discourses, interrogating their different assumptions and claims and exploring (likely or suggested) implications of these discourses in practice. In the process, it becomes possible not only to examine the ethical commitments evident in these discourses but also, more importantly, to reflect on the defensibility of the practices they encourage. To what extent are alternative accounts ultimately consistent with encouraging practices geared towards genuinely addressing the problem of climate change itself, and in particular the threat posed to those most vulnerable to manifestations of it?

As noted, here I make a case for an ecological security discourse in approaching the relationship between climate change and security. Such a discourse, focused on the resilience of ecosystems themselves, encourages practices geared towards addressing the threat climate change poses to the most vulnerable: populations in impoverished countries, other living beings and future generations. Agency and responsibility for addressing climate change is conceived broadly (as all those who contribute to the problem itself), with differentiation of responsibility related to capability. The nature of the threat is also understood in broad terms: not simply in terms of the possibility of climate change contributing to the likelihood of armed conflict but also the direct threat of increased temperatures for the functionality of

44

ecosystems and the protection of their inhabitants, present and future. And, most importantly, the referent objects of security here are ecosystems themselves, not human collectives (or institutions claiming to represent them) whose welfare is frequently considered separately from the ecological conditions of their existence.

The contours, commitments and challenges associated with embracing and implementing an ecological security discourse in practice will be addressed in detail in subsequent chapters. These will outline what ecological security is (Chapter 3), what sets of practices it encourages (Chapter 4) and how it might be advanced or realized within (or indeed beyond) existing sets of institutions and practices (Chapter 5). Before this, however, and by way of providing context to the defence of this means of conceiving and approaching the climate change–security relationship, it is important to explore how engagement with this relationship has evolved over time and to examine the contours of alternative discourses of climate security. That is the task of this chapter.

This chapter is divided into three sections. The first explores engagement with the relationship between climate change and security in theory and practice, noting evolution of this engagement over time and situating it in broader engagement with the relationship between the environment and security. The emphasis here is on capturing key developments and shifts in the way analysts, civil society organizations, policymakers and policy practitioners have approached the intersection between climate change and security. The second section makes a case for a discursive approach: locating various (and differentiated) engagement with the climate change–security relationship in different discourses of climate security. I elaborate on how discourses are defined and categorized in the book, noting that climate security discourses here are organized according to their choice of referent object: their conceptualization of whose security is threatened by climate change. While outlining boundaries between forms of engagement with climate change and security is inevitably partial, reductionist and imperfect, it nonetheless provides a useful means of differentiating between the contours – and ethical commitments – of different approaches to the climate change–security relationship. The third section, and the bulk of the chapter, goes on to identify and examine three discourses of climate security: national, international and human security. It identifies the key contours of these discourses, outlines the ethical assumptions upon which they are based and identifies (and interrogates) the practices they encourage. In the process, this section provides a foundation for the subsequent defence of an ecological security discourse: one built on a more defensible ethical foundation and encouraging progressive sets of practices in response to the challenge of climate change.

## Security, the Environment and Climate Change

The environment – particularly environmental change – was not initially prominent in the way in which analysts, policymakers or practitioners approached 'security' in international relations thought or in practice. In their account of the development of security studies as a discipline, for example, Buzan and Hansen (2009:128–9) note that it was only in the 1980s that analysts began to take the notion of environmental security seriously, prompted largely by developing concerns around environmental change. The continued emphasis of major state powers on the threat and use of force in a Cold War context, however, ensured these nascent concerns remained marginal to security considerations in global politics.

Of course, to the extent that environmental security extends to the use and control of resources, territory and space, the environment has always been a component of security considerations, at the analytical and practical level. States have always been concerned with the control (from preservation to acquisition) of territorial space, and the material resources in the environment have always been central to the capacity of militaries to be built, fuelled and fed. But this largely geopolitical image of the environment is, of course, one of a broader material context to be accounted for or a source of material resources to be used to sustain the defence apparatus (see Agnew 1998; Dalby and O'Tuathail eds. 1998; Dalby 2007). The environment here is at once the goal and means of material power central to traditional geopolitical conceptions of security.

Arguments that environmental *change* might be a genuine security consideration, or even that the challenges of effectively utilizing (particularly scarce and non-renewable) resources might warrant the attention of security scholars and practitioners, arose much more recently. While in the 1970s we saw some attempts to identify the environment as a national security issue, particularly evident in a Worldwatch

Institute publication by Lester Brown (1977), it was ultimately in the 1980s that attention to the environment–security relationship became relatively prominent. This was, of course, driven significantly by the apparent opportunity that the waning and end of Cold War tensions seemed to provide. With the threat of superpower conflict and, in particular, nuclear use appearing less imminent, it became possible to suggest alternative sources of threat and alternative priorities for advancing (even national) security (see Buzan and Hansen 2009; Dumaine and Mintzer 2015:8).

Arguments linking the environment and security that emerged in this agenda-setting period largely followed one of two logics. In the first logic, the role of the natural environment in sustaining (long-term) life on the planet was linked directly to security, with the suggestion that security needed to be expanded or redefined to include environmental issues. The argument here was simple, if unsophisticated: we cannot continue to exclude issues central to human survival from the way we understand and approach security. Authors such as Jessica Tuchman Mathews (1989), Norman Myers (1989), Lester Brown (1986) and Richard Ullman (1983) all called for redefining security on these grounds, suggesting in the process that the narrow and atavistic under-standing of security tied to the possibility of armed conflict missed fundamental existential challenges posed by environmental degrad-ation in particular, including to the nation state. In the process, while these proponents sought to redefine security on analytical grounds, they were driven by normative concerns of promoting priority, atten-tion and funding for environmental issues by elevating them to the 'high politics' realm of security (see Warner and Boas 2019). This involved a series of (problematic) assumptions about the implications of 'securitization' and the politics of security more broadly, as noted in Chapter 1. Nicole Detraz (2015) refers to this approach as an environ-mental security discourse, while in other contexts it has been defined as the first wave (Levy 1995b) or first generation (Ronnfeldt 1997) of environmental security scholarship.

The second environmental security logic (or wave, generation or discourse in the characterizations above) emphasized the centrality of the environment to traditional security concerns of conflict. Rather than attempting to redefine security (as survival) or even fundamen-tally challenge the association of security with the territorial preserva-tion of the nation state from (external) military threat, a range of analysts sought to illustrate the ways in which either environmental degradation or competition over the use or exploitation of natural resources could actually serve to trigger armed conflict. This was perhaps most prominently associated with the work of Thomas Homer-Dixon (1991a, 1991b, 1999). Potential pathways imagined by Homer-Dixon and others included the possibility of interstate conflict over access or use of transboundary water resources ('water wars') or environmental degradation (such as deforestation and/or the lack of arable land), leading to economic hardship and, in turn, either general civil unrest or population movement and subsequent conflict (see, e.g., Starr 1991; Gleick 1993; Uvin 1996; Homer-Dixon 1999). These themes were embraced and echoed in the apocalyptic visions of Robert Kaplan (1994) in his account of a 'coming anarchy'. Here, he envisaged a world (or impoverished parts of it, at least) in which environmental change would drive widespread social upheaval, displacement, conflict and anarchy (see Dalby 2002:27–40).

As will be noted, a number of the pathways noted above have been more recently envisaged in the particular context of climate change. Indeed the spectre of water wars (with dwindling freshwater supply and increasing demand in the context of climate change), civil war and the destabilizing effects of large-scale population displacement and movement have all been suggested effects of climate change and its manifestations (see Mazo 2010; Parenti 2011; Welzer 2012; Selby and Hoffman eds. 2017). It is striking that in this original formulation, however, the role of environmental *change* was often limited, with axes of environmental conflict regularly focused on resource use and exploitation rather than broader processes of change. And while avoiding the charge of advancing a normative position on (shaky) analytical grounds, proponents of this linkage were particularly susceptible to claims of smuggling in Realist or Malthusian assumptions about the inevitability of conflict over dwindling or degraded resources. By this logic, as critics have argued, the possibility of cooperation or even the intersection of broader sets of political and economic factors tend to be either downplayed or dismissed.[1] In the context of

---

[1] Of a substantial range of scholarship, see, e.g., Barnett (2000, 2001); Dalby (2009, 2002); Gleditsch (1998); Levy (1995a); Salehyan (2008); Ide (2017). This has also been a central thrust of so-called environmental peacebuilding literature, whose advocates have pointed not only to the possibility of cooperation in addressing environmental challenges but also to the likely flow-on effects such

'water wars', for example, Aaron Wolff's (1998) analysis of the management of transboundary water resources indicated that developing contestation over these resources was more likely to produce interstate cooperation than conflict (see also Katz 2011). Again, criticism of similar linkages made between climate change, more specifically, and conflict (on the grounds of assumptions made and methodology utilized) has been prominent in recent literature on the security implications of climate change.[2]

As Keith Krause and Michael Williams (1996) have argued, it is striking that in these interventions on the relationship between the environment and security or conflict, those contributing to this literature often did not engage directly with the *meaning* of security. Those attempting to link security and the environment on the grounds that security should be associated with survival (the 'security equals importance' argument) engaged less with the meaning of security itself than the scope of security threats. And the absence of a sustained examination and critique of traditional accounts of the meaning of security was even more evident in literature pointing to the relationship between the environment and conflict. Here, the association of security and (protection from) armed conflict remained, while in both sets of logics the ultimate focus was the security of the nation state. In part, this appeared to aid the political purchase and take-up of some of these concerns in practice, in particular environment-conflict interventions. Robert Kaplan's 'The Coming Anarchy' article in *The Atlantic* was a case in point. As Alex de Waal (1997) noted,

One reader in the US department of global affairs faxed copies of Kaplan's article to American embassies across the globe; it is widely credited with influencing President Clinton's reluctance to intervene to halt the genocide of the Rwandan Tutsis three months later.

Even as the environment – and environmental change – began to warrant engagement as a security issue in theory and practice, climate change was not prominent in early accounts of this relationship. This was, of course, significantly a product of the fact that climate change

---

cooperation could have for positive relations between actors. See, e.g., Conca and Dabelko (2002); Dresse et al. (2019).

[2] See, e.g., Selby and Hoffman eds. (2017), and debates in the journal *Political Geography* (2017) over the role of climate change in recent conflict in Syria. See also Ide (2017).

itself did not emerge as a major international political issue until the late 1980s. And, of course, as noted, early accounts of the environment–security relationship were more likely to focus on control of or access to natural resources than broader issues of the environmental conditions underpinning (even exclusively human) survival.

To be sure, some earlier interventions on environment security touched on the role of climate change. For Peter Gleick (1993), for example, writing on the prospect of contestation and conflict over transboundary water resources, climate change would serve to decrease the supply of freshwater while simultaneously increasing demand (see also Lonergan and Kavanagh 1991). And Jessica Tuchman Mathews's (1989) case for redefining security also noted the potential impact of climate change on the meaning and scope of security. But attention to the relationship between climate change and security developed significantly in the mid-2000s, driven at least in part by growing international political concern about climate change itself. Following extreme weather events in the northern hemisphere, the publication of the 2007 Intergovernmental Panel on Climate Change (IPCC) report, the release of high-profile films with a climate-change theme or focus – *The Day After Tomorrow* and Al Gore's *An Inconvenient Truth* – and the publication of the 2006 *Stern Review* into the global economic implications of climate change, international attention and concern regarding climate change reached something of a high point (see Dalby 2009:150–1; Mazo 2010:9–10). This encouraged a range of scholars to explore the intersection between climate change and security but, in particular, seemed to drive engagement with this relationship in policy circles. International organizations, states and public-policy think tanks all turned their attention to the intersection of climate change and security (see Mazo 2010:31–5; Dalby 2015a). Indeed, for Selby and Hoffman eds. (2017:3), and in contrast to earlier engagement with the security implications of environmental change more broadly, 'the international debate on climate security (has been) led mostly by policy, military and NGO actors'.

International organizations, in particular the United Nations, played a prominent role in this context (see Dellmuth et al. 2017). In 2007, the UN Security Council held its first discussion on the security implications of climate change, sponsored by permanent member the UK. This was followed by subsequent discussions in 2011, 2018, 2019,

2020 and 2021 (sponsored by Germany, Sweden, the Dominican Republic and the UK, respectively), while informal (Arria-formula) meetings on climate security have taken place since 2013 (see Scott 2015; Conca et al. 2017; Conca 2019; Maertens 2021). The 2011 discussions led to an agreed presidential statement, concluding that climate change should be considered and discussed by the Council 'when such issues are drivers of conflict, represent a challenge to the implementation of Council mandates, or endanger the process of consolidation of peace' (UNSC 2011b:2). In 2009, the UN General Assembly also discussed the security implications of climate change and agreed a resolution that 'invited the major organs of the United Nations, including the Security Council, to intensify their efforts to address the challenge, as appropriate and within their respective mandates' (UNGA 2009b).

The bureaucratic and research arms of the United Nations also played a role here, with the United Nations Environment Programme (2007) and then UN Secretary-General Ban Ki Moon (2007) linking ongoing conflict in Darfur to the effects of climate change. The argument presented was that the loss of arable land had contributed to population displacement, in turn bringing populations into contact and, ultimately, conflict with each other. The UNDP and UNEP, together with the UN Office for Political and Peacebuilding Affairs, also established the Climate Security Mechanism in 2018, a small office designed to assist the UN in systematically addressing climate security risks. Meanwhile, some regional organizations (from the African Union to ASEAN and the OSCE) provided a forum for states to discuss the security implications of climate change specific to their regions and in some cases (most notably with the European Union) develop regional positions and responses to the relationship between environmental change and security (see Krampe and Mobjork 2018).

Of course, states themselves often prompted international and regional organizations to engage with questions of climate security and, in a number of cases, sought to integrate climate-security considerations into existing security planning and perspectives. The US military had long identified climate change as a potential future security consideration, though whether this was a product of a process of forward-planning and assessment necessary for defence organizations or a (more cynical) attempt to underwrite the relevance and therefore justify the continued budgets of US security instruments after the end of the Cold War has been a subject of debate (see, e.g., Floyd 2010; Dalby 2015a; Abrahams 2019). While a range of vulnerable states (especially low-lying island states) supported international efforts to identify, engage and prepare for the security effects of climate change (see, e.g., Morgan 2018), Western states were particularly prominent in embracing this perspective. European states have sponsored all but one of the six UNSC debates on climate security, while the governments of the UK, Germany, France, the Netherlands, Sweden, for example, all sought to formally integrate a climate perspective into formal security planning and operations (see Schäfer et al. 2016; Maertens 2021). As Shirley Scott (2015) has noted, by 2015 more than 70 per cent of states producing national security assessment documents had identified climate change as a security threat.

Finally, and while at times straddling the policy-academic divide, public policy–oriented think tanks both responded to and drove states' concerns with the security implications of climate change. Think tanks throughout the world published analyses pointing to various dimensions of the climate-security threat and the imperatives of response. Think tanks have attempted to map the human security effects of climate change, assess the regional and international security implications of climate-induced migration, explore the implications of natural disasters and examine the institutional arrangements needed to incorporate a climate security perspective effectively, for example (Dalby 2015a). US-based think tanks across the political spectrum were particularly prominent in advancing the case that climate change can and should be viewed as a national security challenge (e.g., Brookings, CNA Corporation, Council on Foreign Relations, Centre for a New American Security, Center for Strategic and International Studies, Wilson Center, Center for Climate and Security etc.; see Mazo 2010:33–4). Of these, the CNA Corporation's (2007) report, National Security and the Threat of Climate Change, was perhaps the most influential. This report conceptualized climate change as a 'threat multiplier': not necessarily causing a direct threat to (national) security but creating conditions in which instability and conflict were more likely (CNA 2007). This conceptualization has subsequently been invoked in assessments and in policy statements on the climate–security (and especially climate-conflict) relationship by the European Union, the US Government, NATO, the UN Environment Program and the UN Secretary-General, among others.

The above interventions will be addressed in more detail in the subsequent discussion of discourses of climate security, not least given already evident choices about whose security is to be prioritized and addressed. The central role government and policy-oriented analysis has played in debates about the relationship between climate change and security is worth noting and reflecting on at this stage, however, not least as this provides a window into the challenging trade-offs involved in linking climate change and security. In simple terms, the role of these actors in promoting this link can be viewed as a double-edged sword. While this engagement has ensured 'built-in' policy relevance in which key actors in the international system have engaged directly with the security implications of climate change, this has arguably come at a price. For some, this price is largely in terms of the failure (possibly inherent to any form of political intervention) to develop adequately sophisticated and nuanced accounts of the relationship between climate and security generally, and climate and conflict specifically (see Dalby 2015a; Selby and Hoffman eds. 2017). As Joshua Busby (2018:5) has argued, in the context of 'complex, contingent, and not fully understood' connections between climate change and security, 'for policy audiences, the nuance can be frustrating'. For critics, built-in assumptions about the relationship between scarcity and violence, and the possibility of cooperation between actors, encourages speculative, politicized arguments. These, in turn, are not necessarily borne out in practice, nor do they demonstrate sufficient recognition of the range of intervening variables between climate stress and insecurity or conflict (see Selby and Hoffman eds. 2017).

More importantly, for the purposes of this book, the dominance of government and policy-oriented analysis has created a context in which primary articulations of the climate security agenda and responses to climate insecurity are tailored to already existing institutional arrangements and practices (see Floyd 2015). There has been less reflection on whether these institutions are, in fact, fit for purpose or whether our perspective should extend in radical directions to future generations or other living beings, for example. In targeting existing institutions and conforming recommendations to existing arrangements and practices, we almost necessarily fail to step back to ask what practices and institutions would genuinely address the challenge of climate change and the security implications associated with it, particularly when adopting a global perspective. That is the task of this book.

## Climate Security Discourses

It is possible to develop an account of analytical engagement with the relationship between climate change and security that focuses on the evolution of this literature and identifies key themes over time. Joshua Busby (2018), for example, attempts to 'take stock' of the literature on climate change and security in terms of key themes as it has evolved, albeit while focusing on literature exploring the relationship between climate change and conflict. But attempting to draw out core themes in this literature as it has evolved risks eliding key differences. These differences are evident in the way in which different analysts, theorists and practitioners approach the climate–security relationship and even address (and answer) the same questions: the relationship between climate change and conflict, for example. In this book I suggest that a more useful examination of key themes – and crucially, a more useful explication of key points of difference in approaching the climate security relationship – draws out the contours of and differences between *discourses* of climate security.

A discourse is a framework of meaning that conditions the way we view and approach the world. As noted in Chapter 1, here I endorse Hajer's (1995:44) conceptualization of discourse as 'a specific ensemble of ideas, concepts and categorizations that are produced, reproduced and transformed in a particular set of practices and through which meaning is given to physical and social realities'. Crucially, for Hajer, multiple discourses may exist simultaneously and in opposition or competition with each other. In his account, discourses (and the actors advancing them) may compete to become dominant or hegemonic, ultimately conditioning the way political communities at large conceive and approach reality (see also Dryzek 2005; McDonald 2012). This latter conceptualization – of a dominant or hegemonic discourse – is closer in orientation to a Foucauldian (Foucault 1977) approach to discourse: as a monolithic and unitary account that imposes a partial vision of reality as timeless and universal, constructing, in turn, the interests and identity of that community and the possibilities for political action.[3] In this book I argue that we can discern multiple discourses of climate security in engagement with this

---

[3] On these points and distinctions, see also Hansen (2006); Dunn and Neumann (2016). For an example of such an approach, see Campbell (1992).

relationship in academic literature, policy engagement and practice. Some of these discourses are more likely to find political and practical purchase than others and are more likely to become dominant or hegemonic discourses in the manner envisaged by Foucault.

While the above outlines the manner in which discourses are conceived and approached in broad terms, in this book a *security* discourse is approached as a framework of meaning that serves to define whose security matters, from what threats, by what means it is to be realized or advanced and which actors have responsibility to serve as security agents (see McDonald 2012:10–26, 2013a). This distinction – between alternative accounts of referent, threat, means and agent – is one that can readily be applied to the way in which climate change is conceived. Yet in applying this approach to climate change, here the emphasis – as the key point of distinction – is on the choice of *referent object* of security: of whose security is under consideration.

The focus on the referent object of security as the key point of distinction between alternative climate security discourses reflects two considerations. First, in logistical and organizational terms, such a distinction provides a ready-made means of drawing distinctions between alternative security discourses. Indeed, while not a uniform approach to developing an account or typology of the literature or climate–security engagement,[4] it is an organizing distinction found elsewhere (see, e.g., Diez et al. 2016; Ferguson 2019). Second, and more importantly, this book suggests that the question of whose security is under consideration is the central determinant of the way in which the relationship between climate change and security will be conceived and approached. While a useful means of making distinctions between alternative accounts or discourses of climate security, then, the choice to focus on the referent object follows primarily from the view that the question of whose security is prioritized is most important (see Booth 2007), conditioning the ways in which we subsequently conceive of the nature of the threat, the means of addressing it and the actors capable of and indeed responsible for doing so.

The remainder of this chapter, drawing in part on earlier work (McDonald 2013a), outlines the contours of three distinct climate security discourses on these grounds: national, international and

---

[4] See, e.g., Floyd (2010); Floyd and Matthew (2013); Ronnfeldt (1997); Levy (1995); Cudworth and Hobden (2011).

human security discourses. In the process, it provides a comprehensive account of the central ways in which the relationship between climate change and security is approached. In the case of each discourse, I identify key interventions in academic literature, think tank analysis, policy statements and, in some cases, practices that align to the contours of these discourses. In turn, I note key themes in giving meaning to the constitutive elements of this discourse: the referent object itself (how exactly is the national, the international and the human conceived?), the nature of the threat posed, the means through which it should be addressed and the actors capable or responsible for providing security in this context. In the process, I identify key implications and (in particular) limitations of these discourses.[5] The latter particularly focuses on the sets of ethical assumptions and practical implications of each discourse that militate against significant action focused on addressing the challenge of climate change itself and the rights and needs of those most vulnerable to manifestations of it. In the process, this analysis of climate security discourses serves to provide a foundation and rationale for the case for an ecological security discourse, one outlined and explored in detail in the remainder of the book.

## Climate Change and National Security

In attempts to understand and engage with the link between climate change and security, a *national security* discourse remains the most prominent and powerful discourse. Of course, this reflects the central role of states in the international system and the dominance of a definition of security associated with the preservation of the sovereignty and territorial integrity of the nation state from (usually external and usually military) threat (see Buzan and Hansen 2009). If security is understood and approached in these terms, by extension the national security discourse as applied to climate change is one concerned with the extent to which climate change may pose a threat to the sovereignty and territorial integrity of the state. This would compel that state (and principally its security agencies) to take action

---

[5] Of course, such a distinction between discourses will necessarily be partial and reductionist, and at times risks eliding differences within these discourses and overlap between them. But it remains a useful heuristic device to understand *key* distinctions between approaches to climate change and security, and in providing foundation for the subsequent articulation and defence of ecological security.

to address that threat. In this discourse, the referent object is the state, the threat is (predominantly) an indirect one to the state's territorial integrity and sovereignty, the state retains its central role as security agent and security is to be realized primarily through adaptive responses to manifestations of climate change or the indirect threats arising from it.

Early engagement with the relationship between climate change and security generally oriented towards national security concerns. Here the focus was on the ways in which climate change might complicate states' future security planning and even contribute to axes of conflict and instability with which national security agencies were traditionally concerned. And while key climate security debates involved different central interlocutors to environmental security ones (as noted, public policy oriented think tanks as opposed to environmental organizations), both sets of contributors sought to speak directly to the policy concerns and capacities of states. This focus was despite the fact that climate change is, of course, a global challenge with origins in non-intentional everyday practices rather than the nefarious intentions of an external enemy.

For some cynics, as noted, concern with access to the resources of the state also informed attempts by state agencies themselves to point to the national security implications of climate change and, in the process, to their own capacity to provide security in the face of the threat posed by climate change to the nation state itself (see Floyd 2010). As early as the 1990s, the US Department of Defence has identified climate change as a possible threat, one that could undermine 'DoD's ability to pre-pare for or carry out the National Security Strategy or create instabil-ities that (could) threaten US National Security' (in Floyd 2010:89). Similar concerns have been articulated since by national security estab-lishments through the world, with Western developed states particu-larly focused on the national security implications of climate change (see Schäfer et al. 2016).

In this endeavour, such governments were actively encouraged by policy-oriented think tanks. In the United States alone, and around the highpoint of attention to the climate–security relationship in 2006–8, reports on the national security implications of climate change were produced by the CNA Corporation (CNA 2007), the Center for a New American Security (Burke and Parthemore eds. 2008), the Center for American Progress (Podesta and Ogden 2007–8), the Brookings

Institute (Campbell 2008) and the Council on Foreign Relations (Busby 2007). These all attempted to draw attention to the need for the US Government generally, and the Defence establishment specifically, to take seriously the likely role of climate change as a 'threat multiplier' (CNA 2007:5). Representatives of some think tanks, both within the US and beyond, also sought to publish work in academic journals making the case that climate change posed a threat to national security (see, e.g., Busby 2008; Dupont 2008). Academic literature itself began to address these dynamics too, although arguably has focused less on 'agenda-setting' than exploring specific pathways between the manifestations of climate change on one hand and specific challenges to the state on the other (see, e.g., Selby and Hoffman eds. 2017).

## The Threat

In the national security discourse, the threat associated with climate change is predominantly an indirect one, in which manifestations of climate change might contribute to dynamics that threaten the sovereignty and territorial integrity of the nation state. While distilling a significant literature – encompassing government publications and policy statements, think tank briefs and academic analysis – into a key set of themes is challenging, we can arguably discern three key claims about the ways in which climate change poses a challenge to national security: in increasing the likelihood of armed conflict, in encouraging destabilizing population movements and in undermining the capacity of the state and its security apparatus.

Of literature linking climate change and armed conflict, two forms of conflict are broadly envisaged: civil conflict and (more rarely) interstate conflict. In the former, climate change is viewed as a potential trigger for civil conflict in two key ways. In the first, climate-induced deprivation, deterioration or natural disasters – droughts leading to agricultural decline and, in turn, economic and health problems, for example – may create conditions ripe for citizens attempting to confront and overthrow the government. More nuanced accounts note that for this dynamic to induce civil conflict, it would ultimately need to coincide with existing sets of economic challenges, political and social grievances and/or weak institutions (see Selby and Hoffman eds. 2017). Civil violence in Mali, the ongoing conflict in Syria and the broader Arab Spring movements are frequently invoked as manifestations of this form of climate-induced conflict (see CNA 2014; Dunlop and Spratt 2017:13; Werrell et al. 2017), even if the role of climate change is significantly contested in these cases (see Selby et al. 2017).

In the second image of civil conflict linked to climate change, climate-induced deprivation, deterioration or natural disasters create a context in which population displacement brings groups into contact and ultimately conflict with each other. This brings with it the risk of deterioration into broader civil conflict, contributing to loss of life, state fragility and state failure. Indeed, as noted, both the UNEP (2007) and the UN Secretary-General (Moon 2007) tied ongoing conflict in Darfur to manifestations of climate change that had triggered, even driven, population displacement (see also Brown et al. 2007; Mazo 2010: chapter 3).

On interstate conflict, many of the themes of earlier environmental conflict literature are evident in attempts to point to the potential for interstate war. To reiterate, the imagined pathway here is one in which a climate-induced increase in demand and decrease in supply for a resource (like freshwater, for example) leads to accelerated resource extraction or manipulation, triggering contestation and even conflict. This pathway has been linked to future transboundary water wars and conflict over access to resources found in the global 'commons', such as fishing stocks in oceans (see Gleick 1993; Miller 2000). In his recent analysis of the security implications of climate change, for example, Joshua Busby (2018) sees the potential for tension and future conflict over access to the waters of the Indus, the Mekong and the Nile, and over a scramble for resources in the Arctic. While these accounts are often linked to concern for international security (to be discussed), they also suggest the need for states to prepare themselves for threats to their national interests and even their territorial integrity.

While the threat and use of force commands a central place in considerations of security and, in particular, national security, it is telling that even those states and think tanks that have embraced a national security discourse have been reluctant to directly tie the threat of invasion or attack to climate change. In part, this reflects the difficulty of establishing causal connections between climate change and conflict: the threat, as noted, is an indirect one in which climate change is viewed less as a threat than a 'threat multiplier'.

The second core claim linking climate change to security in the national security discourse is one already noted as a pathway to conflict above – the potential role of climate change in contributing to (large-scale) population movements (see Methmann and Oels 2015:55–6; Oels 2015). For an increasing number of states, the unauthorized or unpredicted arrival of immigrants is viewed as a national security concern (see Boas 2015). For these states, and analysts engaging with this agenda, climate change risks triggering large-scale (and potentially rapid) population displacement (see Myers and Kent 1995; Nansen Initiative 2015). This could be triggered in an immediate sense through either natural disasters – likely to increase in both frequency and severity in the context of climate change – or rising sea levels causing displacement. And, of course, in the longer term, population displacement may result from the loss of arable or indeed inhabitable land through drought, desertification, changing rainfall patterns or water scarcity (see Gleick 2014).

While a range of (particularly Western) countries have expressed concern about the possibility of 'climate refugees', Australia is a particularly illuminating example here, as contributions to a government inquiry into the national security implications of climate change attest. As contributors noted, Australia has a tradition of viewing the issue of unauthorized arrival of asylum-seekers (especially those arriving by boat) through the lens of national security (see McDonald 2021). The Australian Government has formally declared – in the face of the arrival of asylum-seekers arriving by boat – that full control over the movement of people into the country is central to Australia's sovereignty and security; has deployed military forces to intercept boats and prevent them from arriving in Australia; and has used extended offshore detention of asylum-seekers as a means to deter others from attempting to reach Australia this way (Gelber and McDonald 2006). Indeed many have described this example as a key example – even a paradigmatic illustration – of securitization (see McMaster 2002; McDonald 2008, 2011).

In Australia's case, added to the tendency to view irregular population movements through the lens of national security is the fact that its immediate geographical region is particularly vulnerable to manifestations of climate change that may lead to displacement. Low-lying Pacific Island states (such as Kiribati and Tuvalu) are likely to be affected by rising sea levels (see Nansen Initiative 2015), while the region more broadly has been significantly affected by natural disasters, such as cyclones. Indeed, by one recent assessment, the Asia-Pacific is home to 70 per cent of the world's countries most vulnerable to climate change and associated natural disasters, with over forty million people displaced in 2010–11 alone (ADB 2012:viii). While these disasters more directly and clearly pose a threat to those people and their states, this is also viewed as a potential threat to Australia's national security. Indeed this concern – of the danger of large-scale population displacement – emerged as one of the key themes across a range of submissions to Australia's 2017 national inquiry.

Finally, climate change has been presented as a threat to national security more directly in the sense of its potential role in undermining the security capacity of the state and in particular its security apparatus. This has been a prominent theme in the way the US Department of Defence has approached climate change, for example (see Thomas 2017; Abrahams 2019). The concern here is usually twofold. First, defence and security infrastructure may be affected by changing climate conditions, undermining the material power resources of the state. While the immediate threat to low-lying military bases associated with rising sea levels would be acknowledged here, some analysts and policy practitioners have suggested that warmer temperatures generally and natural disasters specifically also risk undermining states' equipment and infrastructure (see Dupont 2008; CNA 2014; MoD 2015; Ruttinger et al. 2015).

Second, changing environmental conditions, operating environments and mission demands for military operations have all been represented as threatening. While conceived less as a direct security threat than as a threat to the state's security capacity, one prominent argument here (following the above) is that manifestations of climate change such as higher temperatures are likely to require potentially costly and significant updating and upgrading of both equipment and infrastructure. Others point out that the increasing demand on military resources to assist with missions related to climate manifestations – such as disaster relief and humanitarian assistance missions – will necessitate changes in equipment acquisition and maintenance along with personnel training (see Thomas 2017; McDonald 2021). The role of the Pakistani military in responding to floods, the US military in responding to hurricanes and European militaries in responding to forest fires – natural disasters likely to increase in frequency and intensity in the context of climate change – point to increasing domestic demands on militaries to aid community responses (Bergin et al. 2013; Sturrock and Ferguson 2015; Dunlop and Spratt 2017). When combined with an increase in international humanitarian assistance and disaster relief missions, these dynamics also – for some analysts – risk undermining the extent to which militaries are readily available for more traditional commitments associated with the defence of the territorial integrity of the state (see Sturrock and Ferguson 2015; Dunlop and Spratt 2017).

This discussion of the ways in which climate change is represented as a threat to national security points to a concern that climate change will trigger new axes of conflict, challenge the state's sovereignty and territorial integrity and undermine the material capacity of the state and its military to provide security. In a number of academic and policy-oriented analyses, these multiple different axes of national security threat are drawn together to paint a picture of looming challenges to the security of the state as traditionally understood (see, e.g., Dunlop and Spratt 2017). It is important to note here that while some of the same challenges associated with climate change are identified as security threats in subsequent discourses (conflict and displacement, for example), the nature of the threat posed and (crucially) the appropriate means of response are often approached in radically different ways.

## Means of Response

The focus in the national security discourse, evident in the previous discussion, is on the *indirect* implications of climate change. The immediate effects of climate change – rising temperatures, increasing frequency and intensity of natural disasters, rising sea levels, changing rainfall patterns and so on – are not in and of themselves generally conceived as security threats.[6] Rather, the focus is on how these dynamics might in turn trigger genuinely threatening developments, undermining the material security resources or capacity of the state or triggering instability, contestation and even war.

---

[6] Rising sea levels in the Pacific constitute a potential exception here, given implications for territory and sovereignty if states are inundated and/ or uninhabitable.

This is an important point to note in helping us make sense of the nature of responses to the climate-security threat in this discourse. Simply put, this focus on indirect implications of climate change associated with instability and conflict – and the nature of their challenge to the nation state – encourages a focus on means of providing security that address *manifestations* of climate change rather than its cause. Put another way, in the national security discourse, the focus is on adaptation rather than mitigation. In his discussion of the national security implications of climate change and responses to them, for example, Busby (2008:500) suggests that 'adaptation and disaster risk reduction strategies should be the priority response for climate security concerns . . .' Other interventions on effective responses to the national security implications of climate change focus on new forms of training and defence acquisition for militaries, forward strategic planning to identify future sites and forms of conflict, more effective management of border controls (in the face of climate-induced displacement) and risk management for defence infrastructure (see, e.g., CNA 2007; Podesta and Ogden 2007–8). With their focus on the development of adaptive capacity to manifestations of climate change, none of these suggested responses involves mitigation – the reduction of greenhouse gas emissions to minimize climate change and its effects. At best, the reduction of emissions as a response to climate insecurity is a by-product of a focus on how militaries can reduce exposure to the changing future availability of fossil-fuel sources (see Floyd 2010).

There is a case, of course, that a focus on the *national* security implications of climate change need not preclude an emphasis on the means through which the problem itself might be addressed at its cause. In articulating the nature of their response to the threat of fundamentalist Islamic terrorism, for example, a range of Western states have emphasized the role of deradicalization initiatives and the importance of creating open, inclusive and multicultural communities in which members of 'suspect communities' (see Breen-Smyth 2014) are less likely to engage in violent acts. While many of these initiatives have been controversial and appear to sit uneasily alongside other practices (from surveillance and extended detention to military interventions, for example, see McDonald 2009), they demonstrate the potential role of preventative measures focused on the origins of the problem rather than responding to manifestations of it (see also Aradau and Van Muster 2007; Horgan and Braddock 2010)

Certainly, a range of analytical accounts of the national security implications of climate change make the case for mitigation directly, while some states have sought to explicitly incorporate mitigation concerns into the climate security response. The UK's 'Whole of Government' response to climate insecurity constitutes one such example, in which significant mitigation commitments are viewed as a component of preparedness for climate insecurity alongside military training and defence acquisition initiatives. In its 2008 National Security Strategy statement, for example, it was noted that when it comes to climate change, 'tackling its causes, mitigating its risks and preparing for and dealing with its consequences are critical to our future security, as well protecting global prosperity and avoiding humanitarian disaster' (UK 2008:18 in Dalby 2009:151).

Yet this integrated approach is the exception rather than the rule. Overwhelmingly, the focus of a national security discourse is the need for military preparedness to better anticipate future axes of (climate-induced) conflict and the need to manage strategic resources in the face of new demands on defence resources. At its most perverse, as will be noted, suggested approaches to preserving national security in the face of climate change not only fail to address the problem of climate change but also risk presenting those most vulnerable to it as threats to national security.

## Agents of Security

In many ways, the question of means and agents of responding to insecurity are mutually reinforcing. The selection of a particular means of response suggests a primary role for a particular actor or set of actors in pursuing those initiatives. Similarly, if we are committed to a particular agent of security, the responses envisaged will largely (if not exclusively) map on to the expertise, capacities and practices of those actors (see Floyd 2015). Most accounts of national security ascribe primary (again, if not exclusive) responsibility for the provision of security to the state, and in particular to security agencies, defence establishments and the military. The above account of the means through which security is to be protected or advanced in the context of climate change clearly implies a central role for these agents.

For states and the military, their role is to ensure the territorial preservation of the nation state and the protection of its sovereignty in the face of threats arising (indirectly) from climate change. The imperative of preserving national borders, preparing for future conflict and ensuring the continued capacity of the state to respond to these challenges clearly positions the state and its military as agents capable of – indeed responsible for – providing (national) security. It is also in this context that broader assumptions about the nature of the international system and the possibility for action between and beyond states is perhaps most readily apparent. Consistent with realist assumptions about the nature of global politics, a national security discourse suggests a central role for states and their security agencies is crucial on that basis that states cannot realistically be expected to cooperate with each other (to pursue absolute gains in the context of climate change), that states are reliant on themselves to provide for their own (national) security and that states are the only consequential actors in the international system (see Walt 1991; Symons 2019a). It is also here that limits to this discourse in terms of the possibility of effectively addressing climate change are again readily apparent.

## Implications and Limitations

In the national security discourse, climate change is presented as an indirect threat to the territorial integrity and sovereignty of the nation state; the state itself (especially its security agencies, the defence establishment and the military) is the key agent through which security is to protected or advanced; and the means envisaged are adaptive responses to manifestations of climate change, with a focus on military preparedness and deployment.

For some, including those eager to see significant and concerted action on climate change, that states are beginning to take seriously the national security implications of climate change is necessarily a good thing (Bergin et al. 2013; CNA 2014). For many advocates of this link, whether explicitly noted or implicit to their analyses, the 'securitization' of climate change at the nation state level means an increase in attention, priority and funding for climate change (Mathews 1989). Some would also note that the national security framing has particular purchase in some contexts and is more likely to speak to or convince audiences within states who might otherwise be unmoved by the imperative to address this issue on behalf of vulnerable outsiders (see McDonald 2013a; Hayes and Knox-Hayes 2014; Dalby 2015a; Diez et al. 2016). Finally, and following both of the above points, addressing this challenge to the key actors and agencies in global politics – states and their security agencies – ensures built-in policy relevance and the promise of drawing on significant state capacity to address the challenge itself.

It is clearly appropriate to consider and prepare for manifestations of climate change – that Western states are increasingly engaging with the question of how to prepare military equipment, infrastructure and personnel for addressing more frequent and severe natural disasters is a good thing. But this cannot be the only means through which climate change is viewed as a threat and certainly not the primary means. As this book suggests, the effects of approaching climate change as a security threat are a product of the choices made in the first instance about whose security matters, and following this from what threats, by what means and through what agents it is to be protected or advanced. In concluding this discussion of the national security discourse, this section identifies key limitations of this discourse in terms of its ethical assumptions and, in particular, its ethical and practical implications. While viewing and addressing climate change as a national security threat may mobilize some resources and audiences, viewing and addressing it through this lens primarily risks encouraging limited, partial and even perverse responses to climate change.

There is, of course, a broad literature on the ethical limitations of traditional nation-state oriented accounts of security. As broadly cosmopolitan accounts have long argued (see Booth 1991, 2007; Burke et al. 2014, 2016), it is difficult to justify the ethical primacy granted to the nation state and fellow citizens, not least as these moral containers are historically recent developments in the human experience; have been arbitrarily constructed and endorsed; deny common membership in the human race (evident elsewhere in commitments to universal principles associated with human rights, for example); and belie substantial international inequalities while justifying and legitimizing these inequalities through endorsing a focus on obligations to the nation state and fellow citizens. Yet ethical limitations are particularly acute in the context of climate change.

Clearly, in focusing on the nation state and its protection from manifestations of climate change, the (ecological) conditions of human survival are presented as separate from security, even (at its most extreme and perverse) as a threat to it (see Kaplan 1994). This separation between humanity and nature, central to modern thought and the discourses of climate security to be discussed in this chapter, is increasingly problematic in the context of the Anthropocene and the particular challenge posed by climate change, as noted (see Harrington and Shearing 2017). While this broad separation is questionable on ethical grounds, not least given the rejection of responsibility to future generations or other living beings, the (communitarian) ethics of drawing ethical boundaries at the nation state is particularly problematic here. Climate change is an inherently global problem, in which national action is insufficient, in which nation states and existing institutions could readily be viewed as part of the problem of climate change and responses to it and even significant unilateral action by states will be insufficient for addressing what is a genuinely transnational and global challenge (see, e.g., Dalby 2009). Like national security discourses broadly, ethical limitations in failing to recognize obligations to outsiders makes it difficult, if not impossible, to imagine effective responses to challenges that transcend boundaries. In the case of climate change, populations of developing states, for example, are excluded from moral consideration in the national security discourses of developed states, while simultaneously being least responsible for the problem and most vulnerable to manifestations of it.

As noted, if viewed through the lens of national security, responses to climate change risk being partial, limited and even perverse. In the context of climate change already being locked in, and a current temperature increase of at least 1 degree Celsius from pre-Industrial levels, a focus on the ways in which people and communities might be in a position to adapt to manifestations of climate change is appropriate. Yet in the national security discourse, adaptation is limited to the particular nation state (not capacity-building for outsiders), while downplaying or excluding mitigation efforts also means a failure to address the problem itself and address the threat to vulnerable communities, beyond the state and even within it.

One particular set of responses to the national security implications of climate change is illustrative here of the problematic ethics underpinning, and perverse practices encouraged by, this approach: border control. In a 2003 Pentagon report on the national security implications of an abrupt climate-change scenario, the authors distinguished between relatively self-sufficient states that might be resilient in the face of the immediate onset of climate change: a product of state capacity, geography and/or ecological context. The report noted that populations of less resilient states (located primarily in the developing world) may be displaced in an abrupt climate-change scenario through a combination of rising sea levels, natural disasters or loss of livelihoods. It further noted that in this context, more climate-resilient states (such as the United States) might seek to build effective boundaries to prevent those displaced by climate change from reaching and/ or penetrating the boundaries of the state (Schwartz and Randall 2003; see also Dalby 2009).

The above example would clearly constitute a perverse response to climate change. A global problem would be viewed in national terms, the responses envisaged will not address the problem itself and those most vulnerable to manifestations of climate change would be viewed as threats to (national) security. While an extreme example, however, it is a response ultimately consistent with the ethics and logics of a national security discourse in which the primary concern is with the sovereignty and territorial integrity of the nation state in the face of manifestations of climate change contributing to these challenges. Contemporary border politics in Western states – from European and Australian efforts to deter asylum-seekers and outsource asylum obligations to the Trump administration's commitment to the construction of a border wall in the United States to prevent irregular migration from Mexico – also suggests a context in which those displaced by climate change might indeed be viewed in such terms (see White 2011). A number of accounts even suggest that India's efforts to construct more effective physical barriers on the border with Bangladesh can indeed be viewed – at least in part – as an effort to prevent an influx of people displaced by flooding from that country, likely to increase in the context of climate change (Banerjee 2010; Chaturvedi and Doyle 2015:122–6).

Ultimately, the ethics and politics of a national security discourse of climate change are fundamentally problematic. Approaching climate change in these terms might mobilize concern for some audiences (Hayes and Knox-Hayes 2014) and have the potential to encourage some useful practices (more effective national preparedness for natural disasters, for example). Yet the problem itself is not addressed, and the necessary whole-of-society and global response to this challenge is evinced in favour of a focus of what the state and its military establishment can do to respond to manifestations of climate change. Such a discourse encourages us to view those most immediately vulnerable to climate change (other living beings, for example) as external to our moral considerations and associated responses, even as potential threats to our national security (those displaced by climate change, for example). While having built-in policy relevance and potentially tapping in to the significant capacity of the state, the responses to climate change this discourse encourages are insufficiently attuned to the rights and needs of the most vulnerable and are inconsistent with addressing the problem of climate change.

## Climate Change and International Security

A focus on the *international* security implications of climate change is an obvious response to the necessarily limited and partial focus on the nature of the threat it poses to nation states. If one of the key limitations of the national security discourse is its focus on the nation state in the face of a genuinely transnational or global problem, a pivot to emphasize the challenges climate change poses to the international system or even international community would seem an appropriate correction, one enabling a focus on cooperative responses to the problem of climate change itself.

A focus on the international security implications of climate change has a less immediately obvious political constituency, especially if Realists are right to reject a meaningful role in global politics for actors or institutions beyond (or, of course, below) the state (see Mearsheimer 1995). Yet this focus has been evident in a range of accounts of the security implications of climate change (e.g., Purvis and Busby 2004; Smith and Vivekananda 2007; Jasparro and Taylor 2008; Garcia 2010; Dodo 2014). And when the climate–security relationship has featured in discussions in international organizations such as the UN Security Council and General Assembly, and in reports from organizations such as the United Nations Environment Programme, the focus on threats to *international* security has been particularly evident. It has also been a point of emphasis for a range of states, especially those eager to see substantive international cooperation and action on climate change and those states that have actively promoted the discussion of climate change in the UN system (e.g., UK, Germany and Sweden; see Maertens 2021). Following this emphasis, it is striking that think tanks with affiliations (or locations) within these (largely European) states also focus more overwhelmingly on international rather than national security, mapping likely future treats to international stability or international institutions and recommending a course of action for a range of states and institutions in responding to these threats (see, e.g., WGBU 2007; Dalby 2015a; Nansen Initiative 2015).

As noted, the designation of the nation state as the referent object of security does not wholly settle or clarify questions of whose security is at stake. We may disagree on the values ascribed to that particular nation state, for example. Yet questions of how to define the referent object of security in terms of 'international' security are more vexed and contested still. Indeed, analysts are right to note the need for suspicion about any claims to represent or protect an 'international community', for example (see Buzan and Gonzalez-Palaez 2005). These are often best viewed as attempts to ascribe a commonality and unanimity of purpose and support for a particular political agenda that are frequently, if not always, missing from the 'international'. In the context of this book and this discussion of international security, I do not attempt to settle or categorically define the 'international' as referent object. Rather, I develop an account that can come to terms with the inherent contestability of the 'international' and in particular the 'international community'. Ultimately, and drawing on English School scholarship (see Dunne 1998), I suggest that the referent object of security in an international security discourse is 'international society', characterized by shared rules and norms of behaviour among states in the international system. As this society is characterized by contestation over the scope and force of those rules and norms, this approach is productive in simultaneously allowing us to account for differences across states while retaining a focus on overarching accounts of an 'international society' whose security is challenged by climate change.

## The Threat

English School accounts of international society suggest that this society of states with a commitment to shared rules and norms is rarely (if ever) settled and is characterized by a core tension between concerns with order or justice (see Bull 1995; Dunne 1998). This is most famously captured by Hedley Bull (1995) in his distinction between pluralist and solidarist accounts of international society. The argument Bull and others advance is that a pluralist account is focused on a concern with the preservation of international order characterized by a shared commitment to sovereignty defined as non-intervention. In this minimalist vision of international society, the agreed principles of that society extend no further than a principle of non-interference (see Jackson 1992). In a solidarist account, meanwhile, international society is viewed as extending to a shared commitment to international justice, in which states can agree on common and universal ethical principles. Advocates of this maximalist vision of international society suggest that the possibility of extending that society to focus on justice has already been validated with a shared commitment to universal human rights (Wheeler and Dunne 1996; Wheeler 2000). For proponents, this shared commitment is evident in the 1948 Universal Declaration on Human Rights and more recently with the unanimous adoption of the Responsibility to Protect (R2P) principle by the UN General Assembly in 2005.[7] This principle constitutes a direct challenge to the minimalist vision of sovereignty and international society, rejecting the idea that recognized statehood enables states themselves to insulate themselves from international criticism and/or sanction (see Bellamy 2014). These two distinct visions of international society amount to different accounts, for our purposes, of who or what is in need of protecting.

The tension between pluralist and solidarist approaches to international society is evident in distinct accounts of the international security implications of climate change and (by extension) the question of who or what requires protection. In a minimalist vision of international security, the central concern is the possibility that climate change will trigger large-scale population movements, instability and/or conflict: a similar agenda to the national security discourse. In this international security discourse, these dynamics constitute a threat to international security to the extent that they pose a threat to the core principle of sovereignty – defined as non-intervention – and the imperative of maintaining international order and stability. This more

---

[7] On the pluralist–solidarist divide in English School thought, see, e.g., Dunne (1998); Bull (1995); John Williams (2005); Linklater and Suganami (2006); Buzan (2004:139–60). As applied to international security, see Bellamy and McDonald (2004); Buzan (2015); Paul Williams (2004).

minimalist vision was evident in the 2011 UN Security Council Presidential statement on the international security implications of climate change, in which it was affirmed that climate change should be considered by the Council 'when such issues are drivers of conflict, represent a challenge to the implementation of Council mandates, or endanger the process of consolidation of peace' (UNSC 2011b:2). It is also evident in analytical accounts that tie (international) security to stability and the absence of conflict (see Purvis and Busby 2004:72).

A maximalist vision of international security differs from this account in two respects. First, while instability and conflict arising from climate change are recognized as potential international security threats, these dynamics are threatening to the extent that they constitute a challenge to core universal principles and norms beyond sovereignty (defined as non-intervention): to imperatives and principles associated with human rights, development and health, for example. Second, a maximalist vision of international security extends beyond conflict and instability to the direct threat climate change poses to communities. In this account, natural disasters and rising sea levels can be viewed as a *direct* threat, not only when leading to instability and conflict. Such an account moves this (maximalist) discourse of international security closer to a human security discourse, to be discussed. It is evident in Jasparro and Taylor's (2008:223) account of climate change as a transnational security threat, characterized as threats 'that cross borders and either threaten the political and social integrity of a state or the health and quality of life of its inhabitants'. Indeed, for them, and consistent with the framing of climate security discourses in this chapter, what they define as a 'transnational' security threat operates 'at the intersection of often competing notions of human security and traditional understandings of state/ national security' (Jasparro and Taylor 2008:223).

Ultimately, the dominant account of threat in the international security discourse depicts climate change as potentially threatening international stability. As noted, similar pathways to those envisaged in the national security discourse, wherein climate change renders large-scale and destabilizing population movements, internal conflict and even transboundary warfare more likely, are viewed as key threats to international security presented by climate change (McLeman 2011; Nansen Initiative 2015). In the context of population movements, for example, one prominent argument is that large-scale displacement can have the effect of challenging existing international norms and institutions associated with managing population movements and asylum, for example (see Biermann and Boas 2010). This argument was prominent in the wake of significant displacement and population movement associated with conflict in Syria, itself linked to climate change (see Baker 2015). Here, concerns were raised that the scale of population movement in this instance (over one million irregular migrants to Europe in 2015 alone) raised the possibility that national, regional and international organizations would revisit their interpretation of and commitment to pre-existing norms and rules around the management of migrants and asylum-seekers (Greenhill 2016). In this sense, norms and rules themselves could be challenged by key manifestations of climate change.

But if the nature of the threat in national and international security discourses bears similarity, the different choice of referent object – the international society as a whole and its constitutive norms and rules – has implications for the way in which both agents and means of response are conceived and approached. The inability to close off or insulate 'international society' from manifestations such as population movements or conflict – a dynamic evident in some accounts of national security – ultimately equates to a more prominent role for two forms of response. The first of these is prevention. If we cannot 'close off' a polity from external threats triggered by climate change, there is, by extension, an increased role for prevention – in this case, mitigation action. Second, given the necessity of international coordination to manage both mitigation efforts and large-scale disruption associated with regional conflict, instability or large-scale population movements, there is a more significant role for international negotiation and cooperation as a means of response.

## Means of Response

The international security discourse positions a combination of mitigation and adaptation measures as appropriate means of responding to the security implications of climate change, with international cooperation central to pursuing both.

The focus on adaptation in this discourse operates at two levels. Most prominently, the first level of adaptation focuses on the specific management of or response to already existing crises related to climate change. This is broadly consistent with the concerns of the UN Security Council. For the most part the organization responds to instances of conflict, violence and instability. The focus here is on international cooperation and coordination to manage instability already evident and/or conflict taking place. This may take the (traditional) form of securing a ceasefire, coordinating negotiations between competing groups and their representatives, keeping the peace on the ground or even coordinating an external intervention (see Scott 2015; Maertens 2021). The latter concern has, of course, been one reason that a range of states have been suspicious of the Security Council's recent discussions of climate change and its security implications (see Eckersley 2007; Hulme 2009; Conca et al. 2017). Indeed, to return to the 'international society' theme, it is telling here that those states most suspicious of – even opposed to – the discussion of international security within the Security Council are non-Western states with a traditional suspicion of an expansive and universalist vision of international society, led by China and Russia (see Scott 2015; Conca 2019; Maertens 2021).

The second means of adaptive response in this discourse is a more traditional focus on building capacity within states to ensure they are better able to deal with the immediate effects of climate change without these effects leading to the types of destabilizing dynamics (population movements and conflict) noted earlier. Traditional development assistance programs are seen as a component of this – as a means of minimizing or warding off state fragility – alongside international programs (such as the Green Climate Fund, for example) directly contributing towards the development of climate resilience (Vanderheiden 2015). A role for this form of response to climate change and the imperative of building resilience in vulnerable communities, often coordinated through UN agencies such as the UNFCCC or the UNDP, is also recognized in the human security discourse, to be discussed (see Matthew et al. eds. 2010).

For its part, the Security Council has, in recent years, also embraced a more proactive role in anticipating and identifying fragility and possible axes of future conflict (see Beardsley et al. 2017). This is evident in the context of the responsibility to protect, for example, with the UNSC increasingly focusing on a prevention agenda and the need to address large-scale violence before it arises (Woocher 2012; Sharma and Welsh eds. 2015). Indeed, in a manner more consistent with a maximalist (solidarist) vision of international society and international security, and drawing explicitly on the 'responsibility to protect' principle, some analysts have suggested the possibility of applying the 'responsibility to protect' principle to climate change (Eckersley 2007; Werrell et al. 2017). Advocates here suggest the need to think of preparation for climate change in terms of a 'responsibility to prepare', focused on climate-proofing security institutions and building a resilient world order in the face of likely security impacts (Werrell et al. 2017).

While adaptive responses to the security implications of climate change are therefore key means of response envisaged in an international security discourse, mitigation efforts are also viewed as playing a significant role. This reflects the inability to wholly protect a self-contained polity from insecurity in the face of a global problem such as climate change. The emphasis here is on negotiation and cooperation, facilitated and coordinated by international instruments such as the UNFCCC. Similarly, technology transfers generally, and the resources provided through the Green Climate Fund specifically, are viewed as means to help developing states transition to low-carbon economies and modes of development less reliant on the burning of fossil fuels.

Simply put, this discourse recognizes the need to focus on measures that try to prevent climate change from taking place or at least minimize the destabilizing effects of climate change through limiting the scale of rises in the global temperature (see also Detraz and Betsill 2009). And while practices of geoengineering (removing greenhouse gases from the atmosphere or managing solar radiation) will be addressed in more detail in Chapter 4 (as a means of advancing ecological security), there is arguably a role here too for these interventions in this discourse.[8]

While discussion of geoengineering as a means of addressing the international security implications of climate change has not been prominent thus far, the combination of adaption and mitigation-oriented responses is evident in a range of accounts. In an International Alert report focused on the international security implications of climate

---

[8] The importance- and challenges- of managing and regulating geoengineering projects, and agreeing on principles that might inform that management and regulation, also suggests a central role for international organizations as agents of security in this context. See Rayner et al. (2013); Symons (2019).

change, some forty states are deemed 'at risk' of climate-induced conflict. Crucially, in the process of making this case, the authors argue simultaneously for the development of adaptive capacity *and* for a rapid transition to low-carbon economies globally (Smith and Vivekananda 2007). Purvis and Busby (2004), meanwhile, suggest that measures oriented towards managing the international security implications of climate change need to focus simultaneously on strengthening mitigation cooperation through the UNFCCC system and monitoring and coordinating responses to future climate-induced conflict through the UN Security Council. In recent work, the Center for Climate and Security has argued that institutions of international security have a 'responsibility to prepare and prevent' in the face of climate change, suggesting a role for both mitigation and adaptation (Werrell and Femia 2016). The simultaneous endorsement of mitigation and adaptation is ultimately a key component of this international security discourse and stands in contrast to the national security focus on the latter.

## Agents of Security

To reiterate a claim made in the preceding discussion of the national security discourse, means of response and agents of security are often mutually constitutive. While the imperative of self-help and management of threats to sovereignty and territorial integrity seemed to compel a focus on what the state and its security establishment could do to secure national security in the face of climate change, the imperative of international cooperation and coordination suggests a central role for international organizations in the context of the international security discourse. Indeed, much of the preceding discussion of means has already identified actors (principally international organizations) deemed as having capacity – even responsibility – for addressing the security threats associated with climate change.[9]

If coordination and cooperation between states is central to responding to a transnational security threat of a genuinely international scale, it stands to reason that instruments and institutions of global governance will play a central role in managing that cooperation. This

---

[9] The nature of responsibility, defined predominantly in terms of capability, will be addressed in Chapter 3.

clearly applies at the level of mitigation, with the UNFCCC taking responsibility for providing a forum in which states can discuss climate mitigation efforts and develop agreements on mitigation targets and timetables. Of course, states still play a central role in this schema: it is ultimately states that pursue substantive mitigation policies and actions, with the UNFCCC serving to develop equitable mitigation targets and timetables commensurate with (complex assessments of ) responsibility (see Ruth 2005:166–76; Bulkeley et al. 2014).

On instability and even conflict arising from climate change, the UNSC has taken on an increasingly prominent role in this space since climate change was first discussed as an international security concern in 2007. Since then, negotiations have taken place in 2011, 2018, 2019, 2020 and 2021, and through informal Arria-formula meetings from 2013. As noted, negotiations within the UNSC have been telling for their different visions of international society and the associated appropriateness of the UNSC's role. While Western states largely sponsored and supported these discussions, and were joined in this position by particularly vulnerable developing states, others objected to the discussions (Scott 2015; Conca 2019).

Even those states most critical of the discussion of climate change as an international security issue within the UNSC, however, did not reject the importance or imperative of international cooperation: most have affirmed the continued primacy of the UNFCCC as the key instrument for managing responses to climate change. In 2007, the Chinese representative noted that 'discussing climate change in the Security Council will not help countries in their efforts towards mitigation ... discussions on climate change should be conducted within a framework accessible to all parties' (UNSC 2007:13). In 2011, meanwhile, the representative of Costa Rica argued that the 'most substantial and decisive actions ... are outside the Council's mandate, and ... should be addressed in accordance with the provisions of the (UNFCCC)' (UNSC 2011a:5). And in 2019, the Indian delegate warned of the dangers of securitizing climate change through discussing it in the UNSC, suggesting that 'thinking in security terms usually engenders overly militarized solutions to problem that inherently require non-military responses to resolve them' (in Maertens 2021). In these contexts, it was not the idea of an international society in need of protection nor even the notion that climate change constituted an international security threat that was questioned: rather the scope of that society, the role of particular institutions as security agents and the appropriateness of particular forms of response (see Croucher and McDonald 2014; Maertens 2021).

In short, key agents of security in the international security discourse are international institutions. These institutions have a role in coordinating and managing the policy and practical responses of states in terms of mitigation efforts (even potentially geoengineering projects) and monitoring and pursuing cooperative responses to instances of conflict and instability (see Moncel and Assalt 2012). Clearly, the central role for these institutions reflects the scale of the problem as presented in this discourse – a genuinely international and transboundary problem necessitating coordination and cooperation by way of response. As Purvis and Busby (2004:72) note, 'climate change will trigger profound global change, and these changes could pose genuine risks to international peace and security. Managing these changes will require well-conceived actions within the UN system'.

## Implications and Limitations

Clearly, the shift to focus on the *international* security implications of climate change is more consistent with recognition of the scale of the issue and the necessity for responses beyond that of an individual nation state. Indeed it raises the prospects of a genuinely international response to the issue targeted (at least substantially) towards addressing the issue itself. To a significant degree, as noted, this follows from recognition of the impossibility of insulating an 'international polity' in any form from the manifestations of climate change. And while this discourse is less immediately able to tap in to the significant security and defence resources and capacity of the state,[10] its resonance with the existing remit of key international institutions ensures some degree of practical purchase and support. Indeed the trajectory and frequency of climate change and international security discussions in the UNSC since 2007 suggests increasing acceptance of the international security implications of climate change at the highest levels of global governance.

---

[10] Though, as noted, some states (e.g., UK, Germany) have explicitly embraced an international security focus and sought to fund research and projects consistent with this emphasis.

Yet this discourse has important limitations in addressing the challenge of climate change, particularly to the extent that it encourages or allows the type of fundamental changes arguably required to respond effectively and equitably to climate change. With the focus here on the preservation of international order and stability, questions necessarily arise about the extent to which that order, or even international society more broadly, is worth preserving. The first article of the UN Charter commits the organization – as its core purpose – to the maintenance of international peace and security (see Conca 2015, 2019). While clearly an ambition preferable to large-scale loss of life witnessed in the world wars of the twentieth century (the context of this article and the formation of the UN itself), and potentially relevant to at least some of the implications of climate change, the commitment to the status quo inherent in this article is problematic on at least two fronts.

First, it arguably predisposes institutions of global governance (in particular the United Nations) to respond to disruption rather than pursue the type of transformation that might be necessary to address the problem of climate change, or a host of other transnational challenges (see Burke et al. 2014). We can realistically expect that the imperative of radically altering patterns of development and economic exchange, or sites and actors involved in securing international agreement and action, would be less likely to come from those institutions that authored and facilitate these arrangements. Indeed, for some analysts, the nature of the international system and international society – the veneration of states and their sovereignty along with a particular (liberal) conception of development and economic exchange – have either rendered any meaningful and coordinated response to climate change acutely difficult or have driven the problem of climate change itself (see Dalby 2009; Burke et al. 2016). And in committing to the maintenance of existing institutions, dynamics and practices, this discourse clearly risks endorsing and validating sources of inequality and/or vulnerability.

Second, the commitment to the preservation of international society in the context of climate change – especially if understood in terms of the maintenance of international stability – positions the acute vulnerability of some populations to climate change as problematic only if this ultimately contributes to instability and disruption. In this discourse, unlike the human security discourse to be discussed, the direct threat that manifestations of climate change pose to human populations is not necessarily recognized as a challenge requiring a response. And, of course, building on this, this discourse pays scant attention to the rights and needs of future generations or other living beings – those most vulnerable to manifestations of climate change.

The ethical limits and problematic practical implications of this discourse are, of course, less evident and concerning in the case of a more maximalist vision of international society. In a solidarist account of international society, in which rules and (in particular) norms of that society extend to those oriented to justice rather than simply order, we can envisage a more central role for mitigation, recognition of the need to address the particular vulnerability of some populations and recognition of the direct effects of climate change on human populations. But aside from the challenges of securing agreement about that vision, one directly evident in debates within the UN Security Council about climate change, there remains a commitment to the international system in some form, in ways that can (if they do not already) constitute limits to responding to climate change. The scope of contemporary debates about and practices associated with R2P is a case in point. The international endorsement of this principle represents a significant development: a revision of norms and even moral boundaries that remind us that these can change and shift towards concerns with international justice (see Bellamy 2014). Yet the conditions in which concern with human rights practices in other states has precipitated large-scale intervention consistent with R2P have been largely limited to genocide.[11] Applied to climate change, it would be reasonable to expect that even if endorsing an expansive definition of international society's constitutive norms, it might only be those instances in which climate change leads to large-scale disruption and loss of life – rather than the everyday diminution of life prospects and chances for vulnerable populations affected by climate change – that trigger concerted international action.

In short, the danger and limitations of an international security discourse are that the practices encouraged will be oriented primarily towards the maintenance of an international status quo in which adaptive responses still take precedence over mitigation. And this international society is also one with inbuilt limitations in addressing

---

[11] And, as critics note, even then only in some instances. See, e.g., Hehir (2011, 2013).

climate change, some degree of responsibility for driving it, and characterized by endemic inequality and differential vulnerability.

## Climate Change and Human Security

If the international security discourse partly corrects the tendency to focus exclusively on the preservation of sovereignty and territorial integrity, and at least recognizes the global scope of the problem itself that necessitates coordination and cooperation across the international system, it is the human security discourse that seeks to decouple the way we think about security from the preservation of existing institutions. This is the third (and final) discourse of climate security to be discussed in this chapter.

The human security discourse has been increasingly prominent in accounts of the security implications of climate change. While articulated and endorsed by critical international relations scholars (see, e.g., O'Brien 2006; Barnett and Adger 2007; Matthew et al. eds. 2010), a focus on the human security implications of climate change was evident in the 2014 IPCC report. This featured a chapter specifically on the human security implications of climate change, featuring lead authors with a research profile in the field of international relations. A range of states have also indicated a concern with and commitment to human security in this context, as evident in the Norwegian government's sponsorship of a large research project committed to exploring global environmental change and human security (Matthew et al. eds. 2010). In 2009, the UN General Assembly Report, Climate Change and its Possible Security Implications, explicitly identified its focus as 'the security of individuals and communities' (UNGA 2009a). In 2007, meanwhile, the UN Development Program's analysis of human security (UNDP 2007) included an extended discussion of climate change as a direct threat to human welfare.

The UNDP's attempt to draw attention to the human security implications of climate change followed their earlier role in developing the 'human security' concept itself. In its 1994 Human Development Report, the UNDP (1994) argued that it was time to move away from approaching security exclusively as the protection of states from the threat and use of force, arguing instead for prioritizing the welfare of people and pursuing both freedom from fear and freedom from want. The latter in particular aligned with the UNDP's concern with promoting international development (see also Page and Redclift eds. 2002), while its purchase in both academic debates and especially political practice followed the new post–Cold War hope for redefining security and prioritizing a range of transnational challenges. Indeed the discourse itself was taken up and embraced by a range of states, including Canada, Norway and Japan (see Paris 2001; McDonald 2002). In its initial formulation, environmental security was recognized as a core component of human security, with climate change identified as a potential direct threat to 'human life and dignity' (UNDP 1994:22).

## What's the Threat?

In their extended discussion of the ways in which environmental change generally could be seen as a threat to human security, analysts associated with the Global Environmental Change and Human Security project defined human security as a situation in which

[i]ndividuals and communities have the options necessary to end, mitigate or adapt to threats to their human, environmental and social rights; have the capacity and freedom to exercise these options; and actively participate in pursuing these options. (Barnett et al. 2010:18)

This represents climate change not only as a direct threat to security but also suggests that existing political, economic and social structures and dynamics of inequality condition the vulnerability of communities (see Dalby 2009:110–12). In situations where groups are already marginalized or economically vulnerable, the effects of climate change are likely to be more immediate and severe. These theorists ultimately argued that 'a holistic and wide-ranging concept such as human security provides a strong basis for developing an integrated view of the multifaceted relationship between material climatic condition and effects, global structures of inequality and community-based understandings of core values in need of protection and adaptive capacity at their disposal' (McDonald 2013a:46). In this discourse, the threat of climate change can be direct, but making sense of the particular vulnerabilities of people and the communities of which they are a part requires an understanding of the broad array of factors that help constitute vulnerability. These extend beyond immediate exposure to manifestations of climate change (see also Barnett and Adger 2007;

Barnett et al. 2010:24; Kumssa and Jones 2010). As Fisher (2011:293) argues, immediate and direct challenges associated with climate change 'merge with preexisting vulnerabilities, creating a hybridized force that ripples through every aspect of society and threatens human security'. These points suggest an important role not only for mitigation efforts but also adaptation.

While the direct threat of climate change to (vulnerable) human communities is emphasized in this discourse, there nonetheless remains a concern with some of the same sets of threats as those identified in the international and even the national security discourse: displacement, instability and even conflict. Here, however, the emphasis is not the flow on effects such dynamics may have for sovereignty, territorial integrity or regional/international stability, but the immediate implications such dynamics have for people, as individuals and groups. This discussion is a feature of the IPCC report chapter on human security (IPCC 2014), while Barnett and Adger (2007) discuss the intersections between climate change, human security and violent conflict. In the process, the authors point out that it is frequently the same societal conditions undermining adaptive capacity and resilience (marginal ecological conditions, poverty, inequality and weak state institutions, for example), those dynamics heightening vulnerability to direct (human) security implications of climate change, that also render conflict more likely.

Accounts of who these dynamics threaten are, of course, more complicated in the human security discourse than in the national security and international security discourse, with follow-on implications for how we might make sense of the nature of the threat itself. Most advocates are eager to make the case that we are talking here about individuals and collectives, with the latter extending from small groups (families) to large ones (ethnic and cultural communities, even nations) (see Barnett et al. 2010:19). Yet, for many, this lacks specificity or clarity and raises fundamental questions over who has responsibility for ensuring security and how powerful actors might be mobilized to act in and for the interests of people across the globe (see, e.g., Paris 2001).

Ultimately, the human security discourse suggests that climate change poses both a direct threat to (especially vulnerable) populations, while also constituting an indirect threat. In already arid areas in which agriculture is marginal and subsistence-oriented, and where populations may already be relatively impoverished and have limited recourse to government support or alternative means of making a living, the effects of dynamics linked to climate change such as desertification, changing rainfall patterns or drought are likely to be immediate and severe (O'Brien 2006; UNDP 2007). Rather than simply assessing whether such dynamics in turn lead to population movements, instability or conflict, a human security discourse suggests that these dynamics are, in themselves, security threats. And indirectly, the human security discourse would also endorse the idea of climate change as a threat multiplier (Barnett and Adger 2007), though in this instance it multiplies and amplifies pre-existing forms of individual and community vulnerability linked to inequality, impoverishment and marginalization.

## Means of Security

Responding effectively to the human security implications of climate change clearly, given the multidimensional nature of the threat outlined previously, involves and indeed necessitates a range of measures. While mitigation action is central here, so too are adaptive measures oriented towards managing the immediate impact of climate change (through changes to infrastructure and its management, for example). Beyond these, there is also clearly a role for broader sets of practices and responses that serve to address the vulnerabilities associated with inequality, impoverishment and marginalization noted earlier (through global aid programs and changing modes of national and international governance, for example). Finally, and in procedural terms, advocates of human security have advocated a role for community-wide participation in decision-making and planning associated with managing the threat of climate change (see Barnett et al. 2010:18).

While geoengineering projects could feasibly play a role in minimizing potential harm to communities associated with the implications of climate change,[12] mitigation has traditionally been represented as the

---

[12] Indeed in his discussion of the limits of international management/ coordination of mooted geo-engineering projects, Julian Symons (2018, 2019a) challenges *restrictions* to geoengineering on grounds that intersect with the ethical commitments of human security. Specially, he argues that we should not deny developing states of the opportunity to unilaterally deploy geoengineering if that has the potential to minimise the direct harm they might otherwise experience.

priority for responding effectively to the human security implications of climate change. Proponents of human security, simply put, are likely to emphasize a central role for urgent mitigation action. The focus on addressing the problem at its source clearly follows from recognition of climate change as posing a direct threat to the referent object identified here: people. Yet the focus on urgent mitigation action also reflects the emphasis on those experiencing particular vulnerability, for whom even slight climatic changes have the capacity to constitute pressing and immediate threats. It is no coincidence that the coalition of vulnerable countries that formed during climate negotiations in Paris in 2015 pushed (ultimately successfully) for a commitment to include the ambition of limiting climate change to no more than 1.5 degrees Celsius. For these communities, most directly the populations of low-lying Pacific Island nations, any temperature increase and associated sea-level rise constitutes an existential security threat, simultaneously threatening territory, livelihoods, health and culture (Wong 2011; Falkner 2016). In the context of environmental security more broadly, Jon Barnett (2001:129) makes the case for practices oriented towards 'peacefully reducing human vulnerability to human-induced environmental degradation by addressing the root causes of environmental degradation'.

Barnett's point also suggests a crucial role for measures orienting towards the reduction of vulnerability in general terms. Vulnerability here is only partly a product of immediate exposure to manifestations of climate change: a large component also relates to the capacity of communities to prepare for such effects, withstand their immediate impact and rebound to functionality in the aftermath (see O'Brien et al. 2007; Dalby 2009:107–12; Fisher 2011:296). The latter is indicative of resilience, to be addressed in Chapter 3. But recognizing this broader conceptualization of vulnerability here is crucial for coming to terms with who will be most affected by climate change and is most in need of protection. In illustrating this point, Paterson (1996:175) has pointed out, for example, that while both Bangladesh and the Netherlands are low-lying countries, one has significant resources and capacity to prepare for and respond to rising sea levels, while the other does not. In its analysis of the human security implications of

Again, the example of geoengineering will be discussed in more detail in Chapter 4.

climate change, meanwhile, the UNDP (2007:3) noted that 'whatever the future risks facing cities in the rich world, today the real climate change vulnerabilities ... are to be found in rural communities ... and in sprawling urban slums across the developing world'.

In the human security discourse, therefore, responding effectively to the security implications of climate change necessitates the development of capacity within and for communities likely to be most affected by climate change (see Renner 1996). It requires adaptive measures that may range from building and rebuilding infrastructure to manage higher temperatures or sea levels, putting in place programs of action and response processes in the instance of natural disasters, even the diversification of livelihoods and economies to help prepare for changing conditions for agriculture or fishing, for example (O'Brien et al. 2007). Some of these would, in turn, be funded through measures such as the Green Climate Fund, with developed states ideally acting to facilitate adaptive measures for those most vulnerable to the problem and least responsible for causing it (UNDP 2007; Kumssa and Jones 2010). While in the past the emphasis on adaptation was downplayed within this discourse due to the sense that it took attention away from mitigation efforts (see Moser 2014), the fact that some degree of climate change is 'locked in' has encouraged a significant focus on how vulnerable communities and populations might prepare for manifestations of climate change.

Finally, as both Paterson's and Barnett's points suggest, there is a clear need to address the systems, processes and contexts that condition vulnerability in the first instance. While readily apparent to the scale of global economic inequality and the functions of the international economic system that serve to propel that inequality, this point is prominent in feminist accounts of (human) security too. Nicole Detraz (2015), for example, points to the ways in which patriarchal structures within societies render women particularly vulnerable to changing climatic conditions, especially regarding agriculture and food security. This point is prominent, too, in Heather Goldsworthy's (2010) account of the particular vulnerabilities confronting women and their human security in the face of environmental change more broadly. Among the (very) wide range of measures that might follow from the recognition of the need to reduce vulnerability are significant international aid programs and the redistribution of global wealth; education programs around health, sanitation and (changing) agriculture; and inclusive and participatory forms of national government and local government, for example (see Ruth 2005:158; O'Brien 2006; UNDP 2007). The scale and variety of measures that might serve the end of human security here are challenging for those seeking to promote human security concerns (as will be noted) and require engagement from a range of actors and agents in the provision of security.

## Agents of Security

Questions of agency are relatively easily settled in the context of the national security discourse, in which the state is both referent and agent of security. And while more diffuse, even the international security discourse suggests that agents of security are principally the United Nations and the broader instruments of global governance. This question is more difficult to settle in the human security discourse (see Dalby 2009:131–2). To continue a theme in the discussion of the previous discourses, means and agents of security are mutually constitutive. Here, the role of a very wide range of measures (from mitigation to adaptation to geoengineering, alongside a raft of practices aimed at minimizing inequality and marginalization) suggests that a wide range of actors and agents have a role to play as agents of human security.

Of course, the necessity of involving a wide range of actors in addressing the (human) security threat of climate change clearly applies to mitigation efforts. Here, and as noted, international organizations have a role to play in coordinating and pushing global action, while states too can and should advance mitigation action through national targets and policies that incentivize mitigation action and disincentivize fossil-fuel use. At the other end of the scale, and recognizing the human security discourse's philosophical location in cosmopolitan thought (Burke 2013), there is also a role here for people throughout the world in reducing their own carbon footprint as a form of (human) security agency.

In the context of adaptation, international organizations and states clearly have a role to play in coordinating and contributing technology, expertise and funding to help facilitate adaptation for local communities. The research community, businesses and civil society groups throughout the world are also in a position to help facilitate adaptive measures through donations, education campaigns and research on the likely impacts and suggested responses to climate manifestations. And in the context of resilience building, the same groups and organizations can advance human security, alongside additional agents. Development organizations and states, for example, need to address poverty, inequality and marginalization through supporting sustainable forms of development, while international organizations, states and civil society groups also have a role to play in promoting and helping to build inclusive societies and decision-making processes. Again in these contexts, people throughout the world – and especially citizens of developed states – have a role to play in supporting actions aimed at building adaptive capacity and resilience. And in all these contexts, vulnerable communities themselves will need to play a role in identifying their own vulnerabilities and capacities, participating in decision-making and coordinating effective local responses to the (human) security implications of climate change. (On these points, see Barnett et al. 2010:19; Matthew and Upreti 2010; Nsiah-Gyabaah 2010.)

In short, the wide-ranging and often direct nature of the threat posed by climate change to human security suggests the need for a wide-ranging set of responses to that insecurity and the vulnerability of people and their communities. This, in turn, suggests a significant number of agents of human security, from international organizations and states to civil society groups, businesses, people throughout the world and vulnerable communities themselves. Such a conception of possible security agents comes closer to acknowledging what the challenge of climate change itself necessitates: the imperative for global action across almost every axis of society. Yet the difficulty of assigning clear security responsibility to one actor or a set of actors also comes with costs.

## Implications and Limitations

In a number of ways, the human security discourse effectively addresses the ethical and practical limitations of the discourses discussed to date. It encourages us to move from a focus on institutions to vulnerable people and groups, draws our attention primarily to the imperative of addressing the problem itself while recognizing a continued role for adaptation measures and involves recognition of the fundamental forms of inequality and marginalization (from discourses and practices associated with gender, development and politics, for example) that ultimately *constitute* vulnerability.

Yet there are two particular challenges or limitations of this human security discourse in the context of climate change that are important to note here. The first concerns agency, the second its ethical limits.

On the challenge of conceptualizing and assigning agency noted above, two distinct problems confront advocates of a human security discourse. On the one hand, the absence of an actor with clear responsibility for providing human security risks creating something of an agency vacuum where no single actors or set of actors acknowledge the imperatives of action (see Newell et al. 2015). This problem is especially acute if particularly powerful actors – states and, to a lesser extent, international organizations – are inclined towards orienting their action towards the preservation of national security or maintenance of international stability, for example (see Paris 2001). On the other hand, some have warned that this discourse provides cover for new forms of liberal interventionism (see Oels 2015) or will be co-opted precisely by states and international organizations, with its ethical commitments compromised in the process (see Chandler and Hynek 2011). Here, the language of human security is embraced, but its imperatives and the fundamental critique it constitutes do not flow from or towards an associated shift in practice. This criticism was applied to the Canadian government's embrace of 'human security', in which the government noted it was focusing exclusively on freedom from fear (not freedom from want), and the embrace of this approach appeared to critics to have minimal effects on its foreign and security policy behaviour (see Booth 2007:323–5; Christie 2010). Both these issues may be characterized as problems associated with the extent to which human security comes to find purchase and resonance among or with existing (powerful) agents and institutions in the international system, with its ethical commitments coming to genuinely inform associated practices. This challenge is even more acute in the context of the ecological security discourse, to be noted.

The second limitation of this discourse concerns its ethical commitments. Critically examining the UNDP's (1994) account of human security, for example, Simon Dalby (2009:131) notes that the environment is positioned as an external condition for human survival, while Audra Mitchell (2014:8) similarly argues that this account views the environment as important not for its (or other species') intrinsic

value but because of its contribution to human survival. More fundamentally, the commitment to currently living (even if vulnerable)
populations does not go far enough in recognizing obligations to those
even more vulnerable: future generations and other living beings.
While some advocates are hopeful or optimistic about the possibility
of aligning human security imperatives and cosmopolitan thought with
obligations to these actors (see Burke et al. 2014), in this book I argue
that a more fundamental and more holistic account of the security
implications of climate change is required: one oriented towards
ecological security.

## Conclusion

There are multiple ways of conceiving and approaching the relationship between climate change and security. These differences are evident
in (changing) engagement with the relationship over time and in the
varied ways different political practitioners, formal institutions, think
tanks, civil society groups and analysts have characterized the climate–
security relationship. I grouped these here into discourses of climate
security: frameworks of meaning with particular sets of assumptions or
prescriptions regarding whose security matters (referent); what constitutes a challenge to security (threat); the manner in which security is to
be preserved in the context of that threat (means); and the actor(s)
capable of or indeed responsible for providing security (agent). These
were organized here according to the choice of referent object, which,
in turn, served to determine (to a significant degree at least) the nature
of the threat, the identification of agents and the appropriate means of
responding to and/or addressing that threat. This account of climate
security discourses (arguably like any typology) is necessarily reductionist and simplistic, eliding important differences within discourses
and similarities between them. And it does not capture all forms or
dynamics of engagement with this relationship in practical or analytical terms. But in this book I suggest it captures central axes of
engagement with this relationship in ways that allows us to appreciate
and interrogate the bases upon which these connections are made and,
crucially, the implications of them in practice. The contours of this
discussion are summarized in Table 2.1.

Distinguishing between accounts of climate security in theory and
practice is an interesting analytical exercise, one reminding us not to

Table 2.1. *Discourses of climate security*

| Discourse | Referent | Threats to | Agent | Response |
|---|---|---|---|---|
| National security | Nation state | Sovereignty, territorial integrity | State | Adaptation |
| International security | International society | Stability, international rules and norms | International organizations | Mitigation and adaptation |
| Human security | People | Life and livelihood, core values | States, NGOs, international community, communities themselves | Mitigation and adaptation |

*Source*: McDonald 2013a

take climate 'securitizations' at face value but to reflect on how climate change is understood and whose security is presented as in need of preservation or advancement. But, more importantly, recognizing the contours and assumptions of different discourses is important at a practical and ethical level precisely because these discourses have different sets of implications for the practices that flow from them. If we view climate change as threatening to the extent that it potentially undermines the territorial integrity and sovereignty of the state via climate-induced population movement or conflict, the security measures we will see in response will be oriented towards responsive practices that better equip the state to adapt to climate effects – not responses oriented towards the direct threats climate change poses to vulnerable people, nor even necessarily to addressing the problem itself (Dalby and Moussavi 2017).

This matters. If different discourses have different implications for the types of practices they encourage, it suggests we should do more than explore whether we have seen 'securitization' of climate change. Of course, we need to reflect on the first principles that underpin choices made to prioritize particular forms of climate security threat and the entity threatened by climate change: the ethical imaginaries that limit our moral universe in communitarian terms to the boundaries of the nation state, extend our imagination to a liberal vision of an international society or develop a cosmopolitan account that compels us to recognize obligations to vulnerable outsiders. More importantly, however, we need to examine and interrogate what practices are encouraged by these different discourses and ask ourselves whether they are genuinely likely to address climate change effectively and in a manner that is ethically defensible.

Ultimately, the preceding typology suggests an inverse relationship between the ethical defensibility of discourses and the effectiveness of practices they encourage in terms of responding to climate change on the one hand and the level of political purchase and take-up in the corridors of power they have on the other. Those discourses speaking most directly to the concerns and capacity of existing institutions – in particular states – are least likely to be underpinned by ethical considerations consistent with basic principles of equity and least likely to encourage practices oriented towards effectively addressing what is a genuinely global challenge. Conversely, those most oriented towards the rights and needs of vulnerable outsiders, and oriented towards addressing the problem of climate change itself in ways that also address other axes of vulnerability and inequality, have limited purchase among key institutions, to the point that identifying key agents with a *responsibility* for providing human security becomes a particularly difficult exercise.

While human security constitutes the most progressive discourse identified above, its ethics and the sets of practices it encourages are still limited in important ways. The focus on vulnerable human populations extends ethical boundaries of consideration and encourages practices oriented towards addressing the problem itself and the broader contexts that condition and affect this vulnerability. Yet it falls short of drawing our attention to the rights and needs of other living beings or future generations. In the context of the Anthropocene in particular, addressing climate change necessitates expanding and altering moral accounts and consideration across both time and space, in the process re-examining the nature of humanity's relationship with (or, more accurately, embeddedness within) broader ecosystems.

Such an approach – consistent with an ecological security discourse – faces a series of challenges associated with clarifying what a focus on ecological resilience means in theory and practice, and in particular outlining how such an orientation might come to provide the lens through which any community or institution conceives and approaches climate change. The radical reorientation of existing institutions and practices necessary for such an approach to be realized, and inform the ways in which the relationship between climate change and security is conceived and approached, is a fundamental challenge. Yet to reiterate a claim made at the start of this book, and one underpinning the book as a whole: if the ethical principles on which this discourse is founded are most defensible, and the practices it encourages most likely to fundamentally address climate change itself, the lack of political purchase cannot be sufficient to dismiss such a discourse. Indeed, our attention can and should turn not to the question of which discourses are most amenable to our institutions but how our institutions might be reoriented to embrace and enact concerns consistent with ethically defensible and practically effective responses to the unprecedented challenge of global climate change. Outlining the contours of this discourse, its implications in practice and the extent to which it might come to find political purchase is the task of the remainder of this book.

# 3 | *Ecological Security*
## *A Definition*

The previous chapters laid a foundation for outlining and defending an ecological security discourse in approaching the relationship between climate change and security. Chapter 1 advanced the claim that security can be viewed as a site of contestation, with multiple actors within a given political community advancing different conceptions or discourses of security. These discourses can be understood as frameworks of meaning with particular claims about whose security matters, from what threats, by what means it is to be provided and by what actors or agents. In the process, the argument advanced here was that the question of which particular discourse of security 'won out' in capturing the way political communities understood and approached security was politically and ethically significant, potentially informing substantive practical responses to a range of issues.

Chapter 2 then applied this particular framework to the question of climate change. Noting the development of engagement with the climate–security relationship over time, the chapter mapped different discourses of security as articulated and advanced by institutions, political actors, think tanks, academics and non-governmental organizations. It sought to identify the key claims made about who or what was to be protected from the threat of climate change, what exactly this threat looked like (direct or indirect, for example), what responses were appropriate to this threat (mitigation or adaptation, for example) and who was responsible for advancing security in the face of this threat. In the process, it identified the ethical assumptions underpinning these discourses and, in particular, their practical and ethical implications in practice.

Ultimately, Chapter 2 presented two key conclusions regarding the discourses of climate security identified – national, international and human security discourses. First, these discourses were underpinned by very different ethical assumptions and encouraged different sets of responses in practice to the challenge of climate change, ranging from military preparedness to large-scale mitigation action. This conclusion underscores the need for a variegated understanding of the implications of 'securitization' (see also Diez et al. 2016) and encourages us to reflect on the practical and ethical defensibility of these discourses. Second, and following this, this exploration demonstrated the limits of these existing accounts of security. This was particularly acute in the context of national security. Here, responses arising from approaching the security implications of climate change as a national security threat were not primarily focused on addressing the problem itself, to the point of positioning those particularly vulnerable to manifestations of climate change as threats to national security (in the context of climate-induced migration, for example). But the other discourses were also limited, with the emphasis on the preservation of currently existing human populations and their institutions failing to come to terms with the rights and needs of the most vulnerable: future generations and other living beings in particular. In the process, the practices encouraged risk falling short of the fundamental and urgent changes required to ensure the functionality of ecosystems and with it the protection of those most vulnerable to manifestations of climate change.

Building on this foundation, the rest of the book outlines the contours of an ecological security discourse. In this discourse, security is understood in terms of a commitment to the resilience of ecosystems themselves and, with it, the rights and needs of vulnerable beings across time (future generations), space (impoverished populations) and species (other living beings). It is a discourse that – if genuinely informing the way political communities understand and approach the relationship between security and climate change – would encourage radical and immediate action to address the problem itself. Yet it is also a discourse posing a series of complicated and challenging questions ranging from the challenge of orienting our moral gaze beyond existing human populations to weighing up the (at times competing) rights and needs of a range of beings (often lacking capacity to communicate these needs as we would understand communication), to the acute uncertainty and complexity associated with the functionality and tipping points of ecosystems and to the lack of a clear political constituency for such a discourse. These are indeed significant challenges, though many are not exclusive to this discourse and significant intellectual traditions can be drawn upon to illuminate answers to these complex questions. And, as noted, if a particular discourse or approach suggests itself as ethically defensible and encouraging practices that address the problem of climate change, the question to resolve should not be 'how do we alter these principles to ensure alignment with existing institutions?'. Rather, it should be 'how can we make institutional arrangements and practices consistent with the most defensible principles?'

The remaining chapters directly engage this question, mapping an ecological security discourse and exploring the conditions in which it might inform substantive approaches to climate change. This chapter outlines the ethical and philosophical foundations of an ecological security discourse, before elaborating on how the referent object of security and the nature of the threat of climate change are conceived. Chapter 4 rounds out the discussion of the components of the ecological security discourse by noting the means and agents of security in this discourse, ultimately engaging the question of what the pursuit of ecological security would look like in practice. Noting that this discourse has even less obvious purchase or resonance with existing institutions in world politics than the human security discourse, Chapter 5 then engages with the challenging question of how an ecological security discourse might ultimately come to provide the lens through which political communities understand and address the challenge of climate change. To return to Linklater's (1998) distinction between a sociological, normative and praxeological imperative for critical theory, if the preceding chapters have provided an account of where we are (the sociological), the remaining chapters concern themselves with the normative and the praxeological: why is this approach to the relationship between climate change and security needed, and how might we get there?

This chapter is therefore definitional in focus. First, the chapter briefly explores engagement with ecological security in theory and practice, identifying parallel discussions of Anthropocene, biosphere and post-human security before providing a definition of ecological security. Second, the chapter locates this discourse in normative context. Here, an ecological security discourse is located in a broadly holistic and pluralist account of (environmental) ethics, one that attempts to move beyond tired and unhelpful anthropocentric-ecocentric binaries. Third, the chapter specifies the way in which the referent object of security in this discourse is understood, along with the nature of the threat posed. It provides a definition of ecosystems and makes a case for this emphasis on ecosystems in the context of the

Anthropocene and, in particular, as a means of ensuring due consideration for the rights and needs of the most vulnerable. This section concludes with a discussion of the need to emphasize the *direct* threat climate change poses to ecosystems and their resilience.

In the process of advancing a particular definition of ecological security, the chapter reaffirms the idea that this discourse should serve to inform the way we conceive and approach climate change as a form of sensibility or orientation rather than as a policy program or definitive set of guidelines. Ultimately, the agents and practices of ecological security – addressed in more detail in Chapter 4 – will be determined in context and through inclusive processes of dialogue and deliberation that draw on local knowledge and are characterized by humility and reflexivity in the interpretation and application of broad ethical principles endorsed here.

## Ecological Security and Its Antecedents

While ecological security is a marginal discourse of climate security, a range of analysts and, in particular, advocates have attempted to make a case for moving beyond existing human populations, collectives and institutions when considering the security implications of climate change. Some have explicitly embraced the term used here – ecological security – while others have framed such a concern in terms of planetary, biosphere, worldly or Anthropocene security, for example. While these framings and the claims made differ across these conceptualizations, they all engage with the question of what security might look like if extended beyond humans and their institutions.

Those explicitly employing the 'ecological security' frame have generally attempted to draw attention to the security implications of climate change for the natural world itself (not simply in terms of subsequent effects on human populations) but have done so in a range of ways. For Patricia Mische (1989, 1994), one of the first to use this framing in exploring the connection between security and environmental change, it was imperative to break down the distinction between the natural world on the one hand and human society or welfare on the other. She suggested the impossibility of decoupling any form of security from the conditions of survival, addressing in turn the mutually constitutive threat posed by deleterious human activity and a changing environment (Mische 1989:391–2). In another theme evident in later accounts of ecological security, and with parallels to ecofeminist research (see Plumwood 2002), Mische also noted the links between social and environmental inequality, identifying the particular vulnerability of populations of the developing world to manifestations of environmental change. Similar themes are evident in Katrina Rogers' (1997) account of ecological security, in which multinationals are viewed as potential agents of ecological security via corporate social responsibility. Again, this speaks to a core ecological security concern: the multiplicity of sites and agents of security, a theme to be addressed in more detail in Chapter 4.

In a subsequent invocation of ecological security, Jon Barnett (2001:109) developed an account grounded in 'green' ecological thought, in which it was 'ecosystems and ecological processes that should be secured; the prima facie referent (was) nonhuman'. Here, Barnett flags a potential role for orienting towards resilience, reflecting the reality of (ongoing) environmental change, while also making a case for a 'new version of politics that emphasizes responsibility' (2001:115). Both, in particular the central role envisaged for resilience, are key dimensions of the ecological security discourse as advanced here. Yet while broadly endorsing the philosophical principles and precepts of ecological security, Barnett (2001:121) is ultimately dismissive, in particular of the capacity for this discourse to cut through and find political purchase: its inability to engage in 'the contestation and delegitimization of security itself'.

Finally, Denis Pirages (2005) provides perhaps the most direct and explicit account of ecological security. He argues that

> Ecological security rests on preserving the following four interrelated dynamic equilibriums:
> 1) Between human populations living at higher consumption levels and the ability of nature to provide resources and services
> 2) Between human populations and pathogenic microorganisms
> 3) Between human populations and those of other plant and animal species
> 4) Among human populations

He goes on to suggest that 'insecurity increases wherever any of these equilibriums is disrupted either by changes in human behavior or in nature' (Pirages 2005:4). While a prominent account, Pirages's emphasis on equilibrium and balance risks neglecting the realities of *ongoing* environmental change. His earlier (Pirages 1997) support for population control as an ecological security measure also suggests a less prominent role for integrating ecological and social considerations, or addressing multiple (and mutually reinforcing) axes of vulnerability across species and over time.

Other interventions attempting to make a case for moving beyond exclusively human populations or institutions can be divided roughly into earlier accounts to emphasize the global and the planetary and more recent attempts to point to the scale and imperative of change in the contemporary human condition. In the former, early articulations of biosphere or planetary security (Myers 1993; Dalby 1998; Liftin 1999), for example, emphasized the 'one world' image and the imperative of jettisoning a zero-sum vision of security. These accounts, to be read in contrast to a dominant national security framing, implied the possibility of drawing on recognition of the scale of global environmental change to drive a broader reformulation of security and the way we divide the world and the planet into self-contained units (see also Mische 1989). It is telling that these accounts, while at the opposite end of the scale to human security's emphasis on the individual, often endorsed a broadly (similar) cosmopolitan vision and advocated universal principles in addressing environmental change.

Other accounts have, more recently, made a case for post-human security and Anthropocene security. The former, most readily associated with the work of Erica Cudworth and Stephen Hobden (2011, 2015, 2017), suggests the need to understand the human condition as something that is embedded in and constitutive of our relations with the world, other living beings and the environment (2013:644–5). Proponents note important variations between those images of the 'posthuman' that extend to the material world as a whole, building on insights of new materialism (e.g. Deleuze 1994; Bennett 2010), hybrid accounts of multiple interpenetrations and networks (e.g. Latour 1999) and those (e.g., Lovelock 2000; Dalby 2009) focused on interrelationships between living beings. (On this distinction, see Cudworth and Hobden 2017:68–71; see also Mitchell 2017.) Ultimately, what unifies these approaches is the case made for humanity's embeddedness within (rather than separation from) the natural world, some recognition of obligation to other living beings and the shared (and fundamental) critique of anthropocentrism (see Mitchell

2017; Grove 2019; Newell 2020).[1] In making a case for post-humanism, including as an emancipatory project (Cudworth and Hobden 2018), proponents tend to demonstrate some degree of ambivalence about the desirability or utility of the security framing (see in particular Mitchell 2017). But the broader suggestion of the need to extend ontological and ethical boundaries beyond humans, human collectives and institutions speaks to the need to reconfigure security in the context of environmental change.

A range of conceptualizations seeking to extend security beyond humans and their institutions, including the ecological security discourse advanced here, view and invoke the 'Anthropocene' as a compelling rationale for approaching the security–environment relationship in different ways. To reiterate, the Anthropocene can be conceived as a geological era in which, simply put, human activities have come to affect Earth systems and their functionality (see Steffan et al. 2004). For some, this provides a compelling context for reconceiving existing human–nature distinctions in modern political thought and practice that has important implications for the way we approach security (evident in existing accounts of ecological security or post-human security discussed earlier, for example). Others have made an even more explicit case for redefining security in the context of the Anthropocene. Harrington and Shearing (2017), Hardt (2017) and Dalby (2009) have all suggested that the Anthropocene is a game changer, constituting a fundamental challenge to accounts of security focused on the preservation of human collectives and institutions. Indeed for Harrington and Shearing (2017:25–6), the security of the environment itself has never really been addressed: 'our ideas about security ... are fundamentally anthropocentric and absent of ecological thought'. In making a case for an ethics of care in approaching environmental change, Harrington and Shearing (2017) suggest the imperative of orienting security towards interconnectedness and networks of relationships: a theme consistent with interventions making a case for post-humanism.

Of course, this necessarily brief account does not wholly capture the range of ways that the security implications of environmental change – even

[1] Following Robyn Eckersley (2017:994), anthropocentrism is here understood as 'a form of human chauvinism which rests on the self-serving ideological belief that humans are the pinnacle of evolution and the centre of agency, meaning and value in the world, which renders the rest of the world valueless unless it is useful or valuable to humans or somehow "human-like"'.

climate change specifically – have been framed for those concerned with moving beyond human populations and institutions.[2] Neither does it wholly account for interventions consistent with the commitments and principles of post-human, ecological or Anthropocene security that employ different sets of labels. 'Environmental security', for example, has often been viewed as consistent with a more traditional approach to the environment and security – examining the impact of resource access or environmental change for human communities and institutions. Yet the 'environmental security' of Simon Dalby (2009), for example, pushes in many similar directions to those noted above in encouraging us to both critique traditional security approaches and radically reconsider our ethical commitments to other living beings and future generations, for example (see also Detraz 2009).

All told, the above accounts speak to growing recognition of the limits of traditional approaches to security in the context of the scale and severity of contemporary global environmental change, even while most are perfunctory in their discussion of the contours of their reformulation of security. Indeed most can be viewed as forms of critique of traditional approaches rather than systematic attempts to make a case for an alternative formulation of or approach to security. It is also worth noting here that – in contrast to the discourses outlined in Chapter 2 – the vast majority of accounts and interventions in this context are advocated by analysts and, to a lesser extent, activists: this discourse is largely absent from accounts of the security implications of climate change advocated by states, regional or international institutions or think tanks. This point speaks to Barnett's (2001) concern with the political purchase or salience of formulations such as 'ecological security', a point I will return to later in the book.

## The Ethical Foundations of Ecological Security

The above attempts to position our security register beyond humans, human collectives and institutions clearly build on a range of ethical

---

[2] Among a range of other interventions not addressed explicitly here include Audra Mitchell's (2014) account of worldly security, for example (broadly consistent with a more materialist-inspired account of post-humanism), or the discourse of 'planetary danger' as outlined by Diez et al. (2016:23), a discourse drawing on various elements of the aforementioned accounts.

principles and commitments. While these might be categorized simply as drawing on 'green theory' (see Hough 2014; Newell 2020), in reality the varied sets of ethical commitments evident in these interventions extend from an holistic and ecocentric ethics to a reconfiguration of cosmopolitan human rights: distinctions evident in broader accounts of the relationship between ethics and climate change (see Gardiner et al. eds. 2010). While some endorse the idea of building upon and extending cosmopolitan thought to drive our approach to the climate–security relationship (see Dalby 2009; Burke et al. 2016), others explicitly reject existing ethical and philosophical frameworks tied to humanity in making a case for post-human or Anthropocene security, for example (see Harrington and Shearing 2017). Elements of these debates warrant discussion, before I outline the set of ethical and philosophical commitments that underpin the discourse of ecological security.

The traditional heart of debates about how to conceive the relationship between the natural world and ethics has been the binary between anthropocentric and ecocentric approaches. As Katie McShane argues, 'ecocentrism involves a reorientation of our moral perspective away from a view of the nonhuman natural world as merely a means for satisfying human interests and towards a view of it as something to which we have moral responsibilities'; she further defines ecocentrism as a 'critical attitude' that challenges 'technocratic and instrumentalist approaches to the nonhuman natural world' (McShane 2014:83). Clearly, a position allowing an extension of moral considerations to other living beings and their welfare for its own sake seems intuitively compelling and is indeed endorsed here. Yet there have been a range of pragmatic and ethical challenges to this approach and the capacity it has to inform the way we conceive climate ethics or address the implications of climate change (see Celermajer et al. 2020; Wienhues 2020).

For some, it is simply not possible to know or understand the needs of other beings, not least in the absence of communicative capacity as we would understand it. Robyn Eckersley (1992: chapter 5) makes the latter point in her critique of critical theory (especially that of the Frankfurt School tradition), requiring as it does a form of communicative rationality we cannot reasonably expect from non-humans. And claims to speak 'on behalf' of ecosystems or other living beings are inherently contestable, suggesting some degree of hubris at best and hypocrisy at worst.[3] In the particular context of the connection between environmental change and security, both Audra Mitchell (2014, drawing on Nolt 1994) and Floyd and Matthew (2013) have argued that it is difficult to wholly overcome anthropocentrism by virtue of simply being human, with Floyd and Matthew (2013:9) ultimately suggesting that 'ecological security can be understood as a variant of human security'.

Of course, criticisms of this moral framework on the basis of claims proponents might make to speak on behalf of 'others', or the absence of full and equal participation in dialogue regarding decisions, are criticisms that apply to almost any ethical framework. Do international institutions or nation states really speak for all (whether citizens or the 'international community') they claim to represent? And as those concerned with extending moral consideration to other living beings have long argued, it is difficult to make the case that the challenges of *fully* appreciating the interests and needs of animals, for example, ultimately prevents *any* form of moral consideration regarding their suffering and survival (see Singer 1975; Sunstein and Nussbaum eds. 2004). Finally, Rafi Youatt (2014:210) has argued in response to claims that we cannot avoid anthropocentrism:

There is an important distinction to be made between the unavoidably human perspective that comes from being human, on one hand, and the entirely avoidable content of moral and political frameworks that are expressed through human language. The first is unavoidable (and properly speaking is not anthropocentrism), while the second is not. Just as one is not inescapably a white supremacist in virtue of being white, so one is not inescapably anthropocentric in virtue of being human. The existence of ecocentrism as an alternative (or various versions of 'non-centrism') speaks directly to this point, for example. In the second, more robust sense, then, anthropocentrism is entirely escapable, since it is not an escape from human perspective that is sought but a shift in human moral and political frameworks that orient our relations with other species.

For others sceptical of a shift beyond a moral universe occupied exclusively by humans, the *pragmatic* challenges of such a reorientation are

---

[3] In contestation over development projects in the Brazilian Amazon rainforest in the 1980s and 1990s, some indigenous groups claiming to 'speak for the Indian *and* the forest' (my emphasis) were also participating in illicit logging activities (see McDonald 2012:87).

at least as challenging as the moral ones. As noted, the apparent inconsistency of an ecological security discourse with existing institutions and practices of global politics was at the heart of Jon Barnett's (2001:119–21) criticism of the framework – on pragmatic rather than ethical grounds. More broadly, a range of theorists have pointed out that if recognizing competing needs and responsibilities in the context of an issue like climate change is difficult enough (given varied historical and contemporary contributions to the problem, capacity to respond, exposure to effects and developmental needs), extending our focus to the rights and needs of plants and animals adds yet another layer of complexity to any future, substantive action (see Gardiner 2014). How do we assess and prioritize the needs of different sets of beings, not least (again in the context of climate change) given acute complexity and uncertainty regarding tipping points or an understanding of when ecosystems' functionality begins to be irrevocably compromised? And on ethical grounds, if we focus instead on the integrity of ecosystems as a whole, in the process drawing on holistic thought, is there a danger that the value of beings is determined by their individual contribution to ecosystem functionality?[4] On this criterion, human populations would be *less* worthy of protecting or securing than any other living being, a recognition some view as encouraging either ecofascism or simply misanthropy (see McShane 2014:84–5). The idea that a commitment to ecosystems might mask an underlying dislike or disrespect for humanity and human populations was, of course, central to Murray Bookchin's (1987) critique of 'deep ecology' and in particular 'Earth First' representations of humanity as an infestation on planet earth (see also Dryzek 2005: chapter 9). Critics here would be unsurprised that some advocates of ecological security (e.g. Pirages 1997) view human population control as an appropriate response to ecological crisis.

The continued salience or at least prominence of this anthropocentric–ecocentric binary in engagement with environmental ethics has been a source of frustration for a range of theorists, a number of whom have attempted to either identify a middle way between these positions or transcend the core differences (see Wienhues 2020). More recent

---

[4] Rita Floyd (2019:116) outlines a rationale for recognizing the particular value (for ecosystem functionality) of so-called keystone species. She also notes a tendency for some NGOs to focus on (and thereby prioritize) iconic or 'flagship species' in their conservation campaigns (WWF and pandas, for example).

'pluralist' ecocentrist accounts, for example, suggest that 'the good of individual organisms and ecological wholes both matter and that neither is reducible to the other' (McShane 2014:85). This position is evident in Robyn Eckersley's (1992, 2005) work, for example, which can be viewed as a conscious attempt to move beyond the anthropocentric-ecocentric binary. For Eckersley (2005:365),

Much of the first wave of green political theorists (myself included) had strenuously defended the critique of anthropocentrism and sought to emphasize this as a distinctive and new feature of political thought vis-à-vis so-called 'mainstream' political theories. However, a number of 'second wave' green political theorists are now inclined to reject the anthropocentric/ecocentric distinction as unhelpful and have sought instead to emphasize the humanist credentials of green politics and redirect attention towards questions of human ecological stewardship, ecological virtue, and what might be the legitimate use (or illegitimate abuse) of natural resources and ecosystems.

Similarly, the ecological feminist approach of Val Plumwood (1993) also attempts to transcend the anthropocentric/ecocentric (or human/ nature) divide, suggesting that binaries and dualisms central to modern thought serve to drive multiple axes of domination and subjugation (whether based on gender, race or class, for example) (see also Merchant 1980). For her, the imperative is the development of a sensibility in which other living beings are recognized as different but worthy of ethical consideration. She suggests the need to think of obligations to non-human living beings in terms of '"earth others", in which nature is perceived not as an object for human manipulation but as a subject that deserves recognition and respect' (Kaijser and Kronsell 2014:425; see also Cudworth 2014). This approach has subsequently informed feminist scholars drawing on intersectionality to make a case for an alternative ecological ethics (see Kaijser and Kronsell 2014; Osborne 2015).

Work in the broad tradition of (particularly critical) political ecology also seeks to move beyond an anthropocentric–ecocentric binary, primarily through emphasizing the need to conceive of human–nature relationships in terms of interrelationships and embeddedness (see Peet et al. eds. 2010; Robbins 2012). These approaches also, like Plumwood (1993), emphasize the intersections between 'the domination of nonhuman nature and the domination of subaltern social groups' (Eckersley 2005:373). In the process, they draw attention to the connections and embeddedness that defines the relationship between living beings and the conditions of their survival and challenge those accounts suggesting the possibility, much less desirability, of emphasizing the preservation of ecosystems or human populations at the expense of the other. Jairus Grove (2014, 2019) identifies political ecology as a fruitful way of approaching the study of security, recognizing as it does a complex, interdependent and interconnected world. Svarstad and Benhaminsen (2020) suggest that political ecology draws our attention to the question of how power manifests itself in struggles – both discursive and material – with reference to the environment. Audra Mitchell's (2014) conception of 'worldly security' positions itself as a framework that rejects the binaries between humanity and the natural world assumed in contemporary accounts of security, even in the context of environmental change. And Peter Newell's (2020) application of green theory to global politics similarly emphasizes the limitations of these binaries and the intersections between multiple sites and dynamics of harm.

The approach to ecological security endorsed here is ultimately one that draws upon these accounts and rejects the anthropocentric–ecocentric distinction as a useful means of either coming to terms with the contemporary condition or guiding the way we should respond to it at a normative and practical level. The above accounts draw on holistic and ecological thought in characterizing the contemporary ecological condition, but also (crucially) recognize the importance of engaging human populations and human agency in advancing progressive change, not least through reorienting the human–nature relationship (see Newell 2020). In the process, all the challenges to the anthropocentric–ecocentric distinction noted above make a case for recognizing the intersections and 'entanglements' (Eckersley 2017; Hardt 2017; Newell 2020) between forms and dynamics of subjugation of both the natural world and non-humans on the one hand, and between human populations and groups on the basis of gender, race or class on the other. Ultimately, the attempt to work through or beyond this binary is often presented as a pragmatic imperative in engaging contemporary human populations to orient their behaviour and action towards a form of ecological stewardship. But if there are compelling practical reasons to move beyond the distinctions between human and nature, and between anthropocentrism and ecocentrism, this seems particularly acute in the context of the Anthropocene.

The Anthropocene, as noted, is the mooted term for the contemporary geological era, in which human activities are viewed as so pervasive and significant as to have altered (with the capacity to further alter) the Earth system itself and its processes upon which humans and other life depends (see Steffan et al. 2004:1). The notion that humans have become the dominant geological force shaping the earth and its processes and that we had entered in to an unpredictable and potentially disruptive era in contrast to the stability of the Holocene and other geological era, encouraged some to make a formal case for the Anthropocene label to the International Commission on Stratigraphy and the International Union of Geological Sciences (IUGS). While yet to make a decision on this formal renaming, it was the IUGS' own Anthropocene working group that made this case, suggesting in the process that the mid part of the twentieth century should be identified as the onset of the Anthropocene (Dalby 2009).

For some, and irrespective of debates about whether it is an accurate account of a shift in the geological era from the Holocene (see Lövbrand et al. 2015), the Anthropocene is a dangerous formulation in terms of its political implications. Some suggest that the image of an all-powerful humanity capable of making and remaking the world and the conditions of its own existence stands in direct contrast to the humility and responsibility that should ultimately inform the way we conceive of our relationship with the natural world (Luke 2013).[5] Those holding this view would point to the claims made in a recent 'ecomodernist manifesto' (Lynas 2011; Asafu-Adjaye et al. 2015) and to the (technological) focus of organizations such as the Breakthrough Institute (see Angus 2015; Mann and Toles 2016). These accounts appear to welcome the Anthropocene's arrival as an opportunity to employ technology on an unprecedented scale to manipulate planetary functions (see Malm and Hornborg 2014; Eckersley 2017:987–9). Some also warn of the danger that the Anthropocene framing, with its focus on the geological impact of 'humans', risks drawing our attention away from the significant inequalities between human communities in contribution and vulnerability to ecological change (see Chandler 2013; Malm and Hornborg 2014).[6]

---

[5] For an account of different visions of the Anthropocene, see, e.g., Dalby (2009); Eckersley (2017); Dryzek and Pickering (2018); Lövbrand et al. (2015); Grove (2019:35–48).

[6] Indeed Grove (2019) suggests the need to focus on the 'Eurocene', a framing he presents as one more consistent with the origins or drivers of the contemporary

Others might hold a less benign view of the Anthropocene but tend to view its mooted arrival as an opportunity to usher in the scale of change in existing institutions, practices, mindsets and ethics that might enable us to escape the devastating effects of global climate change. This view is evident in Burke et al.'s (2016) 'Planet Politics Manifesto', an account of the need for an alternative set of frameworks and institutions in international relations thought and practice to come to terms with the contemporary ecological (and geological) condition. Frank Biermann (2018) has argued that the Anthropocene equates to a 'distinct, new and unprecedented epoch in planetary history', one that necessitates a 'revolution in human consciousness'. Clive Hamilton (2015), meanwhile, suggests that the arrival of the Anthropocene necessitates a fundamental change in humans' relationship with and approach to ecosystems, suggesting this should usher in a wholesale change in the way we understand ethical responsibility and our place in the world. This view is also evident in Bruno Latour's (2015) account of the Anthropocene.

While organizations such as the IUGS consider the question of geological era as an ontological and empirical question about Earth system processes and function, the above accounts point to important questions around the *politics* of the Anthropocene (see, in particular, Lövbrand et al. 2015; Wakefield et al. 2020). Indeed, in focusing on the potential (and varied) normative and practical implications of conceiving and approaching the contemporary geological era in particular ways, the above discussions bear parallels to what is at stake in embracing terms such as 'security' or 'resilience', for example (see Dalby 2009; Clark 2014:22–4; Eckersley 2017; Wakefield et al. 2020). Ultimately, and while recognizing the dangers of enabling projects oriented towards the technological manipulation and reconfiguration of Earth systems, here I endorse the broad claim that even the mooted arrival of the Anthropocene points to the impossibility of sustaining the nature–human distinction central to modern thought, providing a compelling rationale for reflecting on those relationships and reconfiguring the (ecological) context in which humans are embedded. It provides a further empirical and ontological rationale, in this

ecological crisis and geological shift. See also Burke et al. 2016. And in emphasizing the role of particular modes of economic exchange in driving the arrival of the Anthropocene, Jason Moore makes a case for conceptualizing this era as a 'capitalocene' (in Newell 2020:15).

book, for approaching the climate change–security relationship through the lens of ecological security.

Ultimately, the above accounts of the nature–human divide, the ethical commitments entailed in approaching environmental change in anthropocentric or ecocentric terms and the apparent arrival of the Anthropocene all provide context to the discussion of ecological security, even a compelling rationale for understanding the climate change–security relationship in these terms. Ecological security in this context is built on an ethics consistent with key insights of holistic and ecological thought but in ways that attempts to transcend the anthropocentric–ecocentric binary. Drawing on insights from ecological pluralism, feminism and critical political ecology, the ethical foundation of ecological security is one in which our focus is embeddedness, entanglement and complex interrelationships between living beings, with a particular focus on human populations and the ecosystems in which they exist. It emphasizes the intersections between multiple forms and sites of domination and subjugation – whether based on humanity, gender, race or class (see Plumwood 1993) – and suggests the imperative of recognizing and addressing these dynamics in concert with each other.

While the ethical imperative of reconfiguring the human–nature relationship is compelling as a means of addressing the ecological crisis, it is particularly compelling in the context of the Anthropocene. This geological era, even its mooted arrival, provides an important opportunity for reimagining humanity's place in the world and the nature of our relationship to other living beings. As Robyn Eckersley (2017:985) argues, we need a 'non-anthropocentric ontology of entangled human and non-human agencies paired with a non-anthropocentric and geopolitan imaginary of time, space and community that repositions and decentres humanity in Earth's geostory'. These claims and commitments constitute the ethical foundations of the ecological security discourse defended here.

## Defining Ecological Security: Referent and Threat

Ecological security, in the specific context of climate change, may ultimately be defined as the resilience of ecosystems. This discourse of security, in orienting towards ecosystem resilience, emphasizes the rights and needs of the most vulnerable to (manifestations of) climate change across space (impoverished populations), time (future generations) and species (other living beings). While meaning given to the constituent parts of this discourse – in terms of agents, means and the nature of threat – will be outlined later in this chapter and in Chapter 4, three particular components of this discourse require further elaboration and definition here: ecosystems, vulnerability and resilience. These will be addressed in turn, as they serve to give meaning to the referent objects of security (ecosystems) and the nature of the threat climate change poses to those referent objects (threats to ecosystem resilience). In the context of introducing these dimensions of the discourse, the emphasis is on the *direct* nature of the threat posed by climate change.

An ecosystem is defined here as composed of three components. It includes the range of living beings in a given area that interact with each other; the non-living components of the physical environment (atmosphere, soil, water, earth) that surround those beings; and their interrelationships. It is a complex of organisms, their environment and their interactive relationship in a particular space. For our purposes, these ecosystems (inevitably) overlap and are defined by significant variation in scale, dynamics and functionality (see, e.g., O'Neill 2001; McShane 2014).

On the face of it, 'ecosystems' represent broad and amorphous referent objects of security (see Fagan 2016). Yet, in fact, this emphasis draws our attention to key components of the contemporary ecological condition, particularly interrelationships and complexity. These are core features of ecosystems themselves and their functionality, while also characterizing flow, interaction and 'relational processes' (Grove 2019:10) between ecosystems. Further, an emphasis on ecosystems as a referent object is no more problematically abstract than alternative accounts of security that focus on the 'nation-state' or an 'international society', for example, which are themselves sites of contestation. And the broader project of making a case for an ecological security discourse is less about specifying discrete and self-contained entities to be preserved as they are (see Kareiva and Fuller 2016) and more about encouraging the development of a sensibility associated with ecological stewardship to advance the concerns of – and reduce harms to – the most vulnerable (see Dalby 2009; Harrington and Shearing 2017).

The focus on ecosystems as the 'referent objects' of security here reflects a series of normative and pragmatic considerations. Of course, in an immediate sense, it addresses the limitations of other discourses or framings of climate security that emphasize the preservation of human collectives and/or the institutions that (claim to) represent them. In these discourses, as noted in Chapter 2, we see a consistent tendency to view the world in anthropocentric terms, with the environment conceived and approached as a resource to be either exploited or preserved to advance human interests.[7] And while the implications of these discourses vary significantly in the way in which climate change is conceived and approached, they all encourage practices insufficiently oriented to long-term considerations and the rights and needs of other living beings. As noted at the outset of the book, these choices – around whose security is prioritized in the context of climate change – significantly define and determine the way in which climate change is addressed, with attendant ethical and practical implications.

As noted earlier in this chapter, we have seen a range of attempts to account for a shift in emphasis from humans and their institutions, employing a range of registers, terms and concepts. While those interested in orienting our concern towards 'the planet' or 'the biosphere' frequently appear motivated by similar sets of normative concerns with avoiding anthropocentric and exclusive, zero-sum accounts of security anathema to addressing an issue such as climate change, these conceptualizations are prohibitively broad. This breadth, in turn, enables the prioritization of interests and practices that serve more specific sets of interests. Indeed, this criticism has been applied to the planetary boundaries literature (see Eckersley 2017) and high-profile representations of 'one planet' (see Peet et al. 2010).

More positively, the ecosystem focus reflects two central considerations in the context of climate change, one empirical and one normative. First, in empirical terms, a focus on ecosystems – given their dynamic, changing, interactive and overlapping nature – allows us to come to terms with notions of interconnectedness and embeddedness central to the contemporary ecological condition and the Anthropocene (Grove 2019; Newell 2020). The in-built emphasis on dynamic interrelationships that comes with a focus on ecosystems encourages us to reject the possibility of distinguishing humans from

---

[7] This criticism is also frequently applied to the 'ecosystems services' framework, which emphasizes the contribution of ecosystems to human communities (see Sikor ed. 2013).

their environment. And the overlapping and complex nature of ecosystems, in turn, encourages a humility and reflexivity that must be central to any attempt to address climate change, points to be drawn out in more detail in Chapter 4 (Kareiva and Fuller 2016). This is particularly the case given the need to reflect upon and incorporate interests of a wide range of human communities across time and space, along with other living beings.

The second (positive) rationale for the focus on ecosystems follows from the above but is more explicitly normative: the emphasis on maintaining the functionality of ecosystems is the best means of ensuring an orientation towards the rights and needs of the most vulnerable over time, space and species. These are conceived here as impoverished and marginalized human populations (space), future generations (time) and other living beings (species). Focusing on the resilience of ecosystems engages with a holistic conceptualization of ethical responsibility but more directly constitutes a *means* of addressing the more specific concerns of particular beings, now and in the future. As McShane notes (2014:86), as loosely and contingently defined systems, ecosystems do not have interests as such. Yet an orientation towards their continued functionality as systems, I argue, is central to encouraging sets of practices most amenable to addressing climate change and the rights and needs of (especially vulnerable) beings through encouraging practices oriented to sustaining the conditions of their existence. In this sense, there are, ironically perhaps, parallels to a national security discourse. Here, advocates would note that the ethical commitment to the preservation of the nation state is not, ultimately, to the nation state itself but to the citizens within that state who are (best) protected by it – this is the nature of the social contract. Yet aside from questions of whether the state continues to fulfil – or indeed has ever fulfilled – that function or viewed its role as a means rather than ends (see McSweeney 1999), the emphasis here remains on exclusive human populations. In the ecological security discourse, the emphasis is on a multiplicity of beings and the best capacity for their survival in the face of a global and long-term threat.

While the ends of ecological security feasibly extend to all living beings present and future, the ultimate orientation is towards the most vulnerable to manifestations of climate change. The understanding of vulnerability endorsed here draws on Neil Adger's (2006:268) definition of vulnerability as 'the state of susceptibility to harm from exposure to stresses associated with environmental and social change and from the absence of capacity to adapt'. This approach clearly conceives of vulnerability not simply in terms of immediate exposure to manifestations of climate change, for example, but also in terms of actors' capacity to minimize risk or respond to that change (see also Barnett et al. 2010). To return to the earlier example of the relative vulnerability of the Netherlands and Bangladesh – both low-lying states – to rising sea levels, it is clear that recognizing the likely impact and danger associated with climate change requires attention not only to their geography but also to relative levels of economic development, for example. Tragically, as a range of analysts have noted, those parts of the world most immediately exposed to the most serious manifestations of climate change tend to also be those least capable of mustering significant economic resources to build adaptive capacity or respond to immediate effects such as natural disasters, for example (Paterson 1996, 2001; Adger 2006; Dalby 2009).

Degrees of exposure and economic capacity for adaptation are not the only determinants of vulnerability, however (Adger 2006). For our purposes, we also need to acknowledge the relative ability that actors have to input into decision-making that will affect their prospects for survival. Of course, as postcolonial theorists and development advocates have long argued, impoverished communities throughout the world – even developing *states* – are less able to influence the mechanisms of global governance or the processes and dynamics of the global economy, for example (see, e.g., Thomas 2000; Chowdhry and Nair eds. 2004; Anievas et al. eds. 2015). This is even more acute in the context of acutely impoverished (and frequently isolated) communities without access to adequate education, information or means of representing concerns to decision-makers at a national, much less international, level. As Michael Sardo (2020) notes, 'the most vulnerable to climate hazards are both dominated by and excluded from meaningful participation in global political and economic structures built on fossil-fuel intensive practices of extraction, production and distribution that intensify climate change'.

Yet, of course, people in the developing world retain communicative capacity as we would understand it. The same does not apply – at least in the same way – to other living beings or to future generations. While a range of theorists have examined the extent to which it is possible to ascribe communicative and agential capacity to other living beings

(Dobson 2010; Sayes 2014) in an immediate sense, these actors are not represented in domestic or international institutions that oversee agreements or coordinate and enact practical responses to climate change. At best, various present human populations make claims, as noted, to speak 'on behalf' of the interests of other living beings or future generations. Most ethical registers, and certainly the dominant accounts of ethical responsibility that underpin key institutions and their legitimacy, fail to account for the rights and needs of other living beings and future generations (see Sunstein and Nussbaum eds. 2004; Wissenberg and Schlosberg eds. 2014; Wienhues 2020). This exclusion is furthered through their lack of capacity to immediately and meaningfully influence policy debate.

The most vulnerable here are therefore broadly conceived as living beings disproportionately exposed to manifestations of climate change, lacking capacity to adapt to manifestations of it, and unable to meaningfully input into decisions that may create harms for them. Many ethical frameworks, even relevant institutional frameworks in the form of the UNFCCC, for example, recognize the particular vulnerabilities of impoverished populations and the developing world to manifestations of climate change, and recognize associated ethical responsibilities towards them (see Gardiner et al. eds. 2010). This is borne of their immediate exposure, limited adaptive capacity (at least in economic terms) and even relative inability to input into (or more accurately influence) decision-making about climate change (see Sardo 2020). Cosmopolitan ethical frameworks have long identified the need to not only recognize ethical obligation beyond the boundaries of the nation state but also actively prioritize the interests of vulnerable populations in this context (Held 1995, 2010; Burke 2013; Burke et al. 2014). And as a range of analysts have noted in the context of climate change, addressing dynamics of economic, social and political marginalization on one hand and addressing exposure to impacts of climate change on the other are frequently mutually reinforcing to the point of being difficult to address independently (see, e.g., Nsiah-Gyabaah 2010; Newell 2020). For the approach to ecological security endorsed here, recognition of the vulnerability of impoverished human populations is central, not least as manifestations of climate change will disproportionately affect those already struggling to secure their survival.

A focus on the rights and needs of other living beings or future generations is far less apparent in existing ethical or institutional frameworks and raises both complex and challenging questions. Clearly, recognizing obligation to a multitude of beings across both time and space means confronting difficult questions – even immediate dilemmas – about prioritizing the rights of some over others and the way these decisions might be made. Yet it is more common in this context to also encounter arguments suggesting that other living beings or future generations are less worthy of ethical consideration (see Celermajer et al. 2020).

In the case of other living beings, some suggest that our ethical register can only feasibly extend as far as other humans. Reasons given for this exclusive focus extend from a simple speciesism, to the absence of reason or intelligence in other living beings, to the inability to genuinely know the interests and concerns of these beings (see, e.g., Soper 1995; Sunstein 2005; Francione 2010; Cavalieri 2012; Floyd 2019). And, of course, over time the tendency to privilege the rights and needs of humans over other living beings, to the point of viewing their exploitation or use as a component of what it means to be human, has become embedded in arguments around the identity or culture of particular communities, for example (Hulme 2009).

In the context of climate change, it is clear that the vulnerability of other species is acute, not least given the scale of species loss related to climate change (and associated changes in ecosystems) to date. By one recent account, commissioned by the WWF and involving fifty-nine scientists, since 1970 humans had wiped out 60 per cent of the world's mammals, birds, fish and reptiles (Carrington 2018). While this cannot wholly be attributed to processes of climate change, the latter significantly accelerates what some scientists describe as the sixth mass extinction event currently under way – an era of 'biological annihilation' (Zielinski 2015; Sutter 2017. See also Burke 2019; Wienhues 2020:108–9).

An orientation towards other living beings, and recognition of obligation towards them, encourages substantive and significant responses to climate change oriented towards maintaining the functions of ecosystems that sustain them. In this sense, and to reiterate, a commitment to ecosystem resilience is viewed as encouraging a sensibility, orientation and associated set of practices through which the rights and needs of other living beings are best protected.

A commitment to future generations has also been less prominent in institutional frameworks governing the politics of climate change and, indeed, in discourses of climate security. While implicit in a range of arguments for the need to act urgently to address the threat posed by climate change, the complex challenges associated with incorporating concerns for future generations in our frameworks have arguably militated against this inclusion (Okereke 2010; Lewis 2018). This clearly applies to advocates of population control as a means of addressing the climate crisis, wherein securing life on the planet necessitates reducing the number of 'future humans'. But it applies too to less controversial (some might suggest less misanthropic) approaches to climate ethics that identify a series of key challenges associated with incorporating a concern for future generations into our ethical frameworks, institutions and practices.

Again, issues arise here with communication and our capacity to *know* the interests and needs of future generations. This challenge has been the focus of a significant scholarship in normative political theory, focusing on both impediments to addressing ethical responsibility to future generations and mechanisms through which these considerations might be feasibly incorporated (see, e.g., Page 2006; Beckman 2008; Heyward 2008; Gardiner 2014). While varied, these accounts note that by definition, future humans are not able to communicate their interests and needs through contemporary processes of deliberation and decision-making. As Clare Heyward (2008) has argued, this poses significant challenges for those ethical frameworks that emphasize the importance of deliberative democracy as a means of ensuring progressive (environmental) practices, in a manner not wholly dissimilar to the challenge of addressing the rights and interests of other living beings.

For those working in the broadly cosmopolitan tradition, the challenge here (of anticipating the rights of *future* humans) may appear less fundamental than incorporating other living beings into our ethical frameworks. Yet while we may consider ourselves to have greater degrees of empathy towards and understanding of future humans than other living beings, for example, continued societal evolution (Beckman 2008) and the pace and scale of technological change in particular challenge our capacity to readily anticipate future needs and desires. Those working in the broadly ecomodernist tradition have long made this case, in the process advocating continued technological progress rather than significant changes to existing lifestyles and practices as a means of addressing climate change (see Lynas 2011;

Asafu-Adjaye et al. 2015). Yet it is also central to the so-called non-identity problem, as articulated by Derek Parfit (1987) and Clare Palmer (2011). Simply put, this refers to the fact that we may be attempting to incorporate considerations for people or collectives who may not exist in the future, depending on contemporary practices.

For others, the challenge is one of existing *institutional* frameworks and the imperative of their alteration. Stephen Gardiner (2014), for example, has argued that the source of our failure to incorporate concerns towards the rights and needs of future generations are our institutions and their short-term orientation, whether capitalist economic systems or democratic states with short election cycles. For Gardiner (2014:303–4), these are 'poor at giving appropriate voice to intergenerational concerns, and even encourage lesser concerns to dominate over them'. While recognizing this dynamic, a component of what Gardiner refers to as a 'perfect moral storm' presented by climate change, the question of institutional realignment or restructuring will be addressed in more detail in Chapter 4, dealing with means and agents of ecological security.

Ultimately, the commitment to the most vulnerable in this instance clearly extends to future generations who are unable to input into contemporary decision-making and whose life prospects are disproportionately harmed by contemporary practices. A commitment to the resilience of ecosystems, which already suggests a focus beyond immediate preservation or protection, is viewed here as a foundation upon which concern for future generations may be incorporated into existing frameworks, institutions and practices. Indeed, as Nolt (2011:703) has argued, 'implicit in nonanthropocentric value theory is a second assumption, which is shared by intergenerational ethics: benefit and harm are not confined to the present or near present'.

This section has made a case for a focus on vulnerability, defined in the context of climate change as the intersection between exposure, adaptive or response capacity and ability to impact on contemporary decision-making. This orients our attention to the rights and needs of impoverished populations, and even more acutely vulnerable future generations and other living beings. The emphasis on the rights and needs of the most vulnerable in the context of climate change clearly faces a range of complex challenges, whether in terms of anticipating or understanding those needs or in terms of weighing up or adjudicating between different sets of needs of different actors. Yet these

challenges cannot constitute a rationale for ignoring the harms contemporary practices and arrangements cause. Ultimately, the commitment to ecosystem resilience is viewed as a foundation for the
incorporation of the rights and needs of the most vulnerable into
perspectives, practices and institutions.

Prioritizing the *resilience* of ecosystems clearly requires explication
and defence, not least given the argument advanced here that the threat
of climate change is best conceived – in an ecological security discourse –
as a direct threat to the resilience of ecosystems themselves. As noted,
Denis Pirages's (2005) earlier articulation of ecological security focused
not on resilience but on balance and equilibrium. Yet this account, with
its associated suggestion of the need to preserve or conserve existing
dynamics and functions of ecosystems, insufficiently comes to terms
with protecting that which is already and always *changing*, not least in
the context of climate change and the Anthropocene. As such, we need
to conceptualize the 'protection' or security of ecosystems in ways that
enables recognition of and accounting for ongoing change. Resilience is
viewed as a means of coming to terms with this change, reflecting as it
does a concern with maintaining core functions of ecosystems themselves in the face of change.

Resilience is here defined as the capacity of ecosystems to sustain life
over time and space, retain their 'organizational structure following
perturbation' (Barnett 2001:110) and to 'absorb change while
retaining essential function' (Adger et al. 2011:696). Given the focus
on functionality in the face of change, it is perhaps unsurprising that
resilience has long been a prominent concept in ecological thought (see
Holling 1973). Yet it is controversial and far from uniformly embraced
as a means of coming to terms with imperatives for conceptualizing
and addressing both what needs protecting and the manner in which it
should be protected.

In general terms, the increasing prominence of 'resilience' as a term
and concept used by policymakers and analysts has been met with
scepticism by a range of critics, in the tradition of international
relations and beyond. Many of these critics view resilience as a concept
that potentially normalizes rather than challenges harmful change;
defaults responsibility for addressing harmful dynamics to its victims
rather than its architects; or simply becomes a new mechanism of or
rationale for neoliberal governance (see Dillon and Reid 2009;
Chandler 2013; Zebrowski 2013; Evans and Reid 2014). Elements of

these criticisms seemed particularly strong in the context of violence and trauma, for example. Here, some authors have suggested that a focus on the resilience of those experiencing trauma after violence places more emphasis on self-development and protection than it does on the circumstances (such as the decision to deploy and use armed forces) in which that trauma came to be experienced (Fierke 2004; Schick 2011).

While the criticism of resilience is strongest in these contexts, and while resilience has a longer tradition in ecological thought, its embrace in the context of environmental or climate change has not been universal (see Methmann and Oels 2015; Oels 2015). For David Schlosberg (2013:13), for example, resilience can suggest the need 'to simply adapt to, rather than understand and resist' climate change, thereby potentially undermining a concerted push for mitigation action. For some the concept of resilience is still too static for the dynamism of change associated with the Anthropocene (Kareiva and Fuller 2016), while for others change itself (including to ecosystem functionality) may not be wholly regressive (see Thomas 2017a). Most starkly, perhaps, in their broader critique of the connection made between climate change and security, Buxton and Hayes (2015:9) argue that

resilience accepts worsening climate change as fact and, rather than seeking to take the radical actions to prevent it, seeks to adapt to it. Used with equal vigour in the military-industrial complex, it embraces 'disequilibrium as a point of organisation', in which populations are helped to 'survive' while corporations and capitalism are supported to 'thrive'.

Clearly, there are dangers associated with a concept such as resilience, particularly if it encourages us to focus our attention on 'dealing with' change rather than redressing it. Yet this is ultimately one among several interpretations or applications of resilience. Indeed a range of scholars have suggested the need to approach resilience in a similar way to that in which the concept of security is approached in this book: as an unsettled concept with different meanings and interpretations, which themselves can have radically different implications in practice. This is evident in Philippe Bourbeau's (2018) expansive genealogy of resilience, in Cavelty et al.'s (2015) account of different meanings and interpretations of resilience as applied in critical security studies, in Olaf Corry's (2014) specific exploration of the role of resilience in accounts of climate change and more directly still in Ingrid Boas and Delf Rothe's (2015) examination of the role of resilience in discourses of climate security (see also Ferguson 2019).

In all the above accounts of resilience, the authors draw attention to the possibility of multiple interpretations and applications of resilience, suggesting in the process that its wholesale rejection follows from positioning a particular interpretation of it as universal and timeless. For my purposes, and building on this insight, resilience gives us crucial resources for conceptualizing protection and even security in the face of ongoing change, drawing our attention to the crucial question of whether ecosystems are capable of functioning to (continue to) sustain life.

Of course, even if ultimately endorsing resilience in this context, it is not necessarily the case that this resolves issues of uncertainty regarding the threat or responses to it. While the ecological security discourse and its focus on ecosystem resilience entails a conceptualization of the threat of climate change as a direct rather than indirect one, with the latter a feature of other climate security discourses, this does not resolve the challenge of coming to terms with threats to resilience. As Clare Palmer (2011:282) has asked,

[W]hat kind of effect could climate change have that would harm ecological systems? This question is difficult to answer, partly because of our uncertainty about the effects of climate change, and, but more deeply, because of the problem, in the context of ecosystems, of identifying any sustainable distinction between changes and harms, especially over extended time scales.

There is also the question of whether our actions should orient towards redressing *any* form of compromise to ecosystem functionality or only fundamental ones, and the associated question of the point at which this capacity is compromised in either case. Ecosystems, as noted, are interrelated, complex and evolving, such that accurately predicting the implications of specific temperature increases, rainfall decreases or sea-level rises over a specific timeframe is impossible.

But while this degree of uncertainty is indeed significant, it is clearly disingenuous to suggest that other accounts of the security implications of climate change eradicate uncertainty about when climate change constitutes a threat, whether to national, international or human security. And as will be noted in Chapter 4, not least when endorsing the concept of precaution, we have frameworks and resources (both intellectual and practical) that allow us to conceptualize and address the possibilities of harm (see Singer 1975) without knowing with absolute certainty where thresholds have been reached or what the implications of action or inaction will be. To reiterate a core theme of the book, what is needed is a change in orientation and sensibility regarding the ways in which our actions should be oriented, rather than specific programs for the realization of ecosystem resilience. Indeed, as will be noted in Chapter 4, an ecological security discourse necessitates and is built upon reflexivity, humility, and a commitment to dialogue about threats to ecosystems in particular places.

In this account, ultimately, climate change is presented as a *direct* threat to ecosystems themselves, and thereby ecological security. Climate change, by definition, directly undermines and threatens ecosystems and the beings reliant upon them. This is evidenced by the contemporary (and worsening) reality of biodiversity loss or species extinction, with one prominent study suggesting one in six species faces extinction as a result of climate change (Urban 2015; Wienhues 2020). While indirect implications of climate change for ecosystems still constitute threats to ecological security – the ecological destruction associated with conflict and war-preparedness, for example (see Grove 2019) – the emphasis in this discourse is on the direct threat that manifestations of climate change have for ecosystems and their resilience and, with it, the rights and needs of the most vulnerable.

## Conclusion

Ecological security can be defined as a concern with the resilience of ecosystems. Viewed through this lens, climate change constitutes a *direct* security threat through undermining this resilience and functionality, in turn creating harms for a multitude of living beings. Grounded in holistic ethics yet attempting to navigate beyond the ecocentric–anthropocentric divide through drawing on insights from ecological pluralism, feminism and critical political ecology, this chapter has made a case for ecological security as a framework that orients our concern and action to the most vulnerable: those most exposed to manifestations of climate change, least able to adapt or respond effectively to it and least able to affect decisions and practices regarding dominant approaches to climate change. In this context, a focus on ecosystem resilience was presented as the best means of ensuring the

security of these most vulnerable across space (impoverished populations), time (future generations) and species (other living beings). Such
an orientation is not only ethically defensible but *necessary* in the
context of the shifting dynamics of the relationship between humans
and nature in the Anthropocene – evident not only in the context of
climate change but also in the coronavirus pandemic.

Clearly, even given the account outlined here of the referent object
and the nature of threat posed in this discourse, it remains somewhat
unclear what a threat to ecological security looks like in practice and
what should be done in response. It is worth noting here that any
suggestion of simple, clear and universally recognized thresholds for
identifying and/or responding to the national, international or human
security implications of climate change are also highly questionable.
Complexity and uncertainty are a feature of climate change, the
Anthropocene and the broader ecological condition, along with societal responses to it.

Chapter 4 confronts this challenge directly, asking how an ecological
security discourse positions or defines agency and means. Who is to
provide security here and what are those actors able (or indeed
obliged) to do to advance or realize it? This chapter has outlined
ecological security's ethical foundations, its designation of whose
security matters and its conception of the nature of the threat posed.
The next step is to engage more concretely with the question of what
the pursuit of ecological security looks like in practice.

# 4 | *Means and Agents of Ecological Security*

Chapter 3 made a case for ecological security, responding to the limits to alternative security discourses identified in Chapter 2. In the process, it located the ecological security discourse within a set of ethical traditions and in the broader context of the Anthropocene. The latter part of that chapter then sought to outline exactly how ecological security should be understood, focusing on how the referent objects are conceived and what the nature of the threats to these referent objects are. To reiterate, ecological security here was conceived as the resilience of ecosystems themselves from (predominantly) direct threats to their functionality, prioritizing in turn the lives of the most vulnerable across space, time and species.

While a necessary foundation, one that makes a case for ecological security as a perspective or sensibility rather than a program of action, this account still leaves us with important questions about what the pursuit of ecological security might look like in practice. This chapter addresses this question directly, exploring the means and agents of ecological security. It examines the question of appropriate *means* of practicing ecological security, one raising difficult ethical and practical questions about the relative role of a wide range of practices (from mitigation action to geoengineering). It then engages with similarly complex questions of responsibility and agency, making a case for a genuine array of actors (from intergovernmental organizations to states, non-state actors, community groups and individuals) as potentially significant agents in the provision of climate security. The chapter also emphasizes the importance of reflexivity, humility and dialogue in ensuring that the ethical thrust of ecological security is realized effectively and sustainably in practice.

This chapter is divided into two broad sections. In the first, I examine what should be done to advance the ends of ecological security. In short, what do the *means* of ecological security look like? I further divide these means into two forms: practical and procedural.

The former outlines practices that are consistent with the ethical imperatives of ecological security and a commitment to ecological resilience. Traditional mitigation action is of course central here, but so too are a range of practices oriented towards adaptation, with a potential role for (radical) interventions such as geoengineering also.

But rather than suggest these as a definitive set of practices that should be applied globally, in this chapter I argue that we need to recognize the complex and contingent nature of ecological resilience. We also need to ensure that practices are sustainable in the long-term by engaging relevant communities in discussions around the form practical responses might take and the ways in which they are implemented. In procedural terms, then, this involves a commitment to dialogue, reflexivity and humility in advancing ecological security concerns. These are viewed as crucial in facilitating the appropriate perspective or sensibility in approaching measures oriented towards ecosystem resilience and in ensuring that such measures are sustainable and broadly endorsed.

The second section of the chapter deals with the question of agency. Of course, this could also feasibly be divided into two sections: who is *capable* of advancing ecological security, and who is *responsible* for this provision? After engaging here with the complex question of *responsibility* for the provision of security in the context of ecological security, I make a case for a broad approach to agency and responsibility. Essentially, agents of ecological security can be found at multiple sites, ranging from individuals to intergovernmental organizations. Responsibility between these agents is differentiated on the basis of capacity to consciously and meaningfully contribute to the advancement of ecosystem resilience and, in particular, the minimization of harm for the most vulnerable. What agency means at these different levels and for these different actors will be addressed in turn.

If discourses of security are composed of particular sets of responses to the questions of whose security matters, from what threats, by what means it is to be promoted or realized and through which actors, this chapter completes the articulation of the contours of an ecological security discourse. The final substantive chapter of the book – Chapter 5 – attempts to go further in addressing the (praxeological) question of how ecological security might come to provide the lens through which communities and their institutions view the security implications of climate change. In recognizing immanent possibilities for the articulation and even institutionalization of this perspective, Chapter 5 directly addresses criticisms of the ecological security perspective as Utopian and disconnected from contemporary political institutions and practices. As noted, however, the current chapter seeks to give content to the question of how ecological security is to be realized in practice and which actors constitute agents in that process.

## Means of Ecological Security

Clearly, a wide range of actions constitute practical responses to ecological resilience – significant mitigation action directly; shifting modes of economic exchange and development to advance mitigation action and adaptative capacity indirectly; adaptive measures oriented towards the most vulnerable, including societal resilience-building; and even radical interventions to ensure resilience, potentially extending to geoengineering.

There are complex ethical challenges associated with all measures that fall within the categories envisaged here, not least the direct challenge of whether and how to prioritize some projects over others and even some beings over others. While recognizing the existence of climate change, for example, Bjorn Lomborg (2001) famously argued that the immediate human rights and developmental needs of existing human populations spoke against significant action to mitigate greenhouse gas emissions. This position has been the subject of strong and sustained criticism (see, e.g., Hamilton and Turton 2001; Cole 2003; Ackerman 2008), of course, but it does speak to challenges of prioritizing certain subjects and actions, challenges even more acute in the context of a concern with ecological security.

Here, questions of how we value the (possible) needs of future generations relative to immediate concerns of current populations are particularly challenging – even if we agree that the latter are more important, for example, what exactly does this mean in terms of prioritizing funding or practical efforts?[1] Are *all* efforts to be oriented to current generations at the expense of future generations or only in instances where lives are directly and immediately threatened? Or should we conceive of prioritization between different actors on more

---

[1] Of a significant literature, see, e.g., Page (2006); Parfit (1987); Caney (2005, 2010b).

of a scale, whereby we allocate a particular quotient of time, attention and funding oriented to certain sets of concerns and actors relative to others?[2]

Clearly, any attempt to establish definitive criteria for such an adjudication is impossible in terms of understanding the nature of ecosystem functionality and its implications and will almost certainly lack political purchase, resonance and sustainability. While some mitigation action offers the possibility of simultaneously addressing the needs of present and future human populations and that of other living beings (through transition to renewable energy, for example), more significant and controversial interventions (such as geoengineering projects, for example) necessitate sustained and reflective consideration of the implications of those interventions across time and space and significant engagement with relevant communities (see Symons 2019a). In this context, reflexivity, humility and a commitment to sustained dialogue must be a component of any project oriented towards ensuring the resilience of ecosystems in the face of climate change.

## Ecological Security Practices

As noted, a wide range of practices could feasibly be considered as promoting or helping to realize ecological security in the context of climate change. The following discussion groups these into three categories: mitigation, adaptation and geoengineering.

### Mitigation

None of the climate security discourses outlined in Chapter 2 would deny the potential role of mitigation as a means of advancing or realizing climate security. As evidenced in the way a range of states have responded to the national security implications of climate change, for example (see Diez et al. 2016; Zhou 2017), even this (national) security discourse recognizes that significant mitigation action would serve to ameliorate the conditions that may subsequently give rise to displacement, instability and/or conflict. But as the focus of our concern shifts from the preservation of existing (and often powerful) institutions to the rights and needs of the most vulnerable – as our emphasis

---

[2] For Val Plumwood (2002), any form of 'ranking' of ethical subjects in this way is inherently problematic. See also Wienhues (2020:40–2).

shifts from national to human to ecological security – the role and significance of mitigation, and the associated ambition of mitigation action, increases.

The primacy of mitigation in the ecological security discourse follows two key considerations. The first concerns the emphasis on *direct* implications of climate change. Rather than emphasize the possibility that manifestations of climate change might create conditions in which instability and conflict could happen – in which the threat posed is diffused and indirect – the focus on direct and immediate implications of a changing climate encourages attention to the problem of climate change itself. In simple terms, if a changing climate is itself viewed as the core threat in the ecological security discourse, we need to orient the nature of our response to addressing the greenhouse gas emissions that drive climate change. We need, in short, to orient to preventing or at least significantly minimizing global climate change (see Moser 2012).

The focus on the rights and needs of the most vulnerable clearly drives the emphasis on mitigation here. Ultimately, the limited capacity of the most vulnerable – in particular other living beings and future generations but also impoverished populations – to effectively insulate themselves from the effects of rising temperatures caused by global climate change means the need to focus on minimizing those rising temperatures and climatic changes. While adaptation needs to play a role in this discourse, as will be discussed, adaptive capacity is significantly influenced by the wealth and power of those tasked with or able to provide it (see Kelly and Adger 2000; Smit and Wandel 2006). The difference between the relative adaptive capacities of the states of the developed and developing worlds in this context is significant, but, of course, this gap widens significantly when our lens shift to other living beings or future generations.

These two commitments in the ecological security discourse – the focus on direct and immediate implications of climate change and the focus on the rights and needs of the most vulnerable – suggest that mitigation must be the central practice associated with realizing or advancing ecological security. As Simon Dalby (2009:92) has argued, 'In the case of climate change "our" actions in the developed affluent world ... are directly threatening to people in poor states who are most vulnerable, and directly threatening to future generations whose options will be drastically curtailed if nothing is done to alter existing trends in greenhouse gas production'.

In simple terms, mitigation refers to the reduction of greenhouse gas emissions. The IPCC (2014b:4) defines it as 'an anthropogenic intervention to reduce the sources or enhance the sinks of greenhouse gases'. It remains the key and central focus of the UNFCCC process and the climate change regime, even while questions of adaptation to climate change (whether conceived as likely or inevitable) have become more central over time. While the reduction in anthropogenic emissions is central – through transitioning from fossil fuel use towards renewable energy or a general reduction in activities contributing to greenhouse gas emissions – mitigation may also be realized through reforestation practices that serve to create carbon sinks, for example. For some, carbon dioxide removal (to be discussed in a subsequent section on geoengineering) also potentially constitutes a mitigation practice (see Wigley 2006).

The articulation of goals for minimizing greenhouse gas emissions has been made in a range of ways, from those emphasizing a global carbon budget (Le Quere et al. 2015; see Matthews et al. 2018) to those making a case for a reduction in emissions to previous historical levels and those focused on limiting warming to a particular temperature increase (Hulme 2016). These are not mutually exclusive positions and range from an emphasis on means to one of goals. They ultimately focus on conceptualizing the goals or imperatives of mitigation action in particular and different ways. All endorse the imperative of mitigation as a means of *harm reduction*.[3]

Of course, endorsing the importance of mitigation and affirming a commitment to the reduction of greenhouse gas emissions is one thing and (while continued rising global emissions might suggest otherwise) has not been particularly controversial. But complex questions almost immediately beset a focus on mitigation, especially when our focus shifts to the issue of what coordinated global action to mitigate climate change should look like. These questions include scientific uncertainties, ranging from 'how much mitigation action is necessary to prevent dangerous climate change?' to 'what timeframes or deadlines do we have to meet to avoid dangerous climate change or climate tipping points?' While we have seen a range of attempts to put forward

---

[3] On harm and its use and application in the context of climate change and ecological security, see, e.g., Cripps 2013:10–11, 58–84; Shue 2015, 2017; Harrington and Shearing 2017.

responses to these questions, including by international scientific organizations like the IPCC (IPCC 2013:70), the complexity of global ecosystems' response to changing temperatures is such that an answer to these questions cannot claim to be definitive and can only be articulated in probabilistic terms (see also Alley et al. 2001; Kriegler et al. 2009; Lenton and Ciscar 2013).

Other questions are political and normative and clearly defy anything approaching a settled or definitive response, certainly not one that would achieve widespread agreement (see, e.g., Rayner and Malone 1998; Gardiner et al. eds. 2010). These include, for example, 'To what extent should the needs or desires of contemporary human populations be curtailed to advance the concerns of other living beings or future generations?' 'How should we allocate responsibility for mitigation action – or financing mitigation action – across and between different states?' While broader questions about climate change that have long been key axes of contestation within the UNFCCC process, these are ultimately questions about mitigation – even if we agree that mitigation is important, how much is appropriate and by whom?

While such questions cannot be wholly resolved, the ecological security discourse provides a framework for navigating these and guiding practical responses oriented towards the rights and needs of the most vulnerable. The commitment to mitigation, as noted, is driven by a concern with the direct implications of climate change and the particular dangers posed to the most vulnerable across time, space and species. The commitment to harm minimization for the most vulnerable also ensures, in combination with a commitment to precaution (to be discussed), that significant mitigation action is endorsed even in the face of scientific uncertainty. And while ethical dilemmas regarding the responsibility for mitigation action will be discussed in more detail below, the focus on the most vulnerable ensures an emphasis on mitigation that orients towards a wholesale transition away from fossil fuel use, one driven by those with a capacity to make and to facilitate this transition without significant harm to their own populations.

Advocates of ecological security are likely to be relatively agnostic on the question of the specific form that mitigation takes if it serves to drive down emissions and does not create harms for vulnerable populations and their ecosystems. The core principles of the discourse do not extend to advocacy of particular forms of energy production, for example, except to the extent that mitigation action does not under-mine the lives or life prospects of vulnerable beings. In this context, an ecological security sensibility would prioritize action that does not have implications for development and poverty eradication in the developing world, for example (see IPCC 2013: chapter 13; Shue 2014). The transfer of funds from developed to developing worlds to facilitate a transition to renewable energy (a commitment in the current climate regime, even if not always practiced) would be prioritized over the immediate eradication of forms of energy production in those countries (see Shue 2014, 2017).

Ultimately, it is the application of principles consistent with an ecological security discourse in practice that determine the means used to further mitigation action and the actors responsible for undertaking them. A commitment to the most vulnerable compels significant miti-gation action as the primary response to the direct challenges of climate change, even in the face of uncertainty about severity and timeframes. And a commitment to engagement with local communities, reflexivity and humility should minimize the danger of the imposition of new or perverse forms of harm in the act of pursuing mitigation strategies.

**Adaptation**
Clearly, mitigation is central to an ecological security discourse as a practical response to the (direct) threat posed by climate change. In engaging the source of the problem of climate change itself, the focus here is on addressing the challenge directly while also ensuring orien-tation towards the needs of those without the capacity to insulate themselves from immediate effects of climate change. Yet the inevit-ability of climate change necessitates some attention to the role of adaptive responses to manifestations of it. While in previous decades any discussion of adaptation was viewed as taking our attention away from the imperative of preventing the problem from occurring (mitiga-tion),[4] the growing realization that climate change is happening and will worsen regardless of current action necessitates some attention to

---

[4] In her discussion of challenges in communicating imperatives associated with adaptation, for example, Susanne Moser (2014:338) reminds us of then US Vice President Al Gore's dismissal of adaptation 'in 1989 as a "lazy" cop – out on fighting the causes of climate change'.

how communities and institutions may protect themselves from the most dangerous manifestations of climate change (see Dalby 2009:89–90; Moser 2012, 2014).

For the IPCC (2014a), adaptation refers to the processes and dynamics of 'adjustment to actual or expected climate and its effects; in human systems, (it) seeks to moderate or avoid harm or exploit beneficial opportunities'. While mitigation focuses our attention on minimizing the severity and extent of climate change, adaptation focuses on measures that aim to protect particular communities or institutions from the effects of climate change.

Adaptive responses to climate change can cover a vast array of practices. In its Fifth Assessment Report, for example, the IPCC (2014a: chapter 14, p. 845) identifies over 100 adaptation 'options' grouped according to structural or physical, social and institutional responses. These range from the development of early-warning systems regarding natural disasters and sea-level rises; land zoning and development legislation; livelihood diversification; infrastructure development and/or changes; sea walls and coastal protection structures; and insurance schemes, for example. All are oriented towards managing the effects of climate change, protecting institutions, communities and even in some instances ecosystems from these manifestations.

As noted in Chapter 2, of course, the national security discourse prioritizes adaptive responses to climate change (see Busby 2007). For some, this association fundamentally and irrevocably compromises the concept of 'adaptation' itself. Marzec (2015:2), for example, argues that 'adaptation provides perfect camouflage for military institutions bent on governing environmental anxieties from the standpoint of national security'. Drawing on insights from political ecology, Mann and Wainwright (2017), meanwhile, suggest that 'adaptation projects ... allow capitalist elites to stabilize their position amidst planetary crisis'. The concern evident here is that powerful institutions and the actors representing them will prioritize measures that insulate themselves and their institutions from the effects of climate change. In the process, they will enable the practices that actually *cause* climate change (and the acute risks to vulnerable communities arising from climate change) to continue.

For the ecological security discourse, the concern with ensuring the resilience of ecosystems necessitates prioritizing mitigation, as noted. Yet clearly the reality of some form of climate change, and the vulnerability of impoverished populations to direct and immediate effects of it, necessitates a focus on how those people and communities might be protected from those effects. Such practices – in a range of forms, from infrastructure redevelopment to disaster relief strategies – are encouraged in the context of ecological security if they minimize the likelihood of harm associated with the effects of climate change and do not compromise the resilience of ecosystems themselves in the process.

While a focus on adaptation of people and communities is potentially consistent with the principles of ecological security, it is also possible to identify a range of measures focused on building adaptive capacity of ecosystems themselves. Indeed the IPCC (2014a: chapter 14, p. 845) noted a range of 'ecosystem-based' adaptive measures in response to climate change in its discussion of options available to institutions and communities in adapting to climate change. These included ecological restoration measures, bushfire reduction, afforestation and replanting, the establishment of ecological corridors, the establishment of seed banks, and adaptive land-use management. All such measures potentially serve to help ensure ecosystem resilience in the face of climate change, while also potentially protecting vulnerable beings from immediate climate effects.

Ultimately, in the face of inevitable climate change and manifestations of it, there is a need for adaptive responses to climate change. The ecological security discourse recognizes and endorses the legitimacy of adaptive measures alongside other measures and if undertaken in a manner consistent with dialogue and engagement with local communities. As Matthias Ruth (2005) notes, adaptation and mitigation are not mutually exclusive, and practices aimed at adaptation are consistent with the principles of the ecological security discourse to the extent that they play a role in 'actively reducing or preventing vulnerabilities'. In the ecological security discourse, the form adaptive responses take must be developed through and with engagement and dialogue at local levels, drawing on local experience and understanding of those ecosystems while also ensuring local awareness of (and sustainable local support for) such initiatives (see Elliott 2006; Petheram et al. 2010; Vogel and Henstra 2015). Such measures need to be funded and resourced by those states and institutions with capacity to do so, usually also those states with disproportionate contemporary and historical responsibility for contributing to the problem of climate change.[5] And such measures need to remain secondary to practices oriented towards mitigation.

The focus in the ecological security discourse on direct and immediate threats of climate change, and the threat to the most vulnerable (particularly future generations and other living beings), necessitates a continued and overwhelming emphasis on mitigation as a practical means of realizing ecological security in the context of climate change. Yet the unavoidability of some form of climate change also necessitates adaptive responses that orient towards the rights and needs of impoverished populations rendered immediately vulnerable to manifestations of climate change. Measures to ensure that small island nations have requisite resources to build infrastructure (whether schools, hospitals, housing or public transport systems) that can withstand sea-level rises, for example, is clearly not mutually exclusive with continued efforts to reduce global emissions. And as the IPCC (2014a) report on adaptive options in response to climate change notes, some measures directly targeted to ecosystem resilience – and with it the needs of vulnerable beings – can be conceived and approached as adaptive responses to climate change.

## Geoengineering

If adaptation risks appearing controversial, suggesting as it does to some a focus on the preservation of the status quo and the interests of powerful actors rather than on addressing the problem itself, geoengineering proposals are more controversial still. Geoengineering refers to attempts to 'artificially change the atmosphere in ways that will counteract the enhanced warming effects of carbon dioxide and methane' (Dalby 2015a). As Simon Dalby notes, in the context of climate change, geoengineering proposals usually take two forms: solar radiation management (dispersal of aerosols in the stratosphere to reflect some of the sun's energy into space, for example) and efforts to remove carbon dioxide from the atmosphere (carbon capture and

---

[5] As will be discussed in the context of agency, these two components (capacity to respond and extent of contribution to climate change) map broadly on to distributive and retributive justice concerns, respectively (aligning broadly with 'ability to pay' and 'polluter pays' principles, respectively). While the endorsement of retributive justice concerns through 'loss and damage' claims in climate negotiations is compelling, in this book I defend a conceptualization of responsibility and agency that emphasizes distributive justice. See Shue (2014, 2017); Caney (2005); Paterson (2001); McDonald (2005).

storage, afforestation or ocean seeding, for example).[6] Of course, the latter, if serving to minimize or reduce the volume of carbon dioxide in the atmosphere, could feasibly be defined as a form of *mitigation* practice. Yet the difference here, from our perspective, is that while this form of geoengineering involves *removing* greenhouse gases from the atmosphere, mitigation involves *preventing* greenhouse gases from being emitted in the first place.

The practices outlined above range from unprecedented, expansive and costly forms of ecological intervention on a regional or global scale (large-scale mirrors, for example) to relatively uncontroversial and even commonplace contemporary local practices (reforestation and afforestation, for example). While a substantial range of practices therefore fall into the broad category of 'geoengineering', a number of analysts have developed compelling criticisms of geoengineering in principle. Others have raised objections to specific forms of geoengineering, while more still have cautioned against its employment in particular forms or by particular agents without further study or advanced oversight.

For some, manipulation of planetary function entails playing God with nature. A line of criticism consistent with broader attacks on the notion of a 'good' Anthropocene (see Dalby 2016; Eckersley 2017), the argument here suggests it is inherently wrong to consider large-scale manipulation of Earth systems (see, e.g., Hamilton 2013; Buxton and Hayes 2015). As Robyn Eckersley (2017:987–9) has noted, the concept of geoengineering is frequently linked to an ecomodernist project

---

[6] While all forms of geoengineering noted could warrant further explication, the example of ocean seeding is worth clarifying here as an intervention that points to the broader logic (and dangers) of geoengineering. Ocean seeding, also known as iron fertilization, entails the stimulation of phytoplankton production. Phytoplanktons, like land-based plants, consume carbon dioxide and process this as oxygen. These phytoplanktons flourish in iron-rich waters; hence, this form of geoengineering involves the fertilization of ocean water with iron to stimulate their growth. It is – in theory – effective to the extent that phytoplankton cells sink to the bottom of the ocean when they die, in the process taking carbon volume with them. While general controversies associated with geoengineering (such as the issue of governance or regulation and potential impact on local ecosystems) also largely apply to this particular form, the extent to which phytoplanktons withdraw substantial amounts of carbon dioxide from the atmosphere and the extent to which the carbon dioxide these organisms do consume never reaches or returns to the atmosphere, have both been challenged in recent analyses. See Fuentes-George (2017); Darby (2009).

in which the embrace of geoengineering resembles an application for the right to 'remake nature', including in 'better' ways (see also Dryzek and Pickering 2018).[7] In this and other contexts, the actors making the case for geoengineering matter. When climate sceptic and former prime minister Tony Abbott made a case for carbon capture and storage in Australia, it was widely (and almost certainly correctly) criticized as an attempt to take attention away from mitigation or any restriction in the expansion of fossil fuel development and exports (see McDonald 2018:172). The broader suggestion that geoengineering constitutes a search for a climate 'solution' that takes our attention away from the imperative of mitigation is prominent in criticisms of a potential role for it in any form (see, e.g., Corner and Pidgeon 2010; Chaturvedi and Doyle 2015). Indeed this is a component of what Duncan McLaren (2016:596) refers to the as the 'moral hazard' effect, with geoengineering projects such as solar radiation management at risk of deterring mitigation action.

Other criticisms of geoengineering suggest inherent challenges of governance (see McLaren and Corry 2021). Who exactly gets to decide how geoengineering is deployed or what forms it should take? Some have attempted to develop principles for the development and regulation of geoengineering, most evident with the so-called Oxford Principles (see Rayner et al. 2013).[8] The challenge of achieving consensus on any set of principles combined with the capacity (in practice) for unilateral use of geoengineering, however, makes geoengineering a particularly challenging space for management and especially oversight (see Corry 2017; Symons 2019a). Frank Biermann (2018) notes that challenges to geoengineering in this context are almost insurmountable. In suggesting that geoengineering technologies would not survive any sustained democratic debate, meanwhile, Clive Hamilton (2013) has suggested that geoengineering represents 'the dictator's technology

---

[7] For a contemporary – and more nuanced – defence of ecomodernism, one locating the ecomodernist project in a broadly social democratic tradition, see Symons (2019a).

[8] In the context of geoengineering, the five Oxford Principles endorse: its regulation as a public good, public participation in geoengineering decision-making, disclosure of geoengineering research and open publication of results, independent assessment of impacts of geoengineering research, and decisions on deployment to be undertaken through robust governance structures. See www.geoengineering.ox.ac.uk/www.geoengineering.ox.ac.uk/oxford-principles/principles/indexd41d.html?

of choice' (in Eckersley 2017:988). Indeed some have argued that engagement with local and affected communities – one of the five Oxford Principles – is unlikely to be a feature of the development of large-scale geoengineering practices (Chaturvedi and Doyle 2015).

Finally, and crucially from the perspective of ecological security, there are challenges associated with the uncertainty of effects and effectiveness of geoengineering practices and, in particular, the potential side effects for (local) ecosystems. The same complexity of ecosystem function that militates against precise assessments of the timescale, location and severity of climate impacts on ecosystems also complicates a clear understanding of what effects some geoengineering interventions will have on different ecosystems. A range of analysts note that geoengineering practices are often profoundly uncertain and experimental, with local ecosystem implications of interventions such as ocean seeding particularly difficult to either predict or immediately assess (see Clark 2014; Dalby 2015b).

From the perspective of its focus on ecosystem resilience, an ecological security discourse would suggest that there may be a role for geoengineering as a means of addressing climate change. The measures suggested would – crucially, if effective – serve to minimize the effects of climate change, in the process serving the end of ecosystem resilience and the rights and needs of the most vulnerable to the effects of climate change. However, in this discourse, recognition of a potential role for geoengineering practice comes with a series of significant 'riders' to this concession. First, it should be given reduced priority relative to mitigation efforts. The goal, ultimately, should be to address the problem at its source. Second, and related to this, geoengineering should be viewed and employed, as Simon Dalby (2015a, 2015b) has argued, as a short-term, stop-gap measure for minimizing the effects of climate change while pursuing and prioritizing significant mitigation efforts. It should not be viewed as a 'silver bullet' for responding to the problem of climate change. This is echoed in Preston's (2016:161) assessment that geoengineering should be approached as 'a supplementary tool providing more time to organize alternative ways of reducing $CO_2$ emissions'.

Third, regulation, governance and oversight should be democratized and engage systematically with local communities (see Szerszynski et al. 2013; Horton et al. 2018). Finally, geoengineering should be undertaken only in contexts where we can be relatively confident – based on available research material and the use of limited trials and case studies – that it will not cause harm to ecosystems themselves.[9] Viewed through the lens of ecological security, this is clearly a crucial consideration. In practice, research also needs to be publicly available and independently assessed. These latter two points broadly endorse the Oxford Principles and their attempt to democratize both decision-making and research into the effects and effectiveness of geoengineering practices (Rayner et al. 2013).

We should be cautious, even suspicious, when it comes to geoengineering. As Nigel Clark (2014:34) notes while making a case for a significant and sustained discussion of a potential role for geoengineering, geoengineering will be a matter of trial and error, with a 'fair chance of failing, falling short or having unintended consequences'. An increasing number of scholars, including many who would traditionally be viewed as critical ecological theorists, have, of late, noted a potential role for geoengineering in response to the catastrophic harm associated with climate change and the questionable ethics of wholly excluding these forms of intervention (see, e.g., Clark 2014; Dalby 2015a, 2015b; Preston 2016; Corry 2017; Eckersley 2017; Dryzek and Pickering 2018; Symons 2019a). In this sense, we cannot dismiss *any* legitimate role for a form of intervention that potentially has the capacity to ameliorate harms for the most vulnerable, even while we should be cautious about its embrace and application in practice.

## Ecological Security Processes

The preceding discussion of geoengineering suggests that deciding whether and how particular practices are employed in the service of ecological security is not simply a case of assessing the appropriateness of these processes in an abstract sense. In this section, I make a case for three central considerations or processes when approaching the means through which ecological security might be furthered or advanced: dialogue, reflexivity and humility. As noted earlier in the chapter, these dynamics are crucial in facilitating the appropriate *sensibility* for

---

[9] Solar radiation management approaches, for example, serve largely to mask the carbon build-up, thereby leading to dangerous outcomes if the practice is abruptly stopped, while enabling ongoing harms through ocean acidification, for example. I am indebted to one of the manuscript reviewers on these points.

engaging in practices oriented towards ecosystem resilience and crucial in ensuring such measures are sustainable and legitimate within the contexts in which they are employed.

### Dialogue

There is a significant literature and tradition focused on the key role of dialogue in responding to environmental issues, including climate change. Driven by theorists such as John Dryzek (1997, 2005) and drawing on insights from the communicative action framework of Jürgen Habermas (1984, 1989), a particular focus here has been on the idea that progressive environmental policy and politics is most likely to develop through processes of deliberative democracy (see also Held and Hervey 2011). In this schema, for Dryzek and others (e.g. Niemeyer 2011), effective and (crucially) socially sustainable environmental policy will be achieved through deliberative processes that allow multiple voices to be heard and varying interests to be considered and accommodated. In his work, for example, Simon Niemeyer (2013) has utilized small-scale 'mini-public' deliberation case studies to make the case that such contexts and processes increase both acceptance of the science of climate change and support for substantive policy responses to it, including by previously opposing voices. (For an alternative account, see Blue 2015.)

Of course, there has been a range of criticisms of the role of dialogue and deliberation in driving progressive environmental or climate policy. For some, the records of democratic states speaks against the faith placed in democratic processes to achieve progressive climate policy, with some going as far as to advocate an authoritarian response to the climate crisis. (See, e.g., Shearman and Smith 2007; Beeson 2010, 2019). And while we may see significant climate action in some democratic contexts, powerful economic considerations (or at least economic calculations), the influence of key lobby groups and/or cultural forces seem to have militated against progressive climate policy in other democracies.[10] While theorists such as Niemeyer (2013) would see this as evidence for the need for a particular *form* of democracy and deliberation in contrast to that evident in most (if not all) existing

---

[10] The respective national-level climate policies of Germany and the UK, for example, in comparison with the US and Australia, speak to the scale of this distinction. On climate leaders and laggards among a range of democratic, developed states, see Tobin (2017).

political systems, others would note that the challenge of 'upscaling' the type of 'mini-public' deliberation he envisages is particularly significant (see Goodin and Dryzek 2006).

Power – and, in particular, power discrepancy – is a central axis of critique for deliberative democracy as a means of advancing progressive climate policy, as it has been for Habermas's framework (see Sanders 1997; Young 2000; Kadlec and Friedman 2007). At its most fundamental, critics here would suggest that no form of deliberation or dialogue can ever be devoid of power relations, and the different capacities that some actors have to speak and be heard necessarily compromises the idea of deliberation as an equalizing space. As Robyn Eckersley (1992) argued in the context of environmental change, communicative action makes problematic assumptions about the capacity for different (and especially vulnerable beings) to actually communicate their needs and interests (see also Cudworth and Hobden 2013; Youatt 2014, 2017). While Eckersley's focus is other living beings, Claire Heyward (2008) argues that deliberative democracy is similarly – even fatally – weak on the question of consideration for the rights and needs of future generations in the context of climate change (see also Thompson 2010). Clearly, this is an important point from the perspective of the ecological security discourse, in which the concern with ecosystem resilience is precisely oriented towards the rights and needs of the most vulnerable: those unable (or at least lacking similar capacity) to speak or be heard.

These are important limitations to the (proceduralist) ethics at the heart of claims around deliberative democracy. As should be clear from the elucidation of 'progressive' principles that should underpin an approach to climate security in Chapters 1–3, however, the ethics underpinning the ecological security discourse outlined here are not wholly procedural.[11] This book retains a concern with outlining a broad vision of 'the good' in the context of how the relationship between climate change and security should be understood and approached. Even given this more consequentialist inclination, however, dialogue itself plays at least three key roles in the context of advancing a concern with ecological security *in practice*.

---

[11] On proceduralist versus consequentialist ethics, see, e.g., Parfit (2011) and Scheffler (1988).

First, dialogue helps in the process of translating broad principles for action into specific measures and instruments, tailored to local contexts (see Rayner and Malone 1998). Engagement with local voices in particular is crucial in ensuring an understanding of the functions and interrelationships within ecosystems, as advocates for Indigenous knowledges in the context of environmental change have long argued (see Green and Raygorodetsky eds. 2010; Mitchell 2014). As noted earlier, the form that mitigation and/or adaptation measures take should always be aligned to local contexts and dynamics, with dialogue a central means for ensuring that takes place.

Second, sustainability of or support for practices oriented towards ecosystem resilience is more likely in the context of open dialogue and deliberation. As Lorraine Elliott (2006:361) has argued, 'decision-making by governments and the implementation of legislative and regulatory frameworks is ... more effective if all stakeholders are represented and if the legitimate interests of actors other than states are recognized' (see also Kloprogge and Van Der Slujis 2006). In the process, Elliott (2006:361) makes a case for genuine public dialogue that minimizes the extent to which those most vulnerable and most affected by practices attempting to address climate insecurity are excluded or treated as mere 'objects to be acted upon, to be educated, consulted and informed'. Such inclusion, from an array of actors and stakeholders, should serve to ensure greater levels of legitimacy of and support for practices oriented towards ecosystem resilience and the actors undertaking them.

Third, dialogue serves the end of continual learning about the effectiveness and implications of practices. In the context of significant uncertainty about how ecosystems will respond to climate change or the practices undertaken with a view to protecting them, open dialogue between locals, policy makers, practitioners and researchers is important (see, e.g., Kloprogge and Van Der Slujis 2006). This should serve to ensure that what constitutes 'best practice' – while still context specific – can be shared with practitioners and communities of actors concerned with ensuring the best possible practical responses are implemented. This position is evident in the Oxford Principles on geoengineering, for example, which endorse the imperative of full and open disclosure of the latest geoengineering research and trials, and open publication of results (Rayner et al. 2013).

Ultimately, dialogue plays a crucial role in ensuring the principles of an ecological security discourse translate effectively and sustainably into practice. Through engaging local communities and knowledges, reflecting on the effectiveness and implications of practices and minimizing exclusion in the process of responding to the security implications of climate change, effective, legitimate and sustainable practices are more likely to follow.

### Reflexivity

A second dynamic key to ensuring the appropriate approach to practices oriented towards ecosystem resilience is reflexivity. As a concept, reflexivity has a strong tradition in sociological thought. While there are many alternative accounts of the concept within sociology, a core dimension of multiple definitions of reflexivity (especially following Bourdieu and Wacquant 1992) is that it concerns critical self-awareness of, and reflection upon, our own biases and commitments. For sociologists, reflexivity was potentially crucial in mediating between structures and agents, capturing an iterative process between pure structural path dependency and individual autonomy (Bourdieu and Wacquant 1992; Archer 2003; Decoteau 2016). This process of self-reflection offered, for proponents, the prospect of change in light of the outcome of performances (see Dryzek 2016).

More recently in research on environmental and climate politics, John Dryzek and colleagues have taken up the concept and applied it to institutions of global environmental governance. Jonathan Pickering (2018:6), building on Dryzek's (2016) engagement with ecological reflexivity, argues that ecological reflexivity can be understood as

the capacity of an entity (e.g. an agent, structure, or process) to: recognise its impacts on social-ecological systems and vice versa; rethink its core values and practices in this light; and respond accordingly by transforming its values and practices.

Robyn Eckersley (2017:994) pushes further still, drawing on the ecofeminism of Plumwood and others in the process, to argue for a hyper-reflexivity defined by 'critical reflection on the conditions for the ongoing reproduction of self and other, broadly conceived to include the human and non-human worlds'. For Eckersley, and to return to a theme of Chapter 3, the Anthropocene provides an opportunity for interrogation not only of our own beliefs and commitments but also for reflection on the broader conditions of existence on the planet. And for Dryzek and Pickering (2018), this, in turn, potentially enables changes in practices, the institutions that drive them and even the principles that underpin them.

Reflexivity is particularly relevant to the pursuit of practices consistent with advancing or realizing ecological security. With uncertainty a defining feature of how ecosystems will respond to climate change or even the practices designed to protect them, there is clearly a need for continual reflection on the extent to which such practices (and the frameworks in which they are embedded) are effective and fit for purpose (see Kareiva and Fuller 2016:115). For Dryzek and Pickering (2018), the imperative of reflexivity particularly applied to institutions of (environmental) governance, which could create path dependencies in terms of the processes and practices they encourage. Linked to the broader themes of the book, I would endorse the claim that we should not be limited in our actions by institutional structures and arrangements as we find them. Rather, we should allow the nature of the problem and the imperative of responding effectively to it to help determine how institutional arrangements could be improved or indeed how alternative institutions might be developed. Reflexivity plays a central role in this process. And while this articulation of reflexivity is relevant to a potentially large range of issues and dynamics, it is particularly applicable to climate change given its global scope and the acute complexity associated with aligning practices and outcomes.

### Humility

Finally, and following the above discussion of reflexivity, we need to acknowledge the limits of what we can categorically claim and practically endorse in response to climate change. This clearly applies to the limits of our understanding of how ecosystems function, how they respond to perturbation, what tipping points might be and/or what timeframes of climate change and response we should orient attention towards (see Maslin and Austin 2012; Kareiva and Fuller 2016). It applies also to the acutely challenging task of managing and prioritizing different sets of commitments to different beings across space and time. We need to recognize in this context the impossibility of setting specific criteria that will apply universally when mediating between existing communities' developmental needs, for example, and obligations to other living beings or future generations. And recognition of limitations should particularly encourage circumspection when it comes to large-scale (and possibly irrevocable) interventions to address climate change such as geoengineering. As Robyn Eckersley (2017:989) has noted, 'the unexpected gravity of what we have already unintentionally produced counsels in favour of caution and humility when thinking about the deliberate manipulation of Earth systems processes to serve human purposes'.

All this speaks to the imperative and importance of humility, in both thought and practice. We need to be humble in regards to what we can claim about climate change and what we can claim about ecosystems and their function.[12] In some senses, this humility is built in to the consensus model of the IPCC. Here, assessments of the science and implications of climate change are tempered by the need for consensus among a genuinely international membership.[13] They are also accompanied by indications of how probable the scientific assessments are and by the inclusion of a genuine range of assessments (whether in terms of temperature increases, timeframes or the impacts of these on dynamics like sea-level rises, for example). And this sentiment, along with the set of practices it encourages, is also arguably found in the Oxford Principles of geoengineering and even in the 'precautionary principle' endorsed at the founding of the UNFCCC at UNCED in 1992. All encourage humility in different ways, while giving us resources for navigating profound uncertainty about the future of ecosystems without giving up on outlining and pursuing substantive action in the face of that uncertainty. These points will be discussed in more detail in Chapter 5, which will make the case that the endorsement of such principles through relatively mainstream institutional

---

[12] Stephen Hobden (2014:181–2) argues that humility should be viewed as central to post-humanism.

[13] For critics, of course, the IPCC's consensus model has a 'lowest common denominator' effect in which the positions of the most sceptical and cautious are more likely to win out, in turn ensuring that the IPCC's assessments are relatively conservative given the scale of the challenge (see Hoppe and Rödder 2019). Scherer (2012), for example, notes that 'a comparison of past IPCC predictions against 22 years of weather data and the latest climate science find that the IPCC has consistently underplayed the intensity of global warming in each of its four major reports released since 1990'. On the IPCC's role in the construction of climate knowledge more broadly, see Hughes (2011).

settings and arrangements gives us hope for the embrace and pursuit of ecological security in practice.

One final point is necessary here before moving from the means to the agents of ecological security. The above endorsement of dialogue, reflexivity and humility might appear to push against the broad thrust of the book itself, concerned as it is with outlining the contours of a progressive security discourse in the context of climate change. Here, a case is made for particular answers to the question of whose security matters, from what threats, by what means it is to be realized and (to be discussed) by what agents. For post-structuralists, the endorsement of a discourse and the 'meta-narratives' on which it is based necessarily involves a form of universalism, an imposition of standards and values and the likelihood of creating new orthodoxies that will always serve some interests while neglecting or indeed threatening others (see Foucault 1977; Lyotard 1984). From this perspective, the idea that discourses can be softened or tempered, or are even constituted through genuinely intersubjective processes, is inherently problematic. Two forms of response can be made to this critique here.

First, and as noted in Chapter 1, the Foucauldian notion of discourse as all-powerful, structural, monolithic and hegemonic is different in important ways from the context in which it is used here. Following Martin Hajer (1995), discourses are approached as multiple and competing rather than monolithic, and as intersubjectively constituted rather than exclusively performative or structural. In this sense, we need to pay attention to the processes through which discourses compete to provide the framework through which particular issues – like climate change – are conceptualized and approached. Recognizing agency in the way in which discourses are translated from precepts to action necessitates engagement with how this translation or application might take place in progressive and effective ways.

Second, and following this, the imperatives of dialogue, reflexivity and humility can minimize the dangers of embracing a particular discourse and can help ensure that principles are not co-opted and imposed. Rather, these principles should be a constant subject of reflection, with recognition of the limits of what we can claim and recognition too of the imperative of engaging in dialogue to develop understanding of the challenge and responses to them, the effective translation of principles to action and sustainable support for policy and practical responses. The question of who or which actors are responsible for enacting these practical responses is the subject of the remainder of this chapter.

## Agents of Security

As noted in the discussion of the conceptual framework and the specific discourses of climate security addressed in Chapters 1 and 2, existing and dominant accounts of security tend towards the conflation of referent and agent of security. In the case of the national security discourse, 'the state' is the answer to the question of both who *needs* protecting and who *does* the protecting. There is an elegant simplicity to the notion of self-help here. It is one that promises to eliminate the dilemma associated with acting on behalf of constituents who fall outside (whether in terms of time or space) the agent's immediate purview. And it can also imply that any alternative arrangement or set of commitments will separate the referent from the agent of security and, in the process, lose the prospect of meaningful agency from states – the most powerful actors in the international system. Of course, even if the ethics of communitarianism and the social contract genuinely underpin states' approaches to national security (see Williams 1998), this serves to exclude non-human subjects and those located outside the territorial boundaries of the nation state.

Yet the idea of the state as its own security provider – the coincidence of referent and agent – is so powerful that the question of agency becomes a site of critique for any alternative choice of referent object (see Thomas and Tow 2002). Who exactly is responsible for providing security 'on behalf' of individuals who are stateless or whose states don't fulfil this role? (See Huysmans 2006a, 2006b.) And who is responsible for providing security on behalf of an 'international community', for example? (See Buzan and Gonzalez-Palaez 2005.) These are challenging questions that have long been raised – and addressed – by those concerned with human rights abuses, refugees or the management of international crises.[14]

---

[14] Of course, the principle of the 'responsibility to protect' is a key example of a recent attempt to challenge the self-help model of security and (to some extent at least) the communitarian ethics at the heart of traditional accounts of national security and sovereignty. While endorsing the social contract in asserting the importance of states providing for the safety of their citizens – as a condition of international recognition of sovereign rights – the principle moves beyond

This question of agency becomes even more complicated when our frame of reference extends to other living beings and future generations. And the stakes are particularly high: if we cannot identify and mobilize agents for the *provision* of security, then surely that conceptualization or discourse of security has little practical relevance or even grounds upon which it can be defended. As noted, this has been central to criticisms (and the ultimate rejection) of ecological security, including by some analysts who express sympathy for the philosophical and normative commitments at the heart of the discourse itself (e.g. Barnett 2001). This is therefore a crucial question for the ecological security discourse, one in need of elaboration and defence.

The remainder of this chapter identifies agents for the promotion and realization of ecological security in the context of climate change. At an analytical level, agency can be divided – broadly speaking – into responsibility and capacity: who is *obliged* to provide security, and who is *able* to provide security. In practice, however, human consciousness draws these two components together: to the extent that a being is able to engage in conscious action that contributes to climate change or its amelioration, that being is viewed here as having at least some degree of responsibility for serving as an agent of ecological security. In short, responsibility is approached here principally in terms of capacity, defined in terms of both the ability to (knowingly) contribute to climate harms and the ability to contribute to the amelioration of climate change and its effects.[15] The extent or degree of that capacity – to contribute to or address climate change – in turn provides us with a framework for ascribing degrees of responsibility.

As may be anticipated, given the above and the commitments of an ecological security discourse, agency is located at multiple and interrelated levels. The central agents of national and international

communitarianism and the social contract in endorsing a 'responsibility' to address suffering and abuse of peoples beyond the boundaries of the state. It is this latter position, however, that has been most challenged in theory and practice, with critics (e.g. Chandler 2004; Cunliffe 2010, 2017; Hehir 2011, 2013) questioning who exactly bears responsibility for addressing external abuse and how we can account for significant inconsistency in the invocation and application of R2P in similar empirical contexts. See Bellamy (2014).

[15] On the role of consciousness in terms of responsibility, see, e.g., King and Carruthers (2012). As will be clear, however, the predominant focus here is on the structural (rather than individual) dimensions of responsibility for climate action (see Sardo 2020).

security – states and intergovernmental organizations – are viewed here as crucial agents for ecological security. In this context, the key challenge is not whether to engage with powerful institutions of world politics as agents but rather how these institutions might be encouraged to orient their actions towards ecosystem resilience and the rights and needs of the most vulnerable. Given the nature of the challenge of climate change and contributions to it, however, we also need to develop a conception of agency that applies to civil society organizations, companies and individuals. In the process of outlining this conception of agency in the remainder of this chapter, I draw on Toni Erskine's (2003, 2008) account of institutional responsibilities and analyses of the role of the 'green state' in world politics (see Eckersley 2004; Barry and Eckersley eds. 2005).

## Responsibility and Ecological Security

As Toni Erskine (2008) notes, 'questions of agency in International Relations need to be recognized as explicitly moral questions'. This is especially the case if the question of agency draws together responsibility and capacity – the 'who should' and 'who can'.

In the discourses of climate security noted, responsibility is addressed most directly in the case of the national security discourse. As noted, the suggestion here is that the state is responsible for providing for the protection (and to some extent for securing the well-being) of its citizens. As the referent object of security becomes more amorphous and less institutional in form – from notions of international society or community to human welfare – questions of agency tend to become more complicated. While those who would advocate recognizing the international security implications of climate change often point to the role that specific institutions like the UN Security Council can and should play in realizing climate security (e.g. Scott 2015; Maertens 2018), there is often limited reflection on how we might make sense of its responsibility in the context of the capacity or duties of other international institutions, states, private sector organizations, civil society groups or individuals, for example. Most recognize that it cannot just be the UNSC that addresses international security implications of climate change (see Cousins 2013; Conca et al. 2017), including state representatives in UNSC debates themselves (see Croucher and McDonald 2014; Scott 2015; Scott and Ku 2018; Conca 2019;

Maertens 2021; Hardt and Viehoff 2020), but beyond that acknow-
ledgement, there is little specification of agency and responsibility. The
same, for the most part, is true in cases made for human security; these
accounts are likely to detail the human security implications of climate
change and make a broad case for action, but it is not always (indeed
not usually) clear which actors should then be tasked with pursuing
that action (see, e.g., Matthew et al. eds. 2010). As noted, this lack of
specificity in discussions of agency tends to give rise to claims that such
discourses are Utopian.

Of course, in the context of the human security discourse, one simple
way to conceptualize agency would be to talk of universal individual
responsibility, as some cosmopolitan theorists suggest (see Singer
2002; Harris 2008; Hiller 2011). If we all as individuals contribute
to climate change and can therefore help address it through our everyday actions, and if obligations by definition extend across boundaries
to all (especially the most vulnerable human populations), then an
obvious strategy would be to universalize the agent of security in the
same way we universalize the referent object. This potentially has
purchase for an ecological security discourse too, given the extension
of referent object beyond the limits or boundaries of existing
institutions.

There are two key limitations with such a strategy, however. First,
and as most cosmopolitan theorists would acknowledge (see, in particular, Shue 2014, 2017 but also Caney 2005), not all individuals are
equally culpable nor (more importantly) capable. This acknowledge-
ment then necessitates the need for further elaboration about how we
assign responsibility in the face of acutely different levels of vulnerability, contribution to the problem itself and (in particular) ability to
redress it.

Second, a focus on individual responsibility elides the ways in which
institutions bear responsibility, along with the structural context of
individual decision-making. While states or private companies often
claim to represent collectives of particular individuals, these institutions still exercise purposive agency in ways that profoundly impact
climate change and responses to it. This extends from industrial practices that directly contribute to climate change, for example, to policy
that incentivizes or disincentivizes practices contributing to mitigating
greenhouse emissions. As Toni Erskine (2008) notes in making a case
for drawing attention to the roles of institutions of global politics as

holders of responsibility, 'explanations of certain harms (such as global warming) cannot be reduced entirely to the individual human constituents of those organizations involved in relevant practices and policies without overlooking an important part of the story'. And as Newell et al. (2015) note, locating responsibility at the level of the individual takes attention away from the ways in which individual choice is conditioned and defined significantly by broader sets of structures and institutional arrangements (see also Sardo 2020, drawing on the work of Iris Marion Young).

In the following discussion of agency in the ecological security discourse, responsibility for addressing climate change, therefore, is viewed as residing with both institutions and individuals. This ranges from international organizations to states, civil society organizations, private companies and people. In making sense of the extent of their responsibilities, the focus here is on capacity, defined in two senses. The first refers to the capacity for *conscious* decision-making and action that either contributes to climate change or serves to help address it. Any actor that could reasonably take account of the effects of their actions in contributing to climate change, for example, bears some responsibility for limiting those actions.[16] This clearly positions some of those most vulnerable to climate change – future generations and other living beings – as not bearing responsibility for advancing ecological security.[17]

The second capacity refers to the ability to bring resources to bear to redress (e.g., through mitigation action) or to prepare for manifestations (e.g., through adaptation) of climate change. This vision of capacity ties to elements of distributive justice or, more simply, equity (see Shue 1993, 1999; Paterson 2001; Weijers et al. 2010; Wienhues 2020). Here, those with the resources to assist in decarbonization without significant cost to quality of life or immediate life prospects (countries that can readily facilitate a transition from fossil fuel to renewable energy use without depriving populations of energy and/or electricity, for example), or those with the capacity to prepare effectively for managing manifestations of climate change (countries with technological and financial resources to undertake large-scale

---

[16] Of course, the 'do no harm' principle is central to cosmopolitan thought. See, e.g., Linklater (2001); Shapcott (2008); Shue (2015).

[17] And in the process, this account consciously delinks the referent and agent of security.

adaptation projects, for example) bear responsibility to help ensure that others without this ability are assisted to develop such capacity (see Saran 2015). As will be discussed in Chapter 5, this is a principle endorsed through the establishment of the Green Climate Fund and through the broader practices of technology transfers, for example. Both initiatives stem from recognition of the need for developed states to ensure developing states are able to minimize damaging practices without significant costs to their populations, and/or pursue forms of resilience building and adaptation that might otherwise be prohibitively expensive.[18]

The following sections address what this conceptualization of agency in the ecological security discourse means in practice for particular types of 'agents': from traditional agents such as states and intergovernmental organizations to non-traditional agents such as private corporations, civil society groups and individuals.

### Traditional Security Agents: States and IGOs

For many, the state is at the heart of the contemporary ecological crisis. Of course, as those drawing on ecocentric thought (e.g., McShane 2014) or advancing a case for planetary or Earth systems governance have noted (e.g., Biermann 2014, 2018), the state system divides global space arbitrarily. This closes us off to recognition of shared inhabitation of one planet and limits genuine connection with ecological spaces and ecosystems in favour of the territorial borders of the state. For others, the problem is a more direct one of the limits of communitarianism and the social contract in restricting moral concern to

---

[18] Of course, in practice, distributive justice considerations (e.g., ability to pay) in the context of climate change often align with retributive justice (e.g., polluter pays) when it comes to articulating or assigning responsibility. In simple terms, those most able to address climate change and cope with manifestations of it are usually those most responsible for the problem itself, in historical terms and in terms of per capita emissions. Yet the rationale for attributing responsibility differs significantly, even while actors in practice often invoke these distinct principles, and the ethical traditions in which they are located, simultaneously or interchangeably. Small island developing states, for example, have been strong advocates of technology and resource transfers to enable stronger mitigation and especially adaptation projects in their countries (consistent with distributive justice), while also making a case for 'loss and damage' in recent negotiations (consistent with retributive justice), whereby developed states commit to compensation to affected developing for their role in causing climate change. See, e.g., Weijers et al. (2010); Caney (2005); Paterson (2001).

fellow (currently living) inhabitants of the nation state (Burke et al. 2014, 2016), or election cycles in democratic states that encourage a short-term orientation (see Gardiner 2014). In these accounts, the state is a part (even the driving force) of the problem, suggesting some degree of scepticism about its capacity to serve as an agent of progressive climate practice.

Of course, for critics of the concept of security, it is precisely the primacy attached to the state as agent of security in global politics that has allowed a traditional, atavistic and narrow conception of security to dominate international relations (see Booth 1991, 2007). For these critics, the success of the state in positioning itself as the only agent capable of ensuring that individuals can achieve some degree of protection or safety in a Hobbesian state of nature is why we are trapped in a state system, with institutions that aren't fit for purpose in addressing pressing global issues (see Burke et al. 2014).

This criticism clearly also has some relevance to the role of the state in addressing security implications of climate change more specifically. Indeed, for some critics, the inherent danger of framing climate change in security terms is that it allows and encourages states to reaffirm a central role for themselves in responding to a problem or challenge that should be viewed as evidence of the failings of these institutions (see Burke et al. 2016). Taken further still, some view this not simply as an unfortunate by-product of a security framing but as the *rationale* for this framing: the securitization of climate change is pursued by states and their agents as a means of securing relevance, budgets and continued primacy for the state and its instruments or institutions of war (see, e.g., Floyd 2010; Buxton and Hayes 2015; Marzec 2015). As noted in Chapter 2, to the extent that states view their role in the context of the threat posed by climate change as their own self-preservation, critics are surely right to suspect that their embrace of security agency will not result in progressive practices.

Yet, also as noted in that chapter, this is but one account of the relationship between climate change and security. Alternative framings suggest that our focus can (and should) shift to international, human or ecological security, with the question of whose security is under consideration and from what threats then determining who or what might serve as security agents and in what way. Further, and importantly for the prospect of advancing or realizing ecological security, we cannot turn our back on a potential agent of security with the resources and capacity of the state. Indeed, if we acknowledge the primacy of states in the international system, including to existing mechanisms for global action to address climate change through the UNFCCC, it becomes difficult to justify denying a potential role for the state as agent (see Lieven 2020). This was at the heart of attempts to conceptualize a 'green state' in ecological thought, undertaken by scholars located in the tradition of critical theory (see Eckersley 2004; Barry and Eckersley eds. 2005).

The focus of this 'green state' scholarship was twofold. First, it articulated what a 'green state' looked like in terms of its political–ecological agenda, internal dynamics or processes and the practices undertaken in its name. Second, it explored how these agenda, dynamics and practices might ultimately come to characterize the ways in which states acted and even conceived their responsibilities in global politics (see, in particular, Eckersley 2004). Applying these insights to the ecological security discourse, our attention here should shift to the questions of what states can and should do to advance ecological security and how they might come to conceive their role – even their responsibilities – in these terms. While the latter will be addressed in more detail in Chapter 5, here it is important to outline what state agency in the context of advancing ecological security ultimately looks like.

What, then, can and should states do? Of course, one simple way to address this would be to focus on the means of advancing ecological security noted earlier and ask which of these means might be under-taken by states. But in assigning some degree of responsibility to states, we need to recognize states' radically different capacities. We can, at an abstract level, endorse the idea of both international cooperation and domestic policy settings oriented towards effective mitigation action, equitable per capita emissions and the development of adaptive capacity, consistent with the imperatives of an ecological security discourse. But what this means in practice, and the scale of commitment from states, will be very different.

Coming to terms with the particular responsibility (and imperatives for action) of particular states means, ultimately, accounting for varied levels of vulnerability and in particular capacity (see Bulkeley and Newell 2015:35–9). For those with limited immediate vulnerability to climate change and strong capacity to address it, obligations extend directly to the most vulnerable. In this case, the obligations of relatively well-protected developed states necessitate significant aid programs, technology and resource transfer and even efforts to alter relationships of unequal economic exchange to states in the developing world to minimize their vulnerability and develop their adaptive and resilience capacity (Paterson 2001; Shue 2014, 2017; Saran 2015;). Other states, might, by contrast, be justified in focusing their attention on domestic action aimed at protecting immediately vulnerable populations and ecosystems from manifestations of climate change. In either schema, which suggest significantly different roles for different states in the international system, states have a crucial role to play as agents of ecological security and bear (albeit differentiated) responsibility to do so. But it applies beyond this (simple) divide, with every state experiencing different levels of exposure to climate change, different costs and effects.

Clearly, national governments are not the only governments or authorities capable of addressing the effects of climate change. Local and regional governments within states can and should play a role in advancing both mitigation and adaptation measures, along with developing public understanding of both contributions to and implications of climate change (see Betsill and Bulkeley 2005, 2006; Okereke et al. 2009; Bulkeley and Betsill 2010). At the subnational level, for example, local and regional governments are often in a position to legislate on issues such as land clearing, building codes and energy infrastructure development, for example: all areas that have potentially significant implications for the volume of greenhouse gas emissions. And in some contexts, these subnational governments also directly oversee ecosystem protection, adaptation projects (whether in the form of infrastructure development or even preparation for storms, cyclones or flooding) and attempts to encourage changes in individual behaviour (e.g., through education campaigns) within these societies (see Vogel and Henstra 2015; Klein et al. 2017).[19] This capacity equates to responsibility to act as an agent of ecological security.

---

[19] In some contexts, the size and jurisdictional reach of subnational governments can ensure a global impact of practices that either contribute to climate change or serve mitigation and adaptation ends. In Australia, a key driver of rising national emissions from 2012 was the Queensland Government's relaxation of land-clearing laws, which led to a spike in emissions (see Slezak 2017). And California's 'cap and trade' program, launched in 2013, is one of the world's

But of course the governments of nation states still enjoy primacy in terms of their capacities to address climate change and are still the primary authority in responding to climate change: responsible for raising and distributing funds through taxation and recognized as the key participants in international climate negotiations. Clearly, endorsing the ecological security discourse involves rejecting the idea of the state as the *sole* legitimate security provider: the capacity to minimize or redress harms associated with climate change, in the process advancing ecosystem resilience, exists at every level of human activity. But as theorists of the green state note, we cannot ignore the power and capacity of states (Eckersley 2004; Barry and Eckersley eds. 2005). And to the extent that they have resource and capacity to be brought to bear to advance ecological security concerns (without significantly undermining the lives and livelihood of existing populations), they bear responsibility to act in ways that advance these concerns. As noted, the (admittedly difficult) task of incentivizing states to view their roles and responsibilities in this way will be taken up in Chapter 5.

Existing international and regional organizations also have a clear role to play in advancing ecological security, in particular through facilitating international cooperation on mitigation and adaptation. Such organizations also serve as sites for mediating between competing claims and for dialogue between state actors, especially through the UNFCCC processes. In the bureaucratic arm of the United Nations, the UNEP and organizations such as UNDP and WHO are responsible for helping to develop, facilitate and share latest research on the dynamics and implications of climate change, furthering our understanding of complex phenomena (see Maertens 2018). And the UN's Climate Security Mechanism – established in 2018 – was set up to help develop risk assessments regarding (largely international) security threats associated with climate change to better inform international responses.

Of course, as noted, a range of scholars have focused on UN Security Council debates regarding the international security implications of climate change, and the potential role and responsibilities of the UNSC in this context. In many ways, the UNSC raises the most complex questions regarding responsibility given its self-defined role

largest carbon markets, with significant implications for global emissions (Sze et al. 2009).

(maintaining international peace and security) and its direct and significant capacity to marshal a response to climate change, including of a potentially coercive nature (see Conca et al. 2017; Conca 2019; Maertens 2021).

For some, the inclusion of climate change on the UNSC agenda alone is significant, raising awareness and providing an opportunity for state actors to share perspectives and understanding of the implications of climate change and the potential role of international institutions in responding to it (see Oels 2012; Scott 2015). Others have advocated extending the responsibility to protect principle to climate change, recast as a 'responsibility to prepare and prevent', in which institutions like the UNSC have a central role to play as (climate) security agents. Mirroring the increasingly prominent preventative agenda in debates on R2P (e.g. Sharma and Welsh eds. 2015; Jacob 2018), Werrell et al. (2017:2) define the responsibility to prepare and prevent as a 'responsibility to build a resilient world order against a more reliably foreseeable future, while also creating a buffer, or governance shock absorber, for those risks that we still cannot imagine'.

Others, meanwhile, are less convinced of the prospect of threat recognition leading to changing broader perspectives or international practices. Rita Floyd (2015), for example, suggests that the way international organizations depict or engage with the security implications of climate change simply (if predictably) tends to map on to the interests of that institution. For others, the significant (coercive) capacity of institutions like the UNSC is an inherent source of concern, raising the possibility of a militarized response to climate change or the broader 'use' of climate-related threats as a justification for intervention (see Eckersley 2007; Conca et al. 2017). Indeed, concerns about an expanded and interventionist role for the UNSC in the context of 'enforcing' international climate standards have not only been articulated by critics but also were outlined by state participants in discussions about the UNSC's role in addressing the international security implications of climate change in deliberations in 2007, 2011, 2018, 2019, 2020 and 2021, as noted in Chapter 2 (see Scott and Ku 2018:10–15; Maertens 2021).

Of course, by some accounts, the UNSC already engages directly with the international security implications of climate change in practice through responding to situations of conflict or instability in which the manifestations of climate change have contributed to that instability. For Scott and Ku (2018:15–16), this is apparent in UNSC involvement in conflicts in Darfur and the Sahel, for example. While the specific role of climate change in these contexts remains a matter of contention (see Selby et al. 2017), it appears clear that the UNSC will retain a role in instances in which large-scale conflict or instability occur. This, alongside its role in providing a forum and mechanism for addressing indirect implications of climate change effects, constitute important responsibilities for the UNSC, even if more closely aligned to an international security discourse than an ecological security one. As a focus on prevention in international security terms becomes more prominent, however, we may see an increased role for the UNSC in promoting mitigation action. In these contexts, the UNSC has responsibility as an agent of ecological security.

A range of interlocutors in UNSC deliberations suggested that discussion of responses to climate change at the international level should remain the purview of the UNFCCC (see Scott and Ku 2018:12; Conca 2019). Clearly, it constitutes the key international institution on climate change cooperation and the cornerstone of the climate regime. And from the ecological security perspective, the UNFCCC constitutes a critical agent for advancing the resilience of ecosystems in the face of climate change, in at least five senses.

First, and most directly serving ecological security ends, the UNFCCC's primary focus is on addressing the problem of climate change directly through coordinating mitigation action. In this sense, the UNFCCC has a crucial role to play in overseeing the minimization of greenhouse gas emissions.

Second, the UNFCCC plays and should continue to play a central role in developing, promoting and securing endorsement for principles central to the global response to climate change. There are clearly limits with the existing institutional framework of the UNFCCC, manifested in occasional failure of talks to secure agreement (as in 2009) and, more substantively, continued emissions rises (Moncel and van Assalt 2012). But the UNFCCC has also endorsed core principles that inform the international response to climate change, including in progressive terms. Principles such as the 'precautionary principle' and 'common but differentiated responsibility', for example, respectively encourage commitment to action in the face of lingering uncertainty around timeframes and effects associated with climate change, alongside more specific institutions aimed at facilitating mitigation, adaptation and resilience-building in developing countries. In this sense, the UNFCCC has enabled the articulation, development and institutionalization of principles that have guided attempts to manage some of the ethical complexities of responding equitably to climate change in an international context (see, e.g., Morgan and Waskow 2013; Bulkeley and Newell 2015; Tomlinson 2015). And as Chapter 5 will show, such principles can ultimately be viewed as consistent with an ecological security discourse emphasizing urgent contemporary action oriented to ecosystem resilience and the rights and needs of the most vulnerable.

Third, and following from this, this institutional framework also has a key role in developing capacity for effective forms of mitigation, adaptation and resilience-building through technology and resource transfer to those states (and their communities) limited in their capacity to pursue these options. Indeed the ethical principles central to the notion of 'common but differentiated responsibility' inform the rationale and practices of the multibillion-dollar Green Climate Fund. Established in Copenhagen in 2009, the Green Climate Fund is the product of an international commitment to ensure developing states are able to transition away from fossil fuels while meeting development needs and minimizing their vulnerability to manifestations of climate change (see Ciplet et al. 2013; Vanderheiden 2015).

Fourth, the nature of the UNFCCC's CoP meetings serves – and should further serve – the end of ensuring dialogue and the articulation of multiple voices and perspectives in considering fair and effective responses to climate change. The inclusiveness of CoP meetings – in involving civil society groups, media outlets and researchers in the same physical space as state representatives while negotiations take place – is crucial for enabling multiple voices to be heard and broadcast (see Lövbrand et al. 2019). It has even been, by some accounts, central to the progressive principles and outcomes that arise from the CoP meetings themselves.[20]

---

[20] This might be applied to the commitment to loss and damage and the (surprising) endorsement of 1.5 degrees as a target for increased temperature levels agreed in Paris in 2015 (see Christoff 2016). And as Lövbrand et al. (2019:580) have argued, 'the ability of the UNFCCC to bring together different actors across time and space, to perform multiple policy tasks, has become one of its notable strengths and is an important facilitative practice that holds the

Finally, for any institutional limitations, the UNFCCC remains the central international mechanism for coordinating global responses to a global problem. In this sense, like states in the national security context, it occupies an unparalleled position in terms of capacity for coordinating international responses to global climate change, which again amounts to responsibility for acting as an ecological security agent. The same applies to the IPCC – the scientific arm of the UNFCCC process. Again, for any faults and limitations (see Hughes 2011), its history and institutional context make it the most authoritative source of knowledge about climate change and its effects. Like the previous discussion of states, this compels those of us interested in promoting strong global action on climate change to work with the UNFCCC process, at least in an immediate sense. As noted here, and as will be expanded upon in Chapter 5, there is also much about the UNFCCC that does or could directly serve the interests of promoting or realizing ecological security.

Beyond the specific instruments of the climate regime, regional institutions can and should serve as ecological security agents in a more minimalist sense, through raising awareness about climate change and its (security) implications, informing state members of research and 'best practice' governance and potentially coordinating cooperation between member states. While a relatively minimalist model in promoting ecological security concerns, regional institutions can also engage in more substantive and significant practices even if not defined in terms of (ecological) security. The European Union, for example, presides over the largest emissions trading system in the world. Involving more than thirty countries, by most analyses the system has served to drive down industrial carbon emissions (see Duggan 2015; Muuls et al. 2016). The member states of the EU have also, in the past, worked through the organization to negotiate as a single entity at climate negotiations (e.g. Kyoto Protocol negotiations in 1997), increasing the likelihood of international consensus in the process and strengthening the voice of states relatively committed to significant mitigation action.[21] And more recently, the EU's support for

polycentric regime complex together'. For an alternative view on the inclusiveness of CoP meetings, in particular the role of NGOs from the global North and South, respectively, see Gereke and Bruhl (2019).

[21] On the role of the EU in the promotion of climate security – as a climate security actor – see Far and Youngs (2018).

post-coronavirus 'green recovery', featuring 'a more sustainable economic model through investment in green industry' (Lidskog et al. 2020:2), also speaks to its capacity to enable a transition away from fossil fuel economies. All these activities point to a significant role for the EU – and potentially other sets of regional organizations – as agents of ecological security.

In a recent survey of the ways in which intergovernmental organizations – from international to regional organizations – had addressed the security implications of climate change, Dellmuth et al. (2017) pointed to two key roles for these institutions: in constituting a site of discussion, deliberation or awareness raising and in promoting governance through risk assessment and communication to member states. While pointing to the relatively nascent development of climate security concerns in these institutional contexts, the authors nonetheless identify key roles for international and regional organizations in addressing the security implications of climate change.[22] These roles – indeed responsibilities – are more significant still when we view urgent global mitigation action as the central means through which we primarily advance ecological security. Viewed in such a light, institutions such as the UNFCCC become central agents of climate security, tasked as it is with coordinating global mitigation efforts and overseeing the distribution of international resources necessary to assist developing states in their movement towards mitigation, adaptation and resilience-building.

## Non-traditional Security Agents: Private Corporations, Civil Society and Individuals

The account of agency noted at the outset of this discussion conceptualized responsibility for advancing ecological security as arising from a capacity to make conscious decisions that may affect (for better or worse) ecosystem resilience (see also Newell et al. 2015).[23] Defined in such terms, there is clearly a role for a wide range of actors in the realization of ecological security – at, above and below the level of the state. And while substate actors may not be traditionally associated

---

[22] International institutions would, of course, also need to play a crucial role in the regulation of geoengineering, especially at a large scale (see Rayner et al. 2013).

[23] The degree of responsibility was, in turn, related to another dimension of capacity: the relative ability to bring resources to bear to further ecosystem resilience (see Caney 2005).

with security agency, they nonetheless have potentially important roles to play in addressing ecological security in the context of climate change.

Private corporations are perhaps the most obvious bearers of responsibility in this context given their significant contribution to the problem of climate change. As Michael Sardo (2020) has argued, agents bear responsibility to address climate change to the extent that 'they participate in and benefit from carbon intensive structures, practices and institutions that constitute the global political and economic system'. One recent analysis suggested that 100 private corporations were responsible for over 70 per cent of the world's greenhouse gas emissions (Griffin 2017; Riley 2017). In this context, and for these companies, a willingness to desist from or significantly alter their activities would make a substantial immediate contribution to addressing the problem of climate change.

But to what extent can we (realistically) expect private companies to orient towards ecosystem resilience or even minimizing their emissions more directly? This appears especially optimistic if the company in question benefits economically – whether directly or indirectly – from practices that contribute to climate change. Many of those 100 companies noted above are fossil fuel companies, for whom a transition away from fossil fuels is either not financially feasible (Griffin 2017) or necessitates significant changes to existing business practices (Skjærseth and Skodvin 2009). For other companies, should movement away from carbon-intensive practices be a product of their own goodwill (in what some might see as a breach of companies' own social contract to shareholders concerned primarily with wealth generation), the result of shareholder and/or consumer demand or as a response to government legislation and incentives for private corporations to engage in particular forms of behaviour? Some might suggest here that company practices are simply the result of what states allow, even what markets and consumers demand.[24]

This account of the role of private corporations – in which responsibility for changing their behaviour is held by others – is too limited. As Toni Erskine has argued (2003), these forms of institutions have agency, capacity and (therefore) responsibility. We cannot simply

---

[24] On the limits of reliance on private company action, and indeed climate capitalism more broadly, see Newell and Paterson (2010: chapter 8).

allocate responsibility for their regulation to another actor, nor can we give in to what Erskine (2003:2–3) refers to as an 'individualist' position, in which 'assigning moral responsibility to a group is (viewed as) either sloppy shorthand for referring to the decisions and actions of individual human beings, or mere nonsense'.

Actions to minimize harm in the context of climate change have also been an increasingly prominent emphasis in work applying corporate social responsibility to climate change (see Moon 2007a; Seck 2018). The case for business self-regulation to reduce harms appears particularly significant in the context of climate change. Clearly, states and consumers can and should regulate the behaviour of companies in the context of their contribution to climate change, whether through legislation or through their purchasing practices. But these companies themselves also bear responsibility to minimize harmful behaviour, and claims of obligations to shareholders cannot trump more fundamental obligations to the most vulnerable.

Of course, civil society groups have played a significant role in promoting action on climate change, including as oriented towards the rights and needs of the most vulnerable. Their capacity to precipitate change – even if primarily via pressure on other sets of actors (states, IGOs and companies, for example) – necessitates taking seriously their role as agents of ecological security (see Wapner 1995). Indeed, it is arguably particularly important in this case because such groups (at least in the case of environmental NGOs) are more likely to explicitly position themselves as speaking on behalf of or representing ecosystems, other living beings or future generations, for example. While we should not accept such claims at face value, we can certainly recognize the relationship between these claims and the central precepts of the ecological security discourse.

In the context of environmental civil society groups, Peter Newell (2008) for example, suggests that such actors are capable of mobilizing to hold companies, states and even international organizations to account for their action or inaction on climate change (see also Park 2005). Such civil society groups may be located within, beyond or across states. Keck and Sikkink (1998), of course, focused significantly on the role of transnational advocacy networks in promoting normative change across a range of issue areas, including environmental issues. A prominent example here – one directly concerned with questions of ecosystem resilience – was the role of environmental

NGOs in campaigning to protect the Amazon rainforest from large-scale deforestation in the late 1980s and early 1990s (Schmink and Wood 1992:112–26). This campaign involved these NGOs, many in the developed world in particular, mobilizing against large-scale deforestation driven or facilitated by development organizations such as the World Bank (see McDonald 2003, 2012).

The Amazon campaign was ultimately hailed as a successful example of mobilization to prevent unnecessary environmental destruction, leading as it did to the withdrawal of proposed international funding for large-scale projects involving deforestation in Brazil (see Kolk 1996; Scholz 2005). It also, however, raises a series of difficult challenges for conceptualizing responsibility, agency and the nature of an appropriate response to ecological harm. While the immediate risk to the forest and its inhabitants was minimized in this context, the developmental needs or imperatives of the people of Brazil were not. Ultimately, forms and structures of international inequality largely remained (see Newell et al. 2015:536–7). Further, some local groups with whom international NGOs were cooperating claimed explicitly to be 'speaking for' the forest while engaged in illegal logging practices (McDonald 2012:158). This serves as an important reminder – indeed practical manifestation – of the inherent limits in claims to speak for others (see Eckersley 1992). Finally, the location in this instance of particular forms of ecological harm – far away from developed states where environmental NGOs were mobilizing – is arguably also problematic. Specifically, it risks representing ecological harm as originating in the developing world, in the process eliding the role of developed states and their citizens in contributing to that harm (Guimaraes 1991:220–3; Barbosa 2000).

All of the above remind us of the need to conceptualize agency in broad terms and multiple spaces. We need to avoid locating agency or responsibility at one level or site to ensure a broad range of voices are heard in informing appropriate response to harm, rather than taking some as authoritative, and to ensure that responses to ecological harms do not worsen (indeed ideally simultaneously address) forms of structural inequality and deprivation in vulnerable populations. Such an approach would serve to address what Newell et al. (2015) refer to as 'governance traps' in the context of climate change agency and responsibility: 'situations where the agency to effect significant change within institutions and civil society becomes severely constrained either by the inherent complexity of the situation and the operation of competing interests or an inappropriate allocation of responsibilities'.

A final point on agency and civil society groups to note here is that the role or nature of agency in this context is clearly very different to that of private companies outlined earlier. In conceptualizing companies as potential agents, we are focusing on their immediate contribution to climate change and their (associated) capacity to further ecological security, whether through particular forms of action or curtailing existing practices. In the context of civil society groups, their role as potential agents of ecological security arises from a capacity to raise awareness and concern among a broader community, who may, in turn, alter their own practices or behaviour or pressure other institutions to do change policy or practices. This is particularly important if, as Frank Biermann argues (2014, 2018), we cannot realistically expect states to willingly address global concerns – they will need to be pressured and compelled to do so. In this context, civil society groups can be viewed as indirect or secondary agents of ecological security: often without necessary capacity to directly implement large-scale policy or practical initiatives oriented towards ecosystem resilience but with a role to play in *encouraging* such change.

Finally, though no less critically, a focus on agency in the context of ecological security must extend to individuals. If we as individuals are capable of making conscious decisions that contribute to climate change or serves to address it, we have at least *some* degree of responsibility to act or curtail our actions to minimize harm. This broad recognition of individual responsibility – and therefore agency – is tempered by at least two considerations.

First, as Newell et al. (2015:537) note, 'individuals do not consciously decide to emit carbon. Rather, emissions are associated with the practices and routines of everyday life'. This suggests the need to recognize and address broader structural dynamics that condition choices available to individuals,[25] and even dominant cultural norms that encourage and normalize particular (deleterious) practices (see Sardo 2020). The related concern here is that locating primary

---

[25] In most cities in Australia, for example, individual households cannot readily go 'off grid' in terms of their access to electricity. Household solar panels feed into the local electricity grid, but what is provided to those households in terms of their own electricity generation is determined by power companies, themselves subjected to government regulation (see Cranenburgh 2019).

responsibility for minimizing greenhouse gas emissions at the level of individuals is both unreasonable and exhausting given the scale of personal effort required to ensure familiarity with all the ways in which our everyday actions contribute to climate change and (presumably) to cease from undertaking those actions. It is difficult to reasonably expect this scale of effort, not least in the context of varied degrees of action (and inaction) from others (see Cripps 2013).

Perhaps more fundamentally, this individual responsibility should not be shared equally (see Shue 1993; Cripps 2013). Drawing on the same principles of equity and distributive justice that characterize the way we allocate differentiated responsibilities to states, for example, the focus here on capacity in particular encourages us to emphasize action that can be undertaken by those individuals with the resources to accommodate changes to their lifestyles. Agarwal and Narain (1991) memorably distinguished between 'luxury' and 'survival' green-house gas emissions in distinguishing between the moral culpability of those engaged in environmentally deleterious practices for different reasons.[26] For them, we cannot (fairly) equate the production of emissions in a developing country undertaken in the process of a person immediately sustaining themselves and families (through slash and burn agriculture, for example) with a person in a developed country, whose lifestyle choices (whether diet, travel or consumption of products generally) produce greenhouse gas emissions.

Given that individuals contribute to climate change through their everyday actions, it is reasonable to recognize the role of individuals as agents of ecological security. But in recognizing this capacity, we also need to be sensitive to varied degrees of capacity across human populations, the structural contexts in which human agency is exercised and the feasibility and sustainability of placing the onus on individual action in addressing climate change.

Ultimately, locating agency and responsibility in the context of an ecological security discourse is acutely challenging. Indeed, by some accounts, the question of how responsibility for action on climate change is conceived and presented is at the heart of the (to date) dysfunctional and partial response to the challenge of global climate change itself (see Newell et al. 2015). Two core points, however,

---

[26] Henry Shue (1993) articulated a similar distinction – between luxury and subsistence emissions.

oriented the preceding discussion of where we might appropriately locate agency and responsibility for advancing ecological security. First, capacity is central. It is also multifaceted and inherently different over space, time and actors. In this context, I made the case for conceiving of responsibility according to consciousness in the first instance (can an actor be realistically expected to be aware of the implications of action or inaction, for example?) and then in terms of relative resources that might be brought to bear in terms of substantive action. Both of the latter follow from a simple (even intuitive) point that not all states, companies or individuals are equally responsible for the problem, nor equally endowed with the capacity to address it. This should clearly inform who acts in any different context and to what degree.

Second, the discussion of agency in the context of ecological security included the need to recognize multiple sites and actors. Individual contribution to or action on climate change is conditioned by government policy, for example. These same governments cannot necessarily compel other states, or private companies, to behave in particular ways. We cannot, in short, limit our discussion of agency to a single discrete actor (on this point, see also Cudworth and Hobden 2013; Barnett 2018). Locating agency at multiple sites, and responsibility for action to multiple actors, is clearly more complicated than would be the case in a national security discourse, for example. But the predominant focus on addressing the problem of climate change itself necessitates a genuinely global and whole-of-society conceptualization of agency.

## Conclusion

When the security implications of climate change are approached through the lens of national security, answers to the questions of the appropriate means and agents of security are relatively straightforward. It is the state that is responsible for providing security, and it is realized primarily through adaptive responses to manage the indirect consequences of climate change. But, of course, the drawback to this simplicity and elegance is a set of responses that fail to address the problem of climate change itself and which (by definition) cannot extend to the range of contributors and contributions to the problem itself. And those most vulnerable to manifestations of climate change – future generations, other living beings and impoverished populations in the developing world – are neglected at best and potentially treated as threats at worst.

By contrast, if we are interested in ecosystem resilience in the context of climate change, and the direct threat posed to the most vulnerable, we need to locate means and agency in a range of sites and contexts, from the global to the everyday. This is necessarily more complicated and challenging than a simpler focus on the adaptive capacity and practices of states. But the preceding discussion of means (exploring mitigation, adaptation and geoengineering) and agents (from states and IGOs to private corporations, civil society groups and individuals) give us resources for recognizing how ecological security might be realized or advanced in practice and by whom. And the focus on dialogue, humility and reflexivity provides orientation in practically applying the core principles of an ecological security discourse.

Together with Chapter 3, we now have an account of the core constituent elements of an ecological security discourse, with a particular conception of referent, threat, agent and means. But how could this approach – radical as it is and foreign to existing institutions and practices of world politics – come to genuinely inform the way political communities think about security in the context of climate change? How does the preceding discussion matter if there is no conceivable way in which these principles might be embraced and enacted in practice? Chapter 5 addresses this question directly. In the process, it provides a praxeological account of how an ecological security discourse might come to be articulated, endorsed and even institutionalized in substantive practical contexts.

# 5 | Towards Ecological Security?

This chapter – the final substantive chapter of the book – engages with the difficult question of how we might realize or advance ecological security in practice. While Chapters 1–4 have developed a normative case for approaching the climate change–security relationship through the lens of ecological security, and outlined what this might look like, there clearly remain important impediments to the articulation, enactment and institutionalization of this discourse in practice. Indeed for some, including some sympathetic to the normative impulse of this discourse (e.g. Barnett 2001), the scale of change required to orient our consideration, practices and institutions towards ecosystem resilience and the rights and needs of the most vulnerable ultimately renders this discourse irrelevant to the discursive contest over the way climate change and security are conceptualized and addressed.

There are two central responses to this criticism. The first is to reiterate a broad point at the heart of this book. Namely, if we believe a particular approach to the climate change–security relationship is normatively defensible and likely to underpin progressive responses to climate change, we cannot allow existing institutional arrangements, norms or practices to rule it out. We need, rather, to think about how such an approach might be enabled and advanced, extending to the question of whether our existing institutional arrangements, norms or practices are ultimately fit for purpose. This is especially the case given the scale of the climate emergency we are facing.

Second, and following this, contemporary arrangements and dominant discourses are not fixed, set in stone or immutable. While powerful impediments may exist to altering forms of economic exchange, political institutions or means of energy production, for example, these should not be taken to constitute irrevocable limits. Like the conceptualization of discourses and their construction advanced in this book, such arrangements should be viewed as constructs that – again, while potentially powerful – can be challenged and changed.

Of course, recognition of these two points still leaves us with the significant challenge of outlining how such change might be possible. That is the task of this chapter. Drawing on the political sociology of Pierre Bourdieu (1977, 1990, 1991, 1992) in coming to terms with the nature of political 'possibility', and critical theoretical insights regarding immanent possibility for change, this chapter outlines the praxeological case for ecological security regarding the climate change–security relationship (Linklater 1998). While identifying institutional, material and even cognitive impediments to a shift towards ecosystem resilience, the chapter nonetheless locates immanent possibilities for building on existing frameworks and norms in international society. It also identifies a role for imagining and pursuing *new* institutional arrangements, norms and practices to advance ecological security concerns.

This chapter is divided into four sections. First, I outline key impediments to the movement towards ecological security, defined in institutional, material and cultural or cognitive terms. Coming to terms with these impediments is crucial for conceiving possible strategies and sites of effective contestation. Second, I outline how political possibility is conceived here. This discussion harks back to the discussion of discursive contestation introduced in Chapter 1, while noting Bourdieu's insights on the ways in which change might be conceived and realized, including in unpromising contexts. Third, I point to immanent possibility as a crucial foundation for change. Defining the concept and locating it in the critical theoretical tradition, I go on to identify a range of contemporary practices and principles that directly endorse or at least move us towards the central concerns of the ecological security discourse. These include the precautionary principle, the principle of common but differentiated responsibility, the growing international focus on threat prevention, the case for geoengineering regulation and (at least some representations of) the Anthropocene. Finally, the chapter discusses the relationship between possibility, progress and end point. In the process, it makes a case for an approach to ecological security that keeps sight of core goals, principles and objectives while recognizing, endorsing and even actively pursuing incremental change through existing (even if imperfect) institutional frameworks.

## Ecological Security: Impediments

As the discussion in all previous chapters has suggested, there are powerful – even profound – impediments to the possibility of a concern with ecosystem resilience genuinely constituting the lens through which political communities view climate change. Indeed, for some, as noted, it is precisely these impediments that fatally undermine the ecological security discourse itself – as morally progressive but practically unimaginable and Utopian (see Barnett 2001). Before mounting something of a challenge to this account of ecological security, however, it is important to identify the nature and force of those impediments, to give ourselves a fuller picture of the challenges that need to be overcome.

The power of existing discourses is a clear impediment here. This is especially the case if the way we see 'security' in the context of an issue such as climate change is itself a site of contestation between different discourses: accounts of our values in need of protection, from what threats, by what means it is to be protected or advanced and by what agents. The dominance of a national security discourse is increasingly challenged by accounts focusing on the international and human security implications of climate change (see Matthew et al. eds. 2010; Rothe 2015; Busby 2018). But the consistent reiteration of the primacy of the nation state as the referent object of security in theory and practice (regarding climate change but more prominently still in the face of a range of other 'threats', including coronavirus)[1] is such that it constitutes an often uncontested orthodoxy or common sense. This is, of course, evidenced in a range of academic accounts of the meaning of security in international relations, but also in security assessments and statements emanating from key actors in global politics: states. I will return to these points – discursive contestation and dominance – briefly in the following discussion of political possibility.

Powerful – even dominant – countervailing discourses of security in the context of climate change are not the only discursive impediments to progression towards ecological security, however. Predominant framings of ethics and ethical responsibility, along with development and economic growth, also push in opposite directions. On the former, communitarian approaches to international relations suggest that ethical consideration and responsibility begin and end at the nation state (see Morgenthau 1952; Walzer 1983; Moore 2010). This has been challenged extensively by cosmopolitan theorists (see Held 1995; Beitz 1999; Pogge 2008; Caney 2010a ), and states themselves appear likely to identify external ethical responsibility in some form (evident in aid

---

[1] On the primacy of national – rather than cooperative, international and global – responses to the coronavirus pandemic, see Lidskog et al. (2020).

programs and commitments to the Refugee Convention, for example). Yet it is harder to shake the impression that obligations to fellow citizens are still prioritized above external obligations regardless of the immediate need and vulnerability of those beyond our borders (see Gibney 2004, 2018). And in a more immediate sense, dominant discourses of ethics at the everyday level encourage and reaffirm the centrality of acting for our own interests or those of immediate family (see Brighouse and Swift 2006). This is clearly a substantial distance away from recognition of obligations to other living beings or future generations, for example.

For many, meanwhile, dominant discourses of development and economic growth have driven climate change itself (Clark and York 2005; Cannon and Muller-Mahn 2010; Klein 2015). For decades, key accounts of development emphasized energy intensive industrialization, encouraging a transition away from sustainable practices (such as subsistence farming, for example). And dominant economic models attributed value to environmental 'goods' to the extent they could be extracted and sold (see Barbosa 2000). Both are certainly changing. In development terms, we have seen an increased emphasis on 'human development' rather than simply GDP growth (UNDP 1994, 2007; Matthew et al. eds. 2010), and the increasing focus on the transition of resources and technology to developing states to facilitate less climate-harmful forms of development (see Ciplet et al. 2013; Vanderheiden 2015). In economic terms, emissions trading or taxation schemes (for all their frequent problems and limitations) are precisely designed to attribute value to global atmospheric 'goods', with incentives for emissions reduction and maintaining ecosystems, for example (Caney 2010b; Aldred 2012). And as noted, there are some signals of post–Covid-19 shifts away from fossil fuel economies and towards sustainable industries (see Heyd 2020; Lidskog et al. 2020).

Yet whether these shifts in discourses and practices of development and economic growth sufficiently address the scale of the climate crisis, or genuinely challenge the core contours of discourses that have served to drive the climate crisis, is open to challenge.

There is also a lingering sense in many contexts – even when economic indicators appear to align with environmental imperatives[2] – that the two represent a stark, binary choice. And for some countries

---

[2] For example, concerns about the long-term economic future of coal extraction and export has fuelled investment in renewable energy and undermined private sector support for large-scale coal-mining projects (see Mikler and Harrison 2013).

where greenhouse gas emissions rises are steepest (e.g. China, India, Brazil), climate considerations are frequently represented as secondary to the imperative of poverty elimination and economic growth (Najam 2005). Indeed, it is striking in this case that while we have come a long way since the North–South split that characterized international environmental talks in Stockholm in 1972 (the UN Conference on the Human Environment), the need to address the developmental concerns of developing states remains central to current climate negotiations (Najam 2005).

Beyond these broad discursive impediments found in dominant accounts of security, ethical responsibility and development or economic growth, institutional arrangements themselves also militate against the realization of ecological security in practice. Of course, this should be no surprise, not least as institutional design both reflects and constitutes dominant discourses. This could be applied, for example, to institutions of economic governance, from the broad structure of the international economic system to the specific arrangements and practice of the International Monetary Fund or World Bank, for example. For many, such institutions are instantiations of a broad discourse of economics and development (see, e.g., Easterly 2009; Clift and Tomlinson 2010).

In broader terms, the state system and institutions for cooperation on climate change within it (such as the UNFCCC) might also be viewed as arrangements that militate against a shift towards ecological security. In making a case for 'earth systems governance', Frank Biermann (2018) has argued that the contemporary state system is ill-equipped to address climate change, given the inherently global nature of the problem and the bounded structure of states. In their planet politics manifesto, meanwhile, Burke et al. (2016) make the case that the contemporary state system – especially if judged against the scale of the ecological crisis – is not fit for purpose in redressing global challenges such as climate change for similar reasons. Dryzek (2016) directly explores the limits of institutional arrangements in the context of the Anthropocene. He ultimately makes the case that the state system broadly and the UNFCCC specifically are insufficiently dynamic and responsive to changing circumstances (see also Dryzek and Pickering 2018; Pickering 2018). For these theorists, the state system constitutes an institutional context inconsistent with fundamentally addressing the challenge of climate change.

Others still focus on the limits of states themselves. Biermann (2018) has little optimism about the extent to which states can or will ultimately orient their concerns to (vulnerable) outsiders. Stephen Gardiner (2014), meanwhile, points to the pathologies of election cycles that encourage an orientation to the short-term and the immediate rather than long-term in democratic states. Indeed, in Gardiner's broader analysis, contemporary international institutions writ large (from states to the state system to capitalism) render an orientation to future generations impossible. For him, such institutions 'are poor at giving appropriate voice to intergenerational concerns, and even encourage lesser concerns to dominate over them' (Gardiner 2014:304). And while outlining the contours of a 'green state' in her work (Eckersley 2004), Eckersley (2017) argues for a shift in forms and dynamics of democracy in the Anthropocene, suggesting the need for 'hyper-reflexive' forms of democracy that engage with a much larger range of voices.

Finally, if ecological security requires a change of sensibility – a change in the way we think about our values in the context of climate change – all the above dynamics and forces have encouraged ways of individual thinking that appear as fundamental impediments to the shift to ecological security. We are encouraged to view the environment as separate from humanity, and other living beings as inherently less worthy of consideration (see Lövbrand et al. 2015). Indeed even when it comes to other humans, we are encouraged to think of ethical responsibility as extending to our fellow citizens at best (Walzer 1983), ourselves and our loved ones alone at worst (Brighouse and Swift 2006). We are encouraged to over-consume and engage in forms of harmful behaviour, whether eating meat, building large houses or taking flights, with these choices variously presented as expressions of individual freedom, appropriate (and desirable) quality of life or recreational choices, even expressions of cultural identity (Newell et al. 2015). As Newell et al. (2015) note, these decisions are not made with climate change in mind – they are the product of broader structural dynamics that in part condition choices available to us and are normalized by cultural forces that serve to render these imaginable, even desirable. And this is a central part of the challenge facing us: how do we realize the possibility of viewing and approaching climate change through the lens of ecosystem resilience in the face of these impediments?

## Conceptualizing Political Possibility

By some accounts, as suggested above, the dominance of a national security discourse almost certainly precludes any realistic prospect of a transition to ecological security when it comes to approaching climate change. This position may be viewed as particularly compelling given apparent challenges to embracing even a focus on international or indeed human security: both discourses with more political purchase and currency than an ecological security framing.[3] More fundamentally still, for some working in the post-structural tradition, the performative and constitutive power of a dominant discourse is such that it doesn't simply provide a central lens through which to view the world: it serves to constitute that world itself (Foucault 1977). Viewed in this way, it is not simply a matter of decoupling security and the nation state: these are inevitably and irrevocably interlinked. This position has encouraged some to actively challenge any linkage between climate change and security on normative grounds (see Buxton and Hayes 2015; Marzec 2015; Oels 2015). And it also informs a broader tradition in critical security studies of contesting, resisting and rejecting the 'meta narrative' of security itself (see Neocleous 2008; Dillon and Reid 2009).

As noted in Chapter 1, however, the concepts of discourse, security and their relationship are understood in this book in less categorical or performative terms. There I endorsed Hajer's (1995) approach to conceiving of discourses as multiple forms of representations of reality that compete with each other to provide the framework through which particular issues are conceived and addressed by particular political communities. While Hajer accepts that it is possible a particular discourse will ultimately have the performative and constitutive effects a Foucauldian account implies, he is eager to emphasize that this happens only when a particular discourse becomes *dominant*. Even then, this discourse requires reiteration and reinforcement (as post-structural accounts themselves acknowledge) and remains in competition with other frameworks of meaning – it is far from stable, timeless or immutable (see Hansen 2006). As applied to climate security, this

---

[3] As discussed in Chapter 2, this is evident in the endorsement of these discourses by consequential political actors – including states – in fora such as the UN Security Council and the UN General Assembly, for example.

approach suggests that while viewing the implications of climate change through the lens of potential threats to the territorial integrity and sovereignty of the nation state might be dominant, alternative articulations of whose security is threatened, by what manifestations of climate change, through what means they might be addressed and by what agents are always possible. The question then becomes how such alternative accounts might ultimately come to provide the framework through which the security implications of climate change are conceived and addressed.

This broad account of political possibility in the context of powerful discourses clearly intersects with the wider debate regarding the relationship between structure and agency. How much capacity do individual agents have to advance their interests in the face of structures – whether institutional, material or discursive – that appear to determine the conditions of possibility? In this context, and in identifying political strategies for enabling change, the work of Pierre Bourdieu – introduced in Chapter 2 – particularly informs how political possibility and constraint are conceived.

Bourdieu's 'structuralist constructivism' (Bourdieu 1990:123) sought to provide an account of political possibility that acknowledged the powerful and conditioning forces of structures without giving up on the possibility that actors may be in a position to advance their interests and/or alter those structures themselves.[4] For Bourdieu (1991:169), discourses could certainly be a form of constraint on individual agency, with discourse defined as 'a structured and structuring medium tending to impose an apprehension of the established order as natural through the disguised imposition of systems of classification and of mental structures that are objectively adjusted to social structures'. But this discourse, for him, did not constitute an inherent and immovable obstacle to agency or to change.

In much of Bourdieu's work, and in much work applying his insights to international relations, the focus is on the conditions for political

---

[4] While Bourdieu's work has been recently embraced (indeed, discovered) in international relations thought more broadly, and applied to a wide range of issues, the latter point clearly intersects with Wendt's (1992) conception of the possibility for agents (states) to influence the meaning and power of structures (anarchy) themselves. On the application of Bourdieu in international relations more broadly, see, e.g., Adler-Nissen (2013); Adler and Pouliot (2011); Williams (2006); Bigo (2011); Leander (2011).

possibility and agency in a given context. For Bourdieu, this involves understanding and working with the social and political contexts (for him, 'fields') in which actors find themselves, in particular how power or resources (for him, 'capital') are distributed within that particular 'field'. Bourdieu (1991:171–202) suggests that the political field, for example, is defined by actors competing to speak and act on behalf of communities they claim to represent, with capital defined in terms of resources available to advance those messages. Effective agents in this space are not simply those with material resources. Rather they may be those with taken-for-granted knowledge informing their actions in a given field (for him, 'doxa') or a feel for the forms of interactions necessary to advance their interests within a given space (for him, 'habitus').[5]

For our purposes, the above account ultimately suggests that alternative frameworks, conceptions and practices – ultimately, alternative discourses – of climate security are possible even in the face of significant political obstacles or impediments. Agents looking to advance such change, for Bourdieu, need a deep understanding of the contexts in which they are operating and an appreciation and use of forms of power and resources within that context. More directly, this framework suggests the importance (evident in the normative thrust of the Green State literature) of strategic engagement with and within existing axes or sites of power rather than escaping them. More directly still, Bourdieu (1991) emphasizes the importance of symbolic power, which can be defined as 'the capacity of actors to articulate – and secure social endorsement for – a compelling vision of the world, a community's role within it, and/or particular actions that advance them' (McDonald 2016). As applied to ecological security, this would suggest that the extent to which advocates of such a discourse can ensure that framework resonates with community values is central to its immediate prospects, while securing broader societal endorsement for this approach is similarly central.

While the scale of change necessitated to shift from a national or international to an ecological security discourse may seem prohibitive, Bourdieu's insights and the broad conceptualization of discourse advanced here suggest it is not impossible or wholly Utopian. Indeed,

---

[5] Didier Bido (2011:241) defines habitus as 'an anticipation of the actions of other agents of the field which does not necessarily imply conscious thinking'.

while the above discussion has outlined broad principles to inform how we conceive political possibility for such change, more immediately it is important to identify those agents, forces and dynamics already advancing principles consistent with ecological security in practical contexts. These forces provide foundation upon which a transition to ecological security may be built. Drawing on critical theory, these might broadly be conceived as 'immanent possibilities' for the advancement and realization of ecological security.

## Immanent Possibility and Ecological Security

The notion of immanent possibility clearly relates to the critical theoretical tradition of immanent critique. The latter can be defined as an approach to locating emancipatory possibility within the existing order, often through identifying contradictions within that order that might provide the foundation for change (Horkheimer 1972; Antonio 1981).[6] It encourages a focus on the contours and logics of existing sets of discourses, institutional frameworks and practices, with the analyst locating bases for progressive change within those arrangements. It is particularly crucial for our purposes because, as Richard Wyn Jones (1999:25) notes, 'if critical theory cannot locate emancipatory potential immanently within the real world, then it must either succumb to a paralyzing pure negation to appeal to some extra-societal basis for critique – thus transposing itself into a metaphysics or even theology'. In this understanding, then, locating immanent possibility for (emancipatory) change is crucial if that change is going to be feasible and sustainable. This approach is also one embraced in Harrington and Shearing's (2017:33) recent account of Anthropocene security.

### The Precautionary Principle

Locating immanent possibilities for the articulation, endorsement or institutionalization of an ecological security discourse in the context of climate change can begin by reflecting on core principles endorsed in and through the climate-change regime. The first to be noted here is the

---

[6] This particular focus on internal contradiction (potentially) precipitating change draws on a Hegelian teleology central to Marxist thought (see Hook 1994).

precautionary principle. This principle was central to a range of international environmental agreements and declarations from the 1980s, including the UNGA's World Charter for Nature in 1982 and the 1987 Montreal Protocol, and was formally adopted as Principle 15 in the Rio Declaration on Environment and Development in 1992 – the meeting at which the climate-change regime (through the UNFCCC) was established (see Conca 2015).

The Rio Declaration (UN 1992) statement on the precautionary principle articulated it as follows:

In order to protect the environment, the precautionary approach shall be widely applied by States according to their capabilities. Where there are threats of serious or irreversible damage, lack of full scientific uncertainty shall not be used as a reason for postponing cost-effective measures to prevent environmental degradation.

Of course, concessions to relative 'capacities' and 'cost-effective' measures were incorporated in response to the concerns of developing and developed states at UNCED (see McDonald 2018). Beyond this, others have pointed to the lack of prescription or clarity about the forms or scope of action/inaction required (see Sunstein 2003), or have suggested that it is insufficient to orient effective and necessary practices in the context of the scale of the climate emergency. Simply put, some view the 'precautionary principle' as an ambiguous or even conservative statement of our commitment to environmental preservation when specific and revolutionary forms of action are needed (see Sandin et al. 2002; Gardiner 2006; Kareiva and Fuller 2016; Symons and Karlsson 2015).

But at its core, the precautionary principle as articulated above involves endorsement of three key themes fundamental to the ecological security discourse. First, it explicitly recognizes ecosystem complexity and uncertainty about ecosystem functionality, positioning these in the process as a reality to contend with rather than a loophole for either inaction or justification for the continuation of harmful action (see Kim 2019). This accords both with the spirit of the ecological security discourse – as a sensibility rather than a template or prescription for action, a point I will return to later in the chapter – and with notions of humility and reflexivity endorsed in Chapter 4. It also accords, of course, with the points noted in Chapter 3 regarding the inherent complexities of ecosystems themselves.

Second, the precautionary principle leaves open – indeed arguably endorses – the possibility that our concerns might orient towards ecosystems themselves and the lives of other living beings. The explicit focus on the imperative of protecting 'the environment' clearly moves beyond an immediate concern with the preservation of existing human communities or institutions in the face of environmental change. At the very least, the principle's ambiguity (while lamentable for some – see Sandin 2002; Sunstein 2003) allows us to recognize the possibility of defining it in such a way as to actively prioritize the rights and needs of vulnerable beings, including non-human ones.

Third, the notion that the precautionary principle should 'be applied by states according to their capabilities' – while a concession to developing states in the context of (at times divisive) UNCED talks – accords with the account of agency and, in particular, responsibility in the ecological security discourse as articulated in Chapter 4. Here, the notion of capabilities was directly tied to responsibility (see also Shue 1993). I will expand on this point below regarding 'common but differentiated responsibility'.

The precautionary principle is significant as a principle that has both been endorsed explicitly as a core component of the climate-change regime and a norm in the context of climate change that few states have genuinely challenged or contested.[7] While some may lament its lack of specificity and (associated) lack of immediate instruction for directing action, it nonetheless provides us with a foundation for that action, while meaning can be built in to the broad commitments evident in the principle, as some authors have already attempted to do (Gardiner 2006). It is telling here that Cudworth and Hobden (2013:659), for example, endorse precaution in the context of their case for recognizing both ecosystem complexity and the imperative of extending our moral universe towards non-human beings (see also Dalby 2009:166; Kim 2019). In this sense, the precautionary principle – a foundational component of the climate-change regime – can be viewed as a basis upon which a concern with the resilience of ecosystems in the face of climate change might be grounded.

---

[7] Of course, a range of states have arguably challenged the norm in the context of interpretation and practical application of it. On the issue of norm interpretation and contestation, see, e.g., Wiener (2014); Betts and Orchard eds. (2014); Deitelhoff and Zimmermann eds. (2019).

## Common but Differentiated Responsibility

The concept of common but differentiated responsibility (CBDR) was, like the precautionary principle discussed above, endorsed at the UNCED Earth Summit in Rio de Janeiro in 1992. But in the case of CBDR, it was from the outset directly applied to the issue of climate change and was formally incorporated into the UNFCCC at the time of its drafting. Article 3 of the UNFCCC notes the following:

The parties should protect the climate system for the benefit of present and future generations of humankind, on the basis of equity and in accordance with their common but differentiated responsibilities and respective capabilities. Accordingly, the developed country Parties should take the lead in combating climate change and the adverse effects thereof.

As a more specific principle than the precautionary principle – attributing responsibility for action on climate change to particular (albeit a broad set of) agents – CBDR has been challenged more directly than the precautionary principle. For some, the scale of the challenge of climate change necessitates a shift away from the language of differentiation, which opens the door for states to lay claim to special circumstances and their reduced responsibility.[8] For others, the concessions to developing countries (especially significant greenhouse gas emitters such as China and India) under CBDR are potentially too great, creating comparative advantages for those states and their industries (see Rajamani 2012).

Yet CBDR remains a central component of the UNFCCC regime and was again endorsed in the wording (and form) in the most recent substantive international agreement in Paris in 2015 (Voigt and Ferreira 2016). While we certainly see contestation over the precise responsibilities particular actors (largely states) actually have, few would question the legitimacy of the idea that not all states are equally responsible for either contributing to the problem of climate change or for addressing it. More directly from the perspective of the ecological

---

[8] This was perhaps most evident in negotiation for the Kyoto Protocol in 1997, which entailed developed (Annex 1) countries committing to different targets on the basis of national circumstance and capacity. In practice, countries such as Australia used this – and the requirement for consensus – as a basis for justifying minimal commitments, even an increase in greenhouse gas emissions from 1990 levels by the 2008–12 target. See McDonald (2005).

security discourse endorsed here, CBDR endorses key components of that discourse.

First and most directly, of course, CBDR embraces a similar notion of responsibility to that outlined in Chapter 4, one defined significantly in terms of capability and broadly consistent with principles of distributive justice. The central component of CBDR validates the idea that responsibility may be universal but not uniform across states. Second, this universality itself is an important point of consistency with the ecological security discourse. A national security framing ultimately positions climate change as problematic to the extent that it poses a challenge to a discrete nation state. By contrast, ecological security is concerned with climate change as a universal problem on a global scale. The commitment to the 'common' and the benefit of 'humankind' in CBDR similarly implies a universal register. And while ecological security's ethical register extends further to other living beings, the global scope of CBDR is an important point of consistency (see Weijers et al. 2010).

Third, in the form endorsed in the UNFCCC wording, CBDR elaborates an important commitment to future generations. This is a crucial concession, one that brings the principle in closer alignment to ecological security than any of the three other climate security discourses advanced in Chapter 2. Finally, and following the above point, CBDR also endorses a distinction between referent object and agent – between those threatened and those responsible for acting. In specifically articulating a role for states (albeit differentiated between states) while simultaneously emphasizing that the threat posed is to 'humankind', extending to 'future generations', CBDR decouples referent and agent. In this sense, CBDR overlaps significantly with the ecological security discourse, suggesting a precedent in existing axes of climate cooperation for prioritizing action undertaken by the powerful on behalf of the vulnerable.

## The Anthropocene

Increasing – and increasingly widespread – recognition of the arrival of a new geological era of the Anthropocene also creates opportunities for advancing and enabling an ecological security discourse in the context of climate change. While not a core component of environmental governance or the climate regime, the Anthropocene framing still has the potential to promote changes in the way we conceive and approach security in the context of climate change (see Chandler et al. eds. 2021).

As discussed at length in Chapter 3, the Anthropocene refers to the (suggested arrival of a) new geological era in which human activity is recognized as having a clear and significant effect on Earth systems themselves. In the process of recognizing this arrival, the traditional distinctions between humanity and nature central to modern thought (even emancipatory variants of progress) are potentially challenged. It is, as Steffan et al. (2007:614) memorably put it, 'an unintended experiment of humankind on its own life support system'.

Of course for some, the scale of this challenge may be overstated or the effects of its embrace problematic. For Madeleine Fagan (2019), for example, the embrace of the Anthropocene and claims of its role in challenging the traditional human–nature binary rely on a modernist view of time and the human subject and ultimately risk endorsing a liberal humanist conception of ethics in the process. For David Chandler (2018, 2019), the problem may be the opposite – that endorsing the Anthropocene involves decentring the human subject from Enlightenment thought and, in the process, undermining the entire project of ethical critique and conceptualizing progress. Still others are more directly concerned, as noted in Chapter 3, about the possibility that endorsing the Anthropocene means positioning humans as all-powerful forces, enabling an ecomodernist project bent on remaking the world in particular ways (see Luke 2013). In this account, Anthropocene framings in the context of climate change may provide opportunities for agents to wheel out dangerous (e.g. geoengineering) projects oriented towards a reconstitution of Earth systems.

Yet for proponents (see Hardt 2017; Harrington and Shearing 2017), or even those critical of sweeping assessments of the negative implications of an Anthropocene 'framing' (see Clark 2014; Dalby 2016; Lövbrand et al. 2015; Eckersley 2017; Dryzek and Pickering 2018), the concept also (at least potentially) serves to encourage a crucial and necessary shift in the relationship with the natural world (Yusoff 2013; Biermann 2018). Here, following Lövbrand et al. (2015), particular readings or interpretations of the Anthropocene provide a foundation for re-examining our place in the world, a concern central to ecological security. To reiterate, at the heart of ecological security is a concern with reorienting our ethical focus from currently existing human populations (especially discrete or self-contained communities of them) and towards other living beings and future generations. The scale of this moral and cognitive shift requires us to think differently about our place in the world and in particular the idea of a separation between humanity and the (environmental) conditions of our existence. And if climate change encourages us to reconsider that relationship, the onset of the coronavirus pandemic – with ecological destruction and (changing) interspecies interaction a core component of its origins – further compels us to revisit the relationship between humanity and the natural world (Heyd 2020). This increases the likelihood that a re-articulation of human–nature relations in ecological terms might resonate with wider sets of audiences.

In this sense, the Anthropocene has significant potential in furthering and encouraging a shift in perspective and consciousness. It can serve this end through repositioning the relationship between human populations and the physical conditions of our existence, as noted in Chapter 3. This need not mean carte blanche for geoengineering projects (a point I will return to below) or the rejection of existing accounts of ethical responsibility within and between existing human communities – a concern for those wary or critical of the Anthropocene framing. While this could well be conceived as a danger of the Anthropocene's embrace, it is, like security more broadly, a concept whose politics is determined by the meaning we give to it.

## Governing Climate, Governing Security

In the context of managing both climate change and security issues at an international level, existing sets of principles and norms also serve to provide foundation for the elaboration and even institutionalization of an ecological security discourse regarding climate change.

While the precautionary principle and CBDR apply broadly to the management of environmental issues and climate change at the level of core principles, more specific suggestions aligning to ecological security can be found in interventions regarding the management, regulation and use of geoengineering, for example. The so-called Oxford Principles – 'the most widely recognized ethical standards governing the research and implementation of geoengineering' (Symons 2019a:170) – constitute one such example of principles for the management of this form of intervention, one which aligns with the commitments of ecological security. In particular, the Principles endorse the importance of dialogue in the process of developing and implementing geoengineering projects, transparency in research, caution in implementation and ongoing examination of the effects of such projects in practice (see Rayner et al. 2013)

Of course, these principles are not universally endorsed or embraced. Jonathan Symons (2019:171), for example, suggests that in potentially serving to curtail or limit the use of geoengineering, the Oxford Principles might ultimately cause disproportionate harm to those most in need of urgent action to address climate change, especially the world's poor. This does not, however, address lingering concerns outlined in Chapter 4 about the dangers inherent in this form of intervention; the need for significant sensitivity to those dangers; and the potential threat to the local ecosystems and communities immediately exposed to them. In response to this, and in the specific form of the Oxford Principles as articulated above we see a commitment to dialogue, humility and reflexivity: all, as noted, core elements of the ecological security discourse advanced here. If geoengineering needs to remain a part of a conversation about how to address the problem of climate change – even if as a stopgap or 'buying time' measure (see Dalby 2015; Preston ed. 2016; Corry 2017) – it needs to be accompanied by sets of principles and practices consistent with harm minimization and ecosystem resilience. In this sense, the Oxford Principles constitute a statement of considerations aligning with the core commitments of an ecological security discourse.

In terms of regulation of international security issues, meanwhile, an increasing focus on prevention in discussions of the management of international security threats (see Ackerman 2003) aligns clearly with the focus on addressing climate change directly at its origins. Some have focused on the prevention of violent conflict arising from contestation and conflict linked to climate change (see Werrell et al. 2017), in which effective forms of adaptation might intervene between stress and outright conflict. Research making a case for environmental peacebuilding, meanwhile, has long suggested the capacity of individuals, communities and institutions to effectively manage contestation over environmental change in the direction of cooperation rather than conflict (see Conca and Dabelko 2002; Ide 2017; Dresse et al. 2019). In the process, such scholarship points to the problematic assumptions evident in traditional accounts of security and conflict (particularly over environmental issues), recognizes the possibility of dialogue and cooperation and emphasizes prevention as the most effective form of engagement with environmental stress and the potential for armed conflict.

An increasing emphasis on prevention carries with it the possibility of focusing on mitigation as a core response to the threats associated with climate change. Indeed, as noted in Chapter 4, even states increasingly identify effective and significant mitigation effort as a means of advancing or realizing climate security (see Diez et al. 2016; Zhou 2017). This focus is clearly consistent with the ecological security discourse, which encourages rapid and significant mitigation of greenhouse gas emissions in order to ensure ecosystem resilience. Again, the endorsement of the 'preventative security' agenda more broadly can be seen as a foundation upon which a transition to ecological security might be grounded.

## Ecological Security in Practice

The preceding discussion has made the case that a range of principles, concepts and norms provide valuable foundation for the elaboration of an ecological security discourse in the context of climate change. But, of course, a range of actors and groups also – in a range of different sites and ways – make a case for a shift to ecological security.

In broad terms, a wide range of environment, development and human rights civil society groups make an active case for a reorientation *towards* the ethical commitments at the heart of ecological security. Organizations advocating for poverty alleviation or effective medical and educational opportunities for impoverished populations in the developing world, for example, encourage a shift in ethical focus towards the vulnerable and the suffering. This applies too to refugee advocacy groups or organizations campaigning on women's' rights or child welfare issues, for example (see Keck and Sikkink 1998).

More directly, a range of environmental organizations and activists have attempted to make a case for action on climate change. (On NGO advocacy, see Keck and Sikkink 1998; Lang 2013.) Of a significant range of organizations advocating strong climate-change action, a number directly promote the rights and needs of other living beings, future generations or even 'nature'. This is central to the recently established Extinction Rebellion movement, for example, which aims to mobilize against biodiversity loss and social and ecological collapse associated with climate change through nonviolent action (Farrell et al. eds. 2019). More specifically, in the lead up to Paris climate talks in 2015, for example, a range of activists created the Climate Games: a challenge for fellow activists to develop innovative and performative forms of protest to draw attention to the climate crisis and the need for action. The games' motto was, 'We are not fighting for nature, we are nature defending itself' (see McDonald 2015). In this sense, organizers directly challenged the human–nature separation: a central component of the ecological security discourse. And the prominence of youth activist Greta Thunberg, who has emphasized the existential nature of the threat posed by climate change to future life on the planet, also points to an orientation towards concerns central to ecological security – especially the vulnerability of future generations.

At what is arguably the other end of the climate advocacy spectrum, it is also significant to note that a range of traditional NGOs (from the WWF to the Australian Conservation Foundation, for example) have shifted their practices and the focus of their advocacy. Such groups have moved increasingly away from preservation and conservation campaigns to emphasize the imperative of changing practices of industry and development to address the vulnerability of other living beings and ecosystems in the face of climate change (McDonald 2016). As noted in Chapter 4, claims of speaking on behalf of the natural world should be endorsed with caution, not least given the inherent difficulty (even impossibility) of authentically representing nature and the rights and needs of other living beings (see Eckersley 1992). Yet whether through the emergence of new NGOs or the reorientation of established ones, the nature of the climate crisis has encouraged forms of advocacy that directly challenge the human–nature separation and orient explicitly towards the rights and needs of the most vulnerable. In this context, NGO and activist groups are increasingly ecological security advocates, capable of influencing both specific policy and broader societal attitudes towards climate change (see Wapner 1995).

In public debate across a wide range of countries, political actors and commentators are also engaged constantly in attempts to promote significant action on climate change and challenge those perpetuating harm. Whether green political parties or local governments, political commentators, artists or journalists, a range of actors throughout the world attempt to make a case for the rights and needs of the most vulnerable in the face of the threat of climate change (see North 2011; Lövbrand et al. 2015). To return to one of the themes of the book – discussed at length in Chapter 1 – security is a site of contestation between actors advancing different accounts of a political community's values in need of protection or advancement. In this sense, identifying and (where possible) amplifying those voices making a case for defining those values in terms consistent with ecosystem resilience is crucial in locating immanent possibilities for change (see Wyn Jones 1999).

And finally, in the academic space, a range of researchers have sought to make a case for a shift towards ecological security. While the defence of ecological security advanced here parts ways with the utilitarian approach to animal rights Peter Singer (1975) advocates, for example, he nonetheless poses direct challenges to established and accepted means of defining ethical responsibility in the context of other living beings (see also Celermajer et al. 2020; Wienhues 2020). And in the field of international relations, Burke et al. (2016) ultimately make an impassioned plea for alternative modes of governance, institutional design and economic exchange in the context of the ecological crisis (see also Newell 2020). In the process, they ask their colleagues to change the way we think about global politics and IR: from a perspective that begins with existing sets of institutional arrangements and asks how these might be civilized in the service of ecological ends, to a focus on the ecological crisis that asks what forms our politics and institutions should take to ensure they can address this crisis. They ask us, ultimately, to focus our attention on the extent to which IR is 'fit for purpose'.

While it might seem obvious – to the point of seeming banal – to acknowledge the existence of actors advancing concerns consistent with ecological security, this recognition serves as a reminder that these concerns *are* being articulated and advanced in the contemporary context. Those interested in advancing ecological security in the context of climate change can ultimately find solidarity with a range of actors engaged in the struggle to advance various elements of this discourse in a range of different sites and contexts.

While by no means an exhaustive account of the range of immanent possibilities for the articulation, endorsement and even institutionalization of ecological security, the above discussion suggests that despite powerful political, social, cultural and economic impediments, the ecological security discourse is not 'Utopian'. In the precautionary principle and common but differentiated responsibility, we can see elements of this discourse already endorsed in key principles of environmental and climate governance. In discussion of the Anthropocene, we can locate recognition of the need to change the way we view the relationship between humanity and the environment towards an embeddedness at the heart of the ecological security discourse. In accounts of the regulation of large-scale climate interventions, we see the endorsement of dialogue, humility and reflexivity: all central to the ecological security discourse as articulated in Chapter 4. The focus on prevention in the maintenance of international security may at times orient towards the conservative, but it lays groundwork for the focus on mitigation that must be at the heart of ecological security. And as we explore existing forms, sites and dynamics of global climate politics, we cannot help but identify a wide range of actors and forms of engagement advancing (in myriad ways) the sets of concerns at the heart of ecological security. What seems foreign and infeasible as a political project at first glance is actually instantiated in various ways in practice. And if this framework and sensibility *needs* to inform the way we consider the security implications of climate change – the lens through which security is viewed – we need to build upon these immanent possibilities rather than accept powerful constraints as timeless and immovable obstacles.

Beyond the crucial task of recognizing immanent possibilities for shifting towards or embracing ecological security, there is also a role for moving beyond existing resources, institutions and practices in contemporary contexts. Indeed the novel approaches and practices of a range of activist groups remind us of the capacity to promote ends consistent with ecological security in new and innovative ways. As Lövbrand et al. (2015:214) note, we should resist the temptation to default to existing sets of institutions and practices in locating responses to the ecological crisis we face. They refer to this potentially conservative and paradoxical tendency – to locate solutions to potentially apocalyptic challenges within existing institutions and policy mechanisms – as 'a post-political ontology of the Anthropocene' (Lövbrand et al. 2015:214). While we can and should build on existing possibilities for movement towards ecological security within the contemporary order, therefore, we should also imagine alternative sets of

principles, practices and institutions not necessarily evidenced in contemporary climate politics.[9]

## Possibility, Progress and End Point

What, then, does the preceding discussion mean in terms of the
praxeological questions that framed this chapter? How exactly do we
confront and overcome the significant impediments to the articulation,
endorsement and even institutionalization of an ecological security
discourse in practice? Possibility, progress and end point are all part
of this story. The preceding discussion has emphasized (immanent)
possibilities for movement towards ecological security, noting the ways
in which existing sets of principles, practices and struggles provide a
foundation to be built upon, and serve in different ways to advance
ecological security concerns.

Central to the endorsement of these possibilities is a conception of
progress. Simply put, we cannot allow the 'perfect to be the enemy of
the good'. Those who would support an orientation towards ecosystem resilience in the ways political communities view their security –
their core values in need of preservation and advancement – should
recognize and support movement *towards* this orientation and/or away
from practices that create harm. In this sense, the articulation and
support for human security evident in accounts of the implications of
climate change emanating from some states and intergovernmental
organizations (see Chapter 2) is progressive, not least given that this
encourages a commitment to mitigation (see Matthew et al. eds. 2010).
Similarly, a focus on the potential implications of climate change for
international or regional stability might not align with the core principles of the ecological security discourse but should also encourage
cooperative efforts to promote adaptive capacity in affected states, for
example. And while existing institutional arrangements and dynamics
consistently fall short of institutionalizing a commitment to humility,
reflexivity and dialogue as endorsed here (see Dryzek and Pickering
2018), they often offer partial variants of these dynamics and (perhaps
more importantly) still constitute the key actors and institutions we
currently have for addressing climate change cooperation in practice.

---

[9] This concern is also at the heart of Burke et al. (2016) 'Planet Politics Manifesto'.

Of course, this creates a key practical dilemma for those keen to promote ecological security: should we work with and speak to existing (powerful) institutional arrangements and actors, or avoid being co-opted into these imperfect arrangements by remaining on the outside? This is a dilemma familiar to political theorists and philosophers (evident in the distinction made between ideal and non-ideal political philosophy)[10] but is ever-present for those interested in the realization of substantive action on human rights, poverty reduction or environmental change generally.[11] For all their imperfections, do we work with powerful institutions like states, the World Bank or the UN Security Council to realize action on these issues, or do we avoid co-option into problematic processes or the interests of these actors by remaining on the outside?

This dilemma is particularly clear in debates about the 'responsibility to protect' in international relations. For some critics, the principle is necessarily compromised by its inconsistent application in practice, with some suggesting it does little more than provide justification for intervention motivated by narrower sets of national interests (see Chandler 2004; Cunliffe 2010, 2017). In this schema, R2P does little to reorient existing state action at best and serves to facilitate harm at worst. But for others, endorsement of this principle not only serves to challenge the idea of sovereignty as non-intervention (in which statehood becomes a 'get out of jail free card' for all manner of human rights abuses) but also provides a normative basis and mechanism through which states' actors and advocates can mobilize for international action in response to abuses of human rights. For these advocates, its application will always be somewhat contingent on political calculations and considerations, but it provides a crucial foundation for the realization of human rights in practice (see Bellamy 2014; Bellamy and Dunne eds. 2016; Ralph 2018).

As should be clear from the discussion and defence of the 'green state' literature in Chapter 4, for the purposes of this book (and in the

---

[10] For an introduction to this distinction, see Gamble (2010). See also Rawls (1999) on the application of 'first principles' to nonideal political contexts.

[11] As discussed in Chapter 4, the 'green state' literature addressed this issue directly, making a powerful case for exploring the contours and possibilities of progressive state environmental policy even while acknowledging concerns about the environmental credentials of states themselves (Eckersley 2004; Barry and Eckersley eds. 2005).

context of the climate crisis), we cannot allow limitations of existing institutional arrangements and actors to preclude working through them. And again for the purposes of this book, recognizing, encouraging and endorsing *progress towards* (rather than simply the realization of) ecological security is crucial for addressing praxeological questions of how we move from existing discourses of climate security to one oriented towards ecosystem resilience and the rights and needs of the most vulnerable. The challenge is clearly one, however, of supporting progressive change without becoming complacent about the nature of the continued challenge or sufficiently reflexive about the pathologies (and dangers) of working in and through existing sets of arrangements and processes.

A conception of possibility and of progress are therefore central to engaging with the praxeological questions that framed this chapter, but we need to retain a conception of what it is we're aiming for. To put it simply, we cannot know what constitutes progress unless we have some conception of what it is that constitutes an end point. This need not come in the form of a clear and distinct project or framework to be applied; indeed, the proceduralist ethics around dialogue endorsed here speak against such a project.[12] Rather, our end point could be conceived in broad and less prescriptive terms: as circumstances in which political communities view climate change through the lens of its implications for ecosystem resilience and with it the rights and needs of the most vulnerable, orienting their practices and actions accordingly. In this sense, and to reiterate, such a discourse serves less as a prescriptive project and more as a sensibility that serves to drive how those communities make sense of the implications of climate change and the necessity of urgent action to address its effects on the most vulnerable.

Ultimately, this book mounts a defence of recognizing, articulating and pursuing progress alongside the elaboration of the core principles upon which an ethically defensible approach to the relationship

---

[12] Ultimately, the vision of 'end point' above does not align with specific articulations of what new forms of institution or their processes should look like. While a range of recent accounts have made a case for progressive forms of institutional design at the level of global governance (see, e.g., Dufek 2015; Cabrera ed. 2018), the approach taken here suggests that appropriate forms of institutional arrangement will follow from the embrace of a particular *sensibility* aligned to ecological security.

between climate change and security is built. This suggests, building on the insights of Chapter 4, an important role for a range of actors and actions at multiple 'sites'. In practical terms, substantively working *towards* ecological security can involve practices ranging from working with national militaries to focus their attention on long-term challenges of national disasters or population displacement, to public campaigns for significant mitigation action. And as scholars, the above suggests the need to both outline broad sets of normative and ethical commitments (e.g., Lövbrand et al. 2015; Burke et al. 2016) alongside projects that identify possibilities for incremental change through and within existing institutions (e.g., Eckersley 2004; Barry and Eckersley eds. 2005). This could be conceived as something approaching a 'division of labour' between different actors in different spaces (or, as Bourdieu would have it, 'fields'). These multiple axes of agency and action will be required to progress towards viewing climate change through the lens of ecosystem resilience.

## Conclusion

There are profound impediments to the scale of shift required. There are related and reinforcing challenges at the level of the way we think about our values and the world in which we live; the power of particular discourses or models of economic growth, development and ethics; and the institutional frameworks in which we operate. Taken together, these constitute powerful limits to the extent to which we can readily imagine a shift towards viewing our security – in the context of climate change – through the lens of ecosystem resilience. As noted, these impediments have been sufficiently serious for some to write off the utility of ecological security despite acknowledging its normative appeal.

While outlining these challenges to give a fuller extent of the impediments faced, this chapter has primarily sought to address this praxeological challenge head-on. Drawing on Bourdieu and critical theory, I developed an account of political possibility that involves building upon core resources, dynamics and practices that endorse central components of an ecological security discourse. The chapter made a case for recognizing these immanent possibilities: from the precautionary principle to common but differentiated responsibility, from representations of the Anthropocene to progressive developments in climate and global governance and from political activism to forms of intellectual intervention that endorse, in radically different ways and sites, the core constituent elements of an ecological security discourse. I also made the case that those interested in advancing this project and this possibility cannot work at the level of meta-theory alone, outlining ideal principles or contours of this discourse. We must also recognize and celebrate the importance of *progress towards* such a sensibility, one that may involve pragmatic and incremental work with existing institutional arrangements and actors to edge closer towards ecological security. This potentially involves, as noted, a division of labour between a range of actors, activists and academics focused on various axes of the status quo, pushing them further towards a concern with the rights and needs of the most vulnerable in the context of climate change.

The two points made at the opening of this chapter are worth reiterating at its close. First, while impediments to the articulation, endorsement and institutionalization of ecological security might be profound, this cannot serve as a rationale for its abandonment. If we are convinced that such an approach to climate security is most likely to lead us towards progressive and effective climate action (and away from harm for the most vulnerable), we need to challenge the tyranny of the status quo and, instead, turn our attention to how such a discourse might be enabled and advanced. Building on the realization that security itself is a site of contestation between competing discourses – of core values in need of protection, threats to them, means of their preservation and agents capable of acting to protect or advance them – we need to ask how such a discourse might come to provide the lens through which communities ultimately view the challenge of climate change. Second, and following this, we need to recognize that impediments are not the same as preventive limits and that resources for pushing further in the direction of ecological security are to be found in a range of contemporary contexts. Building on these forms of engagement will be crucial to advancing this shift in thought and practice, a shift increasingly necessary in the context of the climate crisis.

# Conclusion

The connection between climate change and security is not going anywhere. This linkage is increasingly recognized by analysts and endorsed by political leaders and practitioners. It features in national security strategy statements and UN Security Council deliberations. It has made its way into IPCC reports and internal defence documents. And, of course, it features in a myriad number of policy briefs, opinion editorials and academic analyses, with the focus increasingly shifting from whether climate change constitutes a security concern, to how exactly we should conceive and approach the climate–security relationship.

And here lies the rub. The question of how that relationship is viewed, and in particular whose security is prioritized, remains unsettled. From the perspective of the conceptual framework developed in this book, this isn't surprising. While security language and practice linked to it are ubiquitous, the same forces that compel engagement with it – its political currency and performative power, its capacity to define a community's core values and its centrality to the legitimacy of key actors – necessarily render security a site of contestation. And distinct claims about whose security matters, from what threats, how it is to be protected and by what agents – the constitutive elements of security discourses – have radically different implications for the way issues such as climate change are addressed in practice.

A national security discourse remains dominant, a product (at least significantly) of the nation state constituting our default answer to the question of whose security matters in global politics. But clearly, protecting or insulating powerful institutions from manifestations of climate change, while accepting the exposure of the most vulnerable to these same effects, is ethically indefensible by almost any standard. Even before addressing the (complex) obligations we have to future generations and other living beings, the national security discourse clearly favours the particular concerns of wealthy and powerful states with the capacity to manage and adapt to manifestations of climate change, states disproportionately responsible for the problem itself. Phillip Alston, the UN's Special Rapporteur on Extreme Poverty and Human Rights, memorably noted that the current international response to climate change risks "a 'climate apartheid' scenario where the wealthy pay to escape overheating, hunger, and conflict while the rest of the world is left to suffer" (in Carrington 2019). While no surprise to analysts such as Simon Dalby (1998, 2002, 2009), who has been advancing precisely this argument for at least the last two decades, it nonetheless serves to remind us of the morally objectionable nature of 'business as usual' climate politics that few, if any, ethical frameworks could defend.

In this sense, the increasing shift to recognizing the implications of climate change for international stability and especially human welfare itself is a good thing. Discourses of international security and human security correct the morally perverse, narrow and atavistic tendencies of a national security discourse that risks perceiving those immediately affected by manifestations of climate change as a source of threat to the imagined community of the nation state: as the threat 'multiplied' by climate change rather than the victims of it. Yet the international security discourse risks endorsing an international status quo already characterized by immediate and direct threats to vulnerable human populations, and the human security discourse risks drawing a line around currently living human populations and failing to address the rights and needs of future generations or other living beings. The latter, as has been noted throughout the book, are most vulnerable to climate change, least responsible for it and least able to affect consequential responses to it.

Ultimately, in this book, I made a case for ecological security as the lens through which we should view the security implications of climate change. When we focus on ecosystems and their resilience, we orient towards radical action to address direct effects of climate change by focusing on the challenge at its source. And in the context of the Anthropocene, an era in which humans have become a geological force, the type of shift in thinking that the ecological security discourse encourages is one consistent with the broader need to recognize the nature of our embeddedness and situatedness in (rather than separation from) the natural world. As feminist scholars such as Val

Plumwood (1993) have long argued,[1] in interrogating and addressing
the hubris of the human–nature separation at the centre of modern
thought, we create conditions in which other axes of discrimination
and violence might be overcome.

Clearly, however, pursuing the goal of ecosystem resilience raises a
series of acutely complex questions. How do we weigh the needs of
future generations with present populations or the lives of other living
beings? How do we navigate significant uncertainty around the timeframes of effects, climate-tipping points and the implications of geoengineering on ecosystems, for example? How do we conceive of
responsibility for action in pursuit of ecological security, when ecosystem resilience may be affected by a wide range of practices, extending
to the mundane and every day?

Ultimately, this book made a case for a genuinely multifaceted
approach to the pursuit of ecological security. The goal of ensuring
ecosystem resilience and the rights and needs of the most vulnerable in
the face of the direct and immediate threats posed by climate change
necessitates a wide range of measures and agents: from mitigation and
adaptation to geoengineering (with a predominant emphasis on the
former) and from concerted action by states, IGOs and private
corporations to activism from civil society groups and shifts in individual behaviour. The responsibility for action was tied here to capacity,
with recognition that individual behaviours follow broader structural
and societal arrangements that consequential actors (states in particular) should seek to address (see Newell et al. 2015).

While specifying the nature of the referent object, the nature of the
threat, the means of responding to it and the agents responsible for
doing so, I also outlined core principles that should inform the detail
given to these broad commitments in specific context. Here, the book
outlined a commitment to dialogue, reflexivity and humility. Dialogue
was approached as a crucial means of ensuring that a large range of
(especially local) voices are involved in the development of responses to
climate change, in the process rendering these responses both more
effective and more (politically and socially) sustainable. I also endorsed
the importance of reflexivity, understood as a commitment to constant
reflection upon and interrogation of the appropriateness of means and
institutions of response to the climate crisis (see Dryzek and Pickering

---

[1] See also Kaijser and Kronsell (2014) on intersectionality in this context.

2018). And humility was also endorsed as a central principle for approaching and advancing ecological security. Minimizing the danger of imposing impractical and perverse responses to climate change requires acceptance of the limits of our understanding and capacity.

Taken together, these principles also suggest that the function of ecological security is less a program of action than a sensibility that should inform how we make sense of the world and act in it. But it is a sensibility that clearly encourages significant changes in the way we view the world, existing institutions and practices, and the nature of ethical responsibility. As Robyn Eckersley (2005) has argued, the challenge is

> how to find and develop a mode of argument that encapsulates the idea of respect for nonhuman nature for its own sake; that does not privilege self-serving human attributes over non-human ones; that does not see nature as some passive substance to be acted on or valued by humans but rather recognizes some form of agency in nature; that goes beyond a mere instrumental valuation of nature's services; that is not narrowly confined to particular cultures (e.g. western) and linguistic (e.g. English) communities, but can speak across, and appeal to, a wider variety of human cultures (and languages); that is not misanthropic and can recognize the needs of human communities to sustain their livelihoods from ecosystems.

In the process of making the case for ecological security, we need to acknowledge the fundamental impediments to approaching climate change (and security) in this way. But as noted in Chapter 5, this recognition of limits should not give way to resignation about the prospect for change. Drawing on Bourdieu's (1990) structuralist constructivism to develop an account of political possibility, I made the case that we can identify resources, principles and practices immanent within the contemporary context that can be built upon to realize progressive change. Principles such as the precautionary principle and common but differentiated responsibility endorse, in different ways, a focus on the rights and needs of vulnerable beings, and the imperative for action in the face of countervailing forces (whether uncertainty or relative cost). The Anthropocene reminds us of the need to reflect critically on the separation between humans and nature at the heart of modern thought, a separation that has arguably driven an extractive vision of the natural world at the heart of ecological destruction. Normative cases for changes in forms of climate governance – from the regulation of geoengineering to the re-examination of sovereignty – can also be built upon to advance movement in the direction of ecological security. And, of course, we need to recognize and amplify those voices and practices instantiating ecological security in practice, whether through pragmatic engagement with existing institutions or through radical forms of activism.

In this context I made a case for a practical and intellectual division of labour, one recognizing the importance of working with both contemporary configurations of power to pursue progress on one hand, and articulating a clear vision of where we need to go on the other. And I made the case that by either standard or form of action, we can already see foundations for realizing ecological security in practice in the context of climate change.

Beyond climate change, there is a case to be made for a focus on ecosystem resilience as a progressive discourse of security in the context of a range of global challenges. Clearly this applies to environmental change more broadly, especially on issues such as biodiversity loss (see Burke 2019; Burke and Fishel 2019). But it also has promise as a framework for orienting our response to issues such as nuclear proliferation and use, for example, with the focus on future generations and ecosystem resilience clearly pushing us towards disarmament (Plesch 2018). And, as noted, the role of ecological destruction and changing inter-species relationships in facilitating the coronavirus pandemic – dubbed the 'disease of the Anthropocene' (O'Callaghan-Gordo and Anto 2020) – also suggests that an ecological security discourse has utility in understanding and framing effective responses to one of the most challenging transnational threats experienced in this century (see also Heyd 2020).

In other contexts, on issues such as poverty, other forms of disease or human rights, the broad endorsement of cosmopolitan principles evident in the commitment to the most vulnerable, and rejection of the ethical limits of the nation state, can guide approaches to these issues that address the immediate threat they pose to communities now and into the future. Here, responsibility for addressing such issues is (again) found at multiple sites, with emphasis on those who have the capacity to minimize harm in these contexts (see Burke et al. 2014).

The focus of this book, however, has been the unprecedented global threat posed by climate change. The scale of this threat necessitates radical changes in the way we view and engage with the world, including how we conceive and approach security. Changes in the way we understand and approach security is not just one possible site

for this change, however, alongside others. It is fundamental because
security is central to why contemporary powerful institutions exist,
how communities come to understand what values are ultimately in
need of preserving and advancing and what the core challenges to
those values might be. Engaging with security is therefore not only
possible in the context of climate change, it is imperative.

# References

Abrahams, Daniel (2019) 'From Discourse to Policy: US Policy Communities' Perceptions of and Approaches to Climate Change and Security', *Conflict, Security and Development*, 19:4, pp. 323–45.

Abrahamsen, Rita (2002) 'Blair's Africa: The Politics of Securitization and Fear', *Alternatives*, 30:1, pp. 55–80.

Ackerman, Alice (2003) 'The Idea and Practice of Conflict Prevention', *Journal of Peace Research*, 40:3, pp. 339–47.

Ackerman, Frank (2008) 'Hot, It's Not', *Climatic Change*, 89, pp. 435–46.

Adger, W. Neil (2006) 'Vulnerability', *Global Environmental Change*, 16, pp. 268–81.

Adger, W. Neil, Katrina Brown and James Waters (2011) 'Resilience', in John Dryzek, Richard Norgaard and David Schlosberg eds., *The Oxford Handbook of Climate Change and Society* (Oxford: Oxford University Press), pp. 696–710.

Adler, Emanuel and Vincent Pouliot (2011) *International Practices* (Cambridge: Cambridge University Press).

Adler-Nissen, Rebecca (2013) *Bourdieu in International Relations* (London: Routledge).

Agarwal, A. and S. Narain (1991) *Global Warming in an Unequal World: A Case of Environmental Colonialism* (New Delhi: Centre for Science and the Environment).

Agnew, John (1998) *Geopolitics: Re-visioning World Politics* (London: Routledge).

Aldred, Jonathan (2012) 'The Ethics of Emissions Trading', *New Political Economy*, 17:3, pp. 339–60.

Alley, R. et al. (2001) 'Abrupt Climate Change', *Science*, 299:5615, pp. 2005–10.

Angus, Ian (2015) 'Hijacking the Anthropocene', *Climate and Capitalism*, 19 May. Available at https://climateandcapitalism.com/2015/05/19/hijacking-the-anthropocene/

Anievas, Alexander, Nivi Manchanda and Robbie Shilliam eds. (2015) *Race and Racism in International Relations* (London: Routledge).

Antonio, Robert (1981) 'Immanent Critique as the Core of Critical Theory', *British Journal of Sociology*, 32:2, pp. 330–45.

Aradau, Claudia (2008) 'Forget Equality? Security and Liberty in the "War on Terror"', *Alternatives*, 33:3, pp. 293–314.

Aradau, Claudia and Rens Van Munster (2007) 'Governing Terrorism through Risk', *European Journal of International Relations*, 13:1, pp. 89–115.

Archer, Margaret (2003) *Structure, Agency and the Internal Conversation* (Cambridge: Cambridge University Press).

Asafu-Adjaye, John et al. (2015) *EcoModernist Manifesto*, April. Available at https://static1.squarespace.com/static/5515d9f9e4b04d5c3198b7bb/t/552d37bbe4b07a7dd69fcdbb/1429026747046/An+Ecomodernist+Manifesto.pdf

Asian Development Bank (ADB) (2012) *Addressing Climate Change & Migration in Asia & the Pacific* (Manila: ADB).

Ayoob, Mohammed (1997) 'Defining Security: A Subaltern Realist Perspective', in Keith Krause and Michael C. Williams eds., *Critical Security Studies: Concepts and Cases* (Minneapolis: University of Minnesota Press), pp. 121–46.

Baker, Aryn (2015) 'How Climate Change Is Behind the Surge of Migrants to Europe', *Time Magazine*, 7 September. Available at http://time.com/4024210/climate-change-migrants/

Baldwin, David A. (1997) 'The Concept of Security', *Review of International Studies*, 23, pp. 5–26.

Balzacq, Thierry (2005) 'The Three Faces of Securitization', *European Journal of International Relations*, 11:2, pp. 171–201.

Balzacq, Thierry ed. (2010) *Securitization Theory* (London: Routledge).

Balzacq, Thierry, Stefano Guzzini, Michael Williams, Ole Wæver and Heikki, Patomäki eds. (2015) 'What Kind of Theory – If Any – Is Securitization?', *International Relations*, 29:1, pp. 96–136.

Banerjee, Bidisha (2010) 'The Great Wall of India', *Slate*, 20 December. Available at https://slate.com/technology/2010/12/india-is-fencing-off-its-border-with-bangladesh-what-will-that-mean-for-millions-of-potential-climate-refugees.html

Barbosa, Luis C. (2000) *The Brazilian Amazon Rainforest* (Lanham, MD: University Press of America).

Barkawi, Tarak and Mark Laffey (2006) 'The Postcolonial Moment in Security Studies', *Review of International Studies*, 32:2, pp. 329–52.

Barnett, Jon (2000) 'Destabilizing the Environment-Conflict Thesis', *Review of International Studies*, 26, pp. 271–88.

(2001) *The Meaning of Environmental Security* (London: Zed Books).

(2018) 'Global Environmental Change I: Climate Resilient Peace?', *Progress in Human Geography*. Online first: https://journals.sagepub.com/doi/10.1177/0309132518798077

Barnett, Jon and Neil Adger (2007) 'Climate Change, Human Security and Violent Conflict', *Political Geography*, 26:6, pp. 639–55.
et al. (2010) 'Global Environmental Change and Human Security', in Richard Matthew et al. eds., *Global Environmental Change and Human Security* (Cambridge, MA: MIT Press), pp. 3–32.
Barry, John and Robyn Eckersley eds. (2005) *The State and the Global Ecological Crisis* (Cambridge, MA: MIT Press).
Beardsley, Kyle, David Cunningham and Peter White (2017) 'Resolving Civil Wars before They Start', *British Journal of Political Science*, 47:3, pp. 675–97.
Beckman, Ludvig (2008) 'Do Global Climate Change and the Interest of Future Generations Have Implications for Democracy?', *Environmental Politics*, 17:4, pp. 610–24.
Beeson, Mark (2010) 'The Coming of Environmental Authoritarianism', *Environmental Politics*, 19:2, pp. 276–94.
(2019) *Environmental Populism* (London: Palgrave).
Beitz, Charles (1999) *Political Theory and International Relations* (Princeton, NJ: Princeton University Press).
Bellamy, Alex J. (2014) *The Responsibility to Protect: A Defence* (Oxford: Oxford University Press).
Bellamy, Alex J. and Matt McDonald (2004) 'Securing International Society: Towards an English School Discourse of Security', *Australian Journal of Political Science*, 39:2, pp. 303–30.
Bellamy, Alex J. and Tim Dunne eds. (2016) *The Oxford Handbook of the Responsibility to Protect* (Oxford: Oxford University Press).
Bennett, Jane (2010) *Vibrant Matter: A Political Ecology of Things* (Durham: Duke University Press).
Bergin, Anthony et al. (2013) *Heavy Weather: Climate Change & the Australian Defence Force* (Canberra: ASPI, Special Report 49).
Bertrand, Sarah (2018) 'Can the Subaltern Securitize?', *European Journal of International Security*, 3:3, pp. 281–99.
Betsill, Michele and Harriet Bulkeley (2005) 'Transnational Networks and Global Environmental Governance', *International Studies Quarterly*, 48:2, pp. 471–93.
(2006) 'Cities and the Multilevel Governance of Global Climate Change', *Global Governance*, 12, pp. 141–59.
Betts, Alexander and Phil Orchard eds. (2014) *Implementation and World Politics: How International Norms Change Practice* (Oxford: Oxford University Press).
Biermann, Frank (2014) *Earth System Governance: World Politics in the Anthropocene* (Cambridge, MA: Cambridge University Press).

(2018) 'Politics for a New Earth: Governing in the Anthropocene', in Simon Nicholson and Sikina Jinnah eds., *New Earth Politics: Essays from the Anthropocene* (Cambridge: MIT Press), pp. 405–20.

Biermann, Frank and Ingrid Boas (2010) 'Preparing for a Warmer World: Towards a Global Governance System to Protect Climate Refugees', *Global Environmental Politics*, 10:1, pp. 60–88.

Bigo, Didier (2002) 'Security and Immigration: Towards a Critique of the Governmentality of Unease', *Alternatives*, 27 (Special Issue, 2002), pp. 63–92.

(2011) 'Pierre Bourdieu and International Relations: Power of Practices, Practices of Power', *International Political Sociology*, 5:3, pp. 225–58.

Blue, Gwendolyn (2015) 'Public Deliberation with Climate Change', *Review of European, Comparative and International Environmental Law*, 24:2, pp. 152–9.

Boas, Ingrid (2015) *Climate Migration & Security* (London: Routledge).

Boas, Ingrid and Delf Rothe (2015) 'From Conflict to Resilience? Explaining Recent Changes in Climate Security Discourse and Practice', *Environmental Politics*, 25:4, pp. 613–32.

Bookchin, Murray (1987) 'Social Ecology versus Deep Ecology: A Challenge for the Ecology Movement', *Green Perspectives: Newsletter of the Green Program Project*, nos. 4–5 (Summer).

Booth, Ken (1991) 'Security and Emancipation', *Review of International Studies*, 17:4, pp. 313–26.

(2007) *Theory of World Security* (Cambridge: Cambridge University Press).

Bourbeau, Philippe (2015) 'Resilience and International Politics', *International Studies Review*, 17:3, pp. 374–95.

(2018) *On Resilience: Genealogy, Logics and World Politics* (Cambridge: Cambridge University Press).

Bourdieu, Pierre (1977) *Outline of a Theory of Practice* (Cambridge: Cambridge University Press).

(1990) *In Other Words: Essays towards a Reflexive Sociology* (Stanford: Stanford University Press).

(1991) *Language and Symbolic Power*, edited by John Thompson and translated by Gino Raymond and Matthew Adamson (Cambridge: Polity).

(1992) *An Invitation to Reflexive Sociology* (Chicago: University of Chicago Press).

Bourdieu, Pierre and Loic Wacquant (1992) *Invitation to a Reflexive Sociology* (Chicago: University of Chicago Press).

Breen-Smyth, Marie (2014) 'Theorising the "Suspect Community"', *Critical Studies on Terrorism*, 7:2, pp. 223–40.

Brighouse, Harry and Adam Swift (2006) 'Equality, Priority and Positional Goods', *Ethics*, 116:3, pp. 471–97.

Brown, Lester (1977) 'Redefining National Security', *Worldwatch Paper 14* (Washington, DC: Worldwatch Institute).

(1986) 'Redefining National Security', in Brown et al. eds., *State of the World 1986* (New York: Norton), pp. 195–212.

Brown, Oli, Anne Hammill and Robert McLeman (2007) 'Climate Change as the "New" Security Threat: Implications for Africa', *International Affairs*, 83:6, pp. 1141–54.

Browning, Chris and Matt McDonald (2013) 'The Future of Critical Security Studies: Ethics and the Politics of Security', *European Journal of International Relations*, 19:2, pp. 235–55.

Bulkeley, Harriet and Michele Betsill (2010) 'Rethinking Sustainable Cities', *Environmental Politics*, 14:1, pp. 42–63.

Bulkeley, Harriet and Peter Newell (2015) *Governing Climate Change* (London: Routledge).

Bulkeley, Harriet et al. (2014) *Transnational Climate Change Governance* (Cambridge: Cambridge University Press).

Bull, Hedley (1995) *The Anarchical Society*, 2nd ed. (London: Macmillan).

Burke, Anthony (2001) *In Fear of Security: Australia's Invasion Anxiety* (Sydney: Pluto Press).

(2013) 'Security Cosmopolitanism', *Critical Studies on Security*, 1:1, pp. 13–28.

(2019) 'Blue Screen Biosphere: The Absent Presence of Biodiversity in International Law', *International Political Sociology*, 13:3, pp. 333–51.

Burke, Anthony and Stefanie Fishel (2019) 'Power, World Politics, and Thing-Systems in the Anthropocene', in Frank Biermann and Eva Lövbrand eds., *Anthropocene Encounters: New Directions in Green Political Thinking* (Cambridge: Cambridge University Press), pp. 87–108.

Burke, Anthony, Katrina Lee-Koo and Matt McDonald (2014) *Ethics and Global Security* (London: Routledge).

et al. (2016) 'Planet Politics: A Manifesto from the End of IR', *Millennium*, 44:3, pp. 499–523.

Burke, Sharon and Christine Parthemore eds. (2008) *A Strategy for American Power: Energy, Climate and National Security* (Washington, DC: Center for a New American Century).

Busby, Joshua (2007) 'Climate Change and National Security: An Agenda for Action', *Council of Foreign Relations Report* (Washington, DC: Council of Foreign Relations).

(2008) 'Who Cares about the Weather? Climate Change and US National Security', *Security Studies*, 17:3, pp. 468–504.

(2018). 'Taking Stock: The Field of Climate and Security', *Current Climate Change Reports*, 4, pp. 338–46.

Buxton, Nick and Ben Hayes (2015) 'Introduction: Security for Whom in a Time of Climate Crisis', in Buxton and Hayes eds., *The Secure and the Dispossessed* (London: Pluto), pp. 1–19.

Buzan, Barry (2004) *From International to World Society?* (Cambridge: Cambridge University Press).

(2015) 'The English School: A Neglected Approach to International Security Studies', *Security Dialogue*, 46:2, pp. 126–43.

Buzan, Barry and Ana Gonzalez-Palaez (2005) '"International Community" after Iraq', *International Affairs*, 81:1, pp. 31–52.

Buzan, Barry and Lene Hansen (2009) *The Evolution of International Security Studies* (Cambridge: Cambridge University Press).

Buzan, Barry and Ole Wæver (2003) *Regions and Powers* (Cambridge: Cambridge University Press).

Buzan, Barry, Ole Wæver and Jaap de Wilde (1998) *Security: A New Framework for Analysis* (Boulder, CO: Lynne Rienner).

Cabrera, Luis ed. (2018) *Institutional Cosmopolitanism* (Oxford: Oxford University Press).

Campbell, David (1992) *Writing Security: United States Foreign Policy and the Politics of Identity* (London: UCL Press).

Campbell, Kurt ed. (2008) *Climate Cataclysm: The Foreign Policy and National Security Implications of Climate Change* (Washington, DC: Brookings Institute).

Caney, Simon (2005) 'Cosmopolitan Justice, Responsibility and Global Climate Change', *Leiden Journal of International Law*, 18, pp. 747–75.

(2010a) 'Cosmopolitanism', in Duncan Bell ed., *Ethics and World Politics* (Oxford: Oxford University Press), pp. 146–63.

(2010b) 'Markets, Morality and Climate Change', *New Political Economy*, 15:2, pp. 197–224.

Cannon, Terry and Detlef Muller-Mahn (2010) 'Vulnerability, Resilience and Development Discourses in Context of Climate Change', *Natural Hazards*, 55:3, pp. 621–35.

Carrington, Damian (2018) 'Humanity Has Wiped Out 60% of Animal Populations Since 1970, Report Finds', *The Guardian*, 30 October. Available at www.theguardian.com/environment/2018/oct/30/human ity-wiped-out-animals-since-1970-major-report-finds

(2019) '"Climate Apartheid": UN Expert Says Human Rights May Not Survive', *The Guardian*, 25 June. Available at www.theguardian.com/ environment/2019/jun/25/climate-apartheid-united-nations-expert-says -human-rights-may-not-survive-crisis

Cavalieri, Paola (2012) 'Do We Need Continental Philosophy? Nonhumans, Ethics, and the Complexity of Reality', *The New Centennial Review*, 11:2, pp. 83–113.

Cavelty, Myriam Dunn, Mareile Kaufmann and Kristian Soby Kristensen (2015) 'Resilience and (In)security: Practices, Subjects, Temporalities', *Security Dialogue*, 46:1, pp. 3–14.

Celermajer, Danielle et al. (2021) 'Multispecies Justice: Theories, Challenges and a Research Agenda for Environmental Politics', *Environmental Politics*, 30:1–2, pp. 119–40.

Chandler, David (2004) 'The Responsibility to Protect? Imposing the Liberal Peace', *International Peacekeeping*, 11:1, pp. 59–81.

(2013) 'The World of Attachments? The Post-humanist Challenge to Freedom and Necessity', *Millennium: Journal of International Studies*, 41:3, pp. 516–34.

(2014) *Resilience: The Governance of Complexity* (London: Routledge).

(2018) *Ontopolitics in the Anthropocene* (London: Routledge).

(2019) 'The Transvaluation of Critique in the Anthropocene', *Global Society*, 33:1, pp. 26–44.

Chandler, David and Nik Hynek eds. (2011) *Critical Perspectives on Human Security* (London: Routledge).

Chandler, David and Nik Hynek (2013) 'No Emancipatory Alternative, No Critical Security Studies', *Critical Studies on Security*, 1:1, pp. 46–63.

Chandler, David, Franziska Müller and Delf Rothe eds. (2021) *International Relations in the Anthropocene* (London: Palgrave).

Chaturvedi, Sanjay and Timothy Doyle (2015) *Climate Terror* (London: Palgrave).

Chowdhry, Geeta and Sheila Nair eds. (2004) *Power, Postcolonialism and International Relations* (London: Routledge).

Christie, Ryerson (2010) 'Critical Voices and Human Security: To Endure, to Engage or to Critique?' *Security Dialogue*, 41:2, pp. 169–90.

Christoff, Peter (2013) 'Climate Discourse Complexes, National Climate Regimes and Australian Climate Policy', *Australian Journal of Politics and History*, 59:3, pp. 349–67.

Christoff, Peter ed. (2013) *Four Degrees of Global Warming: Australia in a Hot World* (London: Routledge).

(2016) 'The Promissory Note: COP21 and the Paris Climate Agreement', *Environmental Politics*, 25:5, pp. 765–87.

Ciplet, David, J. Timmons Roberts and Mizan Khan (2013) 'The Politics of International Climate Adaptation Funding', *Global Environmental Politics*, 13:1, pp. 49–68.

Clark, Brett and Richard York (2005) 'Carbon Metabolism: Global Capitalism, Climate Change, and the Biospheric Rift', *Theory and Society*, 34:4, pp. 391–428.

Clark, Nigel (2014) 'Geo-politics and the Disaster of the Anthropocene', *The Sociological Review*, 62:S1, pp. 19–37.

Clift, Ben and Jim Tomlinson (2010) 'When Rules Started to Rule: The IMF, Neo-liberal Economic Ideas and Economic Policy Change in Britain', *Review of International Political Economy*, 19:3, pp. 477–500.

CNA (2007) *National Security and the Threat of Climate Change* (Washington, DC: CNA). Available at http://securityandclimate.cna .org/report/

    (2014) *National Security and the Accelerating Risks of Climate Change*. May. Available at www.cna.org/cna_files/pdf/MAB_5-8-14.pdf

Cole, Matthew A. (2003) 'Environmental Optimists, Environmental Pessimists, and the Real World', *The Economic Journal*, 113:48, pp. 362–80.

Conca, Ken (2015) *An Unfinished Foundation: The United Nations and Global Environmental Governance* (Oxford: Oxford University Press).

    (2019) 'Is There a Role for the UN Security Council on Climate Change?', *Environment*, 61:1, pp. 4–15.

Conca, Ken and Geoffrey Dabelko (2002) *Environmental Peacemaking* (Washington, DC: Woodrow Wilson Center Press).

Conca, Ken, Joe Thwaites and Goueun Lee (2017) 'Climate Change and the UN Security Council', *Global Environmental Politics*, 17:2, pp. 1–20.

Constantinou, Costas (2000) 'Poetics of Security', *Alternatives*, 25:3, pp. 287–306.

Corner, Adam and Nick Pidgeon (2010) 'Geoengineering the Climate: The Social and Ethical Implications', *Environment*, 52:1, pp. 24–37.

Corry, Olaf (2012) 'Securitization & Riskification', *Millennium*, 40:2, pp. 235–58.

    (2014) 'From Defense to Resilience: Environmental Security beyond Neo-liberalism', *International Political Sociology*, 8:3, pp. 256–74.

    (2017) 'The International Politics of Geoengineering: The Feasibility of Plan B for Tackling Climate Change', *Security Dialogue*, 48:4, pp. 297–315.

Cousins, Stephanie (2013) 'UN Security Council: Playing a Role in the International Climate Change Regime?', *Global Change, Peace and Security*, 25:2, pp. 191–210.

Cranenburgh, Nadine (2019) 'Solar Energy Is on the Rise, as Coal-Fired Power Stations Age and Gas Prices Rise', *ABC News*, 10 May. Available at www.abc.net.au/news/science/2019-05-10/solar-energy-power-grid-renewables-policy/11088002

Cripps, Elizabeth (2013) *Climate Change and the Moral Agent* (Oxford: Oxford University Press).

Croucher, Ashleigh and Matt McDonald (2014) 'Contesting the International: UNSC Debates on Climate Change and the Politics of International Security', Paper presented at *Oceanic Conference on International Studies*, Melbourne, July.

Cudworth, Erika (2014) 'Feminism', in Carl Death ed., *Critical Environmental Politics* (London: Routledge), pp. 91–100.

Cudworth, Erika and Stephen Hobden (2011) 'Beyond Environmental Security: Complex Systems, Multiple Inequalities and Environmental Risks', *Environmental Politics*, 20:1, pp. 42–59.

(2013) 'Complexity, Ecologism and Posthuman Politics', *Review of International Studies*, 39:3, pp. 643–64.

(2015) 'The Posthuman Way of War', *Security Dialogue*, 46:6, pp. 513–29.

(2017) 'Post-human Security', in Burke and Parker eds., *Global Insecurity: Futures of Global Chaos and Governance* (London: Palgrave), pp. 65–81.

(2018) *The Emancipatory Project of Posthumanism* (London: Routledge).

Cunliffe, Philip (2010) 'Dangerous Duties: Power, Paternalism and the "Responsibility to Protect"', *Review of International Studies*, 36:1, pp. 79–96.

(2017) 'The Doctrine of the "Responsibility to Protect" as a Practice of Political Exceptionalism', *European Journal of International Relations*, 23:2, pp. 466–86.

Dalby, Simon (1998) 'Ecological Metaphors of Security: World Politics in the Biosphere', *Alternatives: Global, Local, Political*, 23:2, pp. 291–319.

(2002) *Environmental Security* (Minneapolis: University of Minnesota Press).

(2007) 'Anthropocene Geopolitics: Globalisation, Empire, Environment and Critique', *Geography Compass*, 1, pp. 103–118.

(2009) *Security and Environmental Change* (Cambridge: Polity).

(2015a) 'Climate Change and the Insecurity Frame', in Shannon O'Lear and Simon Dalby eds., *Reframing Climate Change: Constructing Ecological Geopolitics* (London: Routledge), pp. 83–99.

(2015b) 'Geoengineering: The Next Era of Geopolitics?' *Geography Compass*, 9:4, pp. 190–201.

(2016) 'Framing the Anthropocene: The Good, the Bad and the Ugly', *The Anthropocene Review*, 3:1, pp. 33–51.

Dalby, Simon and Zahra Moussavi (2017) 'Environmental Security, Geopolitics and the Case of Lake Urmia's Disappearance', *Global Change, Peace and Security*, 29:1, pp. 39–55.

Dalby, Simon and Geraid O'Tuathail eds. (1998) *Rethinking Geopolitics* (London: Routledge).

Darby, Andrew (2009) 'Ocean Seeding Fails on Carbon but Plankton Score', *The Sydney Morning Herald*, 27 March. Available at www.smh.com.au/environment/climate-change/ocean-seeding-fails-on-carbon-but-plankton-score-20141112-9ces.html

Decoteau, Claire (2016) 'The Reflexive Habitus: Critical Realist and Bourdieusian Social Action', *European Journal of Social Theory*, 19:3, pp. 303–21.

De Waal, Alex (1997) 'Anarchy Postponed', *Prospect Magazine*, 20 February. Available at https://prospectmagazine.co.uk/magazine/anarchypostponed

Deitelhoff, Nicole and Lisbeth Zimmermann eds. (2019) *Norms under Challenge*. Special Issue of *Journal of Global Security Studies*, 4:1, pp. 1–16.

Deleuze, Gilles (1994) *Difference and Repetition*, trans Paul Patton (New York: Columbia University Press).

Dellmuth, Lisa et al. (2017) 'IGOs and Global Climate Security Challenges', SIPRI Fact Sheet, December. Available at www.sipri.org/sites/default/files/2017-12/fs_1712_igos_and_climate_security_0.pdf

Detraz, Nicole (2009) 'Environmental Security and Gender: Necessary Shifts in an Evolving Debate', *Security Studies*, 18:2, pp. 345–69.

(2015) *Environmental Security and Gender* (London: Routledge).

Detraz, Nicole and Michele Betsill (2009) 'Climate Change and Environmental Security: For Whom the Discourse Shifts', *International Studies Perspectives*, 10:3, pp. 304–21.

Deudney, Daniel (1990) 'The Case against Linking Environmental Degradation and National Security', *Millennium*, 19:3, pp. 461–73.

Diez, Thomas, Franziskus von Lucke and Zehra Wellmann (2016) *The Securitization of Climate Change* (London: Routledge).

Dillon, Michael (1996) *Politics of Security: Towards a Philosophy of Continental Thought* (London: Routledge).

Dillon, Michael and Julian Reid (2009) *The Liberal Way of War: Killing to Make Life Live* (London: Routledge).

Dobson, Andrew (2010) 'Democracy and Nature: Speaking and Listening', *Political Studies*, 58:4, pp. 752–68.

Dodo, Mahamat (2014) 'Examining the Potential Impacts of Climate Change on International Security', *SpringerPlus*, 3:194, pp. 1–18.

Doty, Roxanne Lynn (1993) 'Foreign Policy as Social Construction', *International Studies Quarterly*, 37:3, pp. 297–320.

Doty, Roxanne (1998–9) 'Immigration and the Politics of Security', *Security Studies*, 8:2–3, pp. 71–93.

Dresse, Anais, Itay Fischhendler, Jonas Ostergaard Nielsen and Dimitrios Zikos (2019) 'Environmental Peacebuilding: Towards a Theoretical Framework', *Cooperation and Conflict*, 54:1, pp. 99–119.

Dryzek, John (1997) *The Politics of the Earth: Environmental Discourses* (New York: Oxford University Press).

(2005) *The Politics of the Earth: Environmental Discourses*, 2nd ed. (New York: Oxford University Press).

(2016) 'Institutions for the Anthropocene', *British Journal of Political Science*, 35:4, pp. 937–56.

Dryzek, John and Jonathan Pickering (2018) *The Politics of the Anthropocene* (Oxford: Oxford University Press).

Dufek, Pavel (2013) 'Why Strong Moral Cosmopolitanism Requires a World State', *International Theory*, 5:2, pp. 177–212.

Duggan, Jill (2015) 'Has the EU's Carbon Trading System Made Business Greener?', *The Guardian*, 16 July. Available at www.theguardian.com/sustainable-business/2015/jul/15/eu-carbon-trading-system-made-business-greener

Dumaine, Carol and Irving Mintzer (2015) 'Confronting Climate Change and Reframing Security', *SAIS Review of International Affairs*, 35:1, pp. 5–16.

Dunlop, Ian and David Spratt (2017) *Disaster Alley: Climate Change, Conflict & Risk* (Melbourne: Breakthrough). Available at www.breakthroughonline.org.au/disasteralley

Dunn, Kevin C. and Iver Neumann (2016) *Undertaking Discourse Analysis for Social Research* (Ann Arbor: University of Michigan Press).

Dunne, Tim (1998) *Inventing International Society* (London: Macmillan).

Dupont, Alan (2008) 'The Strategic Implications of Climate Change', *Survival*, 50:3, pp. 29–54.

Easterly, William (2009) 'The Ideology of Development', *Foreign Policy*, July/August.

Eckersley, Robyn (1992) *Environmentalism and Political Theory: Toward and Ecocentric Approach* (Albany: State University New York Press).

(2004) *The Green State: Rethinking Democracy and Sovereignty* (Cambridge, MA: MIT Press).

(2005) 'Ecocentric Discourses: Problems and Future Prospects for Nature Advocacy', in John Dryzek and David Schlosberg eds., *Debating the Earth: A Reader*, 2nd ed. (Oxford: Oxford University Press), pp. 399–407.

(2007) 'Ecological Intervention: Prospects and Limits', *Ethics and International Affairs*, 21:3, pp. 275–96.

(2017) 'Geopolitan Democracy in the Anthropocene', *Political Studies*, 65:4, pp. 983–99.

Elliott, Lorraine (2006) 'Cosmopolitan Environmental Harm Conventions', *Global Society*, 20:3, pp. 345–63.

Eroukhmanoff, Clara and Matt Harker eds. (2017) *Reflections on the Posthuman in International Relations* (Bristol: E-International Relations).

Erskine, Toni (2003) *Can Institutions Have Responsibilities?* (Berlin: Springer).

(2008) 'The Problem of Moral Agency in International Relations', in Christian Reus-Smit and Duncan Snidal eds., *Oxford Handbook of International Relations* (Oxford: Oxford University Press), pp. 699–707.

Evans, Brad and Julian Reid (2014) *Resilient Life: The Art of Living Dangerously* (Cambridge: Polity).

Fagan, Madeleine (2016a) 'Security in the Anthropocene', *European Journal of International Relations*, 23:2, pp. 292–314.

Falkner, Robert (2016b) 'The Paris Agreement and the New Logic of International Climate Politics', *International Affairs*, 92:5, pp. 1107–25.

(2019) 'On the Dangers of an Anthropocene Epoch', *Political Geography*, 70, pp. 55–63.

Far, Shahrazad and Richard Youngs (2018). 'The EU's Distinctive Approach to Climate Security', in Shirley Scott and Charlotte Ku eds., *Climate Change and the UN Security Council* (Cheltenham: Edward Elgar), pp. 147–61.

Farrell, Clare, Alison Green, Sam Knights and William Skeaping eds. (2019) *This Is Not a Drill: An Extinction Rebellion Handbook* (London: Penguin).

Ferguson, Peter (2019) 'Discourses of Resilience in the Climate Security Debate', *Global Environmental Politics*, 19:2, pp. 104–26.

Fierke, Karin M. (1998) *Changing Games, Changing Strategies: Critical Investigations in Security* (Manchester: Manchester University Press).

(2004) 'Whereof We Can Speak, Thereof We Must Not Be Silent', *Review of International Studies*, 30:3, pp. 471–91.

Fisher, P. Brian (2011) 'Climate Change and Human Security in Tuvalu', *Global Change, Peace and Security*, 23:3, pp. 293–313.

Floyd, Rita (2010) *Security and the Environment* (Cambridge: Cambridge University Press).

(2015) 'Global Climate Security Governance: A Case of Institutional and Ideational Fragmentation', *Conflict, Security and Development*, 15:2, pp. 119–46.

(2019) *The Morality of Security: A Theory of Just Securitization* (Cambridge: Cambridge University Press).

Floyd, Rita and Richard A. Matthew (2013) 'Environmental Security Studies: An Introduction', in Floyd and Mattthew eds., *Environmental Security: Approaches and Issues* (London: Routledge), pp.1–20.

Francione, Gary L (2010) 'Animal Welfare and the Moral Value of Nonhuman Animals', *Law, Culture and the Humanities*, 6:1, pp. 24–36.

Foucault, Michel (1977) *Discipline and Punish* (New York: Pantheon Books).

Fuentes-George, Kemi (2017) 'Consensus, Certainly and Catastrophe: Discourse, Governance and Ocean Iron Fertilization', *Global Environmental Politics*, 17:2, pp. 125–43.

Gamble, Andrew (2010) 'Ethics and Politics', in Duncan Bell ed., *Ethics and World Politics* (Oxford: Oxford University Press), pp. 73–92.

Garcia, Denise (2010) 'Warming to a Redefinition of International Security: The Consolidation of a Norm Concerning Climate Change', *International Relations*, 24:3, pp. 271–92.

Gardiner, Stephen M. (2006) 'A Core Precautionary Principle', *Journal of Political Philosophy*, 14:1, pp. 33–60.

(2014) 'A Call for a Global Constitutional Convention Focused on Future Generations', *Ethics and International Affairs*, 28:3, pp. 299–315.

Gardiner, Stephen M., Simon Caney, Dale Jamieson and Henry Shue eds. (2010) *Climate Ethics: Essential Readings* (Oxford: Oxford University Press).

Gelber, Katharine and Matt McDonald (2006) 'Ethics and Exclusion: Representations of Sovereignty in Australia's Approach to Asylum-Seekers', *Review of International Studies*, 32:2, pp. 269–89.

Gereke, Marika and Tanja Bruhl (2019) 'Unpacking the Unequal Representation of Northern and Southern NGOs in International Climate Change Politics', *Third World Quarterly*, 40:5, pp. 870–889.

Gibney, Matthew (2004) *The Ethics and Politics of Asylum* (Cambridge: Cambridge University Press).

(2018) 'The Ethics of Refugees', *Philosophy Compass*, 13:10, p. e12521.

Githens-Mazer, Jonathan and Robert Lambert (2010) 'Why Conventional Wisdom on Radicalization Fails', *International Affairs*, 86:4, pp. 889–901.

Gleditsch, Nils Petter (1998) 'Armed Conflict and the Environment: A Critique of the Literature', *Journal of Peace Research*, 35:3, pp. 381–400.

Gleick, Peter (1993) 'Water and Conflict: Fresh Water Resources and International Security', *International Security*, 18:1, pp. 79–112.

Gleick, Peter H. (2014) 'Water, Drought, Climate Change, and Conflict in Syria', *Weather Climate and Society*, 6, pp. 331–40.

Goldsworthy, Heather (2010) 'Women, Global Environmental Change, and Human Security', in Richard Matthew et al. eds., *Global Environmental Change and Human Security* (Cambridge, MA: MIT Press), pp. 215–36.

Goodin, Robert and John Dryzek (2006) 'Deliberative Impacts: The Macro-Political Uptake of Mini-Publics', *Politics and Society*, 34:2, pp. 219–44.

Green, D. and G. Raygorodetsky eds. (2010) *Indigenous Peoples' Knowledge of Climate and Weather*. Special Issue of *Climatic Change*, 100:2, pp. 239–354.

Greenhill, Kelly (2016) 'Open Arms behind Barred Doors', *European Law Journal*, 22:3, pp. 313–32.

Griffin, Paul (2017) The Carbon Majors Database. CDP Report, July. Available at https://b8f65cb373b1b7b15feb-c70d8ead6ced550b4d 987d7c03fcdd1d.ssl.cf3.rackcdn.com/cms/reports/documents/000/002/ 327/original/Carbon-Majors-Report-2017.pdf?1499691240

Grove, Jairus Victor (2014) 'Ecology as Critical Security Method', *Critical Studies on Security*, 2:3, pp. 366–9.

   (2019) *Savage Ecology: War and Geopolitics at the End of the World* (Durham: Duke University Press).

Grove, Kevin (2013) 'Security beyond Resilience', *Environment and Planning D*, 35:1, pp. 184–94.

Guillaume, Xavier (2018) 'How to Do Things with Silence: Rethinking the Centrality of Speech to the Securitization Framework', *Security Dialogue*, 49:6, pp. 476–92.

Guild, Elspeth (2009) *Security and Migration in the Twenty-First Century* (Cambridge: Polity).

Guimaraes, Roberto (1991) *The Ecopolitics of Development in the Third World* (Boulder, CO: Lynne Rienner).

Habermas, Jürgen (1984) *The Theory of Communicative Action Volume 1*. Translated by Thomas McCarthy (London: Heinemann).

   (1989) *The Theory of Communicative Action Volume 2* (London: Heinemann).

Haftendorn, Helga (1991) 'The Security Puzzle', *International Studies Quarterly*, 35:1, pp. 3–17.

Hajer, Maarten (1995) *The Politics of Environmental Discourse: Ecological Modernization and the Policy Process* (Oxford: Oxford University Press).

Hamilton, Clive (2013) *Earth Masters: The Dawn of the Age of Climate Engineering* (New Haven, CT: Yale University Press).

   (2015) A New Kind of Human Being: A Reply to Steve Fuller', *ABC Religion and Ethics*, 17 September. Available at www.abc.net.au/reli gion/articles/2015/09/17/4314453.htm

Hamilton, Clive and Hal Turton (2001) 'With Friends Like Bjorn Lomborg, Environmentalists Don't Need Enemies', *Pacific Conservation Biology*, 7:3, pp. 214–17.

Hansen, Lene (2000) 'The Little Mermaid's Silent Security Dilemma and the Absence of Gender in the Copenhagen School', *Millennium*, 29, pp. 285–306.

(2006) *Security as Practice: Discourse Analysis and the Bosnian War* (London: Routledge).

(2011) 'Theorizing the Image for Security Studies', *European Journal of International Relations*, 17:1, pp. 51–74.

Hardt, Judith (2017) *Security in the Anthropocene* (London: Routledge).

Hardt, Judith and Alina Viehoff (2020) *A Climate for Change in the UN Security Council? Member States' Approaches to the Climate-Security Nexus*. Hamburg: Institute for Peace Research and Security Policy. Available at www.climate-diplomacy.org/publications/climate-change-un-security-council

Harrington, Cameron and Clifford Shearing (2017) *Security in the Anthropocene* (Bielefeld: Transcript).

Harris, Paul (2008) 'Climate Change and Global Citizenship', *Law and Policy*, 30:4, pp. 481–501.

Hartmann, Betsy (2009) 'Lines in the Shifting Sand: The Strategic Politics of Climate Change, Human Security and National Defence'. Paper presented at *Rethinking Security in a Changing Climate Conference*, Oslo, June 2009.

Hayes, Jarrod and Janelle Knox-Hayes (2014) 'Security in Climate Change Discourse: Analyzing the Divergence between US and EU Approaches to Policy', *Global Environmental Politics*, 14:2, pp. 82–101.

Hehir, Aidan (2011) 'The Responsibility to Protect in International Political Discourse, *International Journal of Human Rights*, 15:8, pp. 1331–48.

(2013) 'The Permanence of Inconsistency: Libya, the Security Council and the Responsibility to Protect', *International Security*, 38:1, pp. 137–59.

Held, David (1995) *Cosmopolitanism: An Agenda for a New World Order* (Cambridge: Polity).

Held, David (2010) *Cosmopolitanism: Ideals and Realities* (Cambridge: Polity).Held, David and Angus Hervey (2011) 'Democracy, Climate Change and Global Governance', in David Held, Angus Fane-Hervey and Manika Theros eds., *The Governance of Climate Change* (Cambridge: Polity), pp. 89–110.

Heyd, Thomas (2020) 'Covid-19 and Climate Change in the Times of the Anthropocene', *The Anthropocene Review*. Online before print: https://doi.org/10.1177/2053019620961799

Heyward, Clare (2008) 'Can the All-Affected Principle Include Future Generations?', *Environmental Politics*, 17:4, pp. 625–43.

Hiller, Avram (2011) 'Climate Change and Individual Responsibility', *The Monist*, 94:3, pp. 349–68.

Hobden, Stephen (2014) 'Posthumanisim', in Carl Death ed., *Critical Environmental Politics* (London: Routledge), pp. 175–83.

Holland, Jack (2012) *Selling the War on Terror* (London: Routledge).

(2013) 'Foreign Policy and Political Possibility', *European Journal of International Relations*, 19:1, pp. 49–68.

Holling, C. S. (1973) 'Resilience and Stability of Ecological Systems', *Annual Review of Ecology and Systematics*, 4, pp. 1–23.

Homer-Dixon, Thomas (1991a), 'Environmental Security, Mass Violence and the Limits to Ingenuity', *Current History*, 95:604, pp. 359–65.

(1991b) 'On the Threshold: Environmental Changes as Causes of Acute Conflict', *International Security*, 16:2, pp. 76–116.

(1999) *Environment, Scarcity, and Violence* (Princeton, NJ: Princeton University Press).

Hook, Sidney (1994) *From Hegel to Marx: Studies in the Intellectual Development of Karl Marx* (New York: Columbia University Press).

Hoppe, I. and S. Rödder (2019) 'Speaking with One Voice for Climate Science – Climate Researchers' Opinion on the Consensus Policy of the IPCC', *JCOM Journal of Science Communication*, 18:3, A04.

Horgan, John and Michael Boyle (2008) 'A Case against "Critical Terrorism Studies"', *Critical Studies on Terrorism*, 1:1, pp. 51–64.

Horgan, John and Kurt Braddock (2010) 'Rehabilitating the Terrorists?', *Terrorism and Political Violence*, 22:2, pp. 267–91.

Horkheimer, Max (1972) 'Traditional and Critical Theory', in M. O'Connell ed., *Critical Theory: Selected Essays* (New York: Herder and Herder), pp. 198–238.

Horton, Joshua B. et al. (2018) 'Solar Geoengineering and Democracy', *Global Environmental Politics*, 18:3, pp. 5–24.

Hough, Peter (2014) *Environmental Security* (London: Routledge).

Hughes, Hannah (2011) 'Bourdieu and the IPCC's Symbolic Power', *Global Environmental Politics*, 15:4, pp. 84–104.

Hulme, Mike (2009) *Why We Disagree about Climate Change* (Cambridge: Cambridge University Press).

(2016) '1.5 Degrees and Climate Research after the Paris Agreement', *Nature Climate Change*, 6, pp. 222–4.

Huysmans, Jef (2006a) 'Agency and the Politics of Protection', in Jef Husymans, Andrew Dobson and Raia Prokhovnik eds., *The Politics of Protection* (London: Routledge), pp. 1–18.

(2006b) *The Politics of Insecurity: Fear, Migration and Asylum in the EU* (London: Routledge).

Ide, Tobias (2017) 'Space, Discourse and Environmental Peacebuilding', *Third World Quarterly*, 38:3, pp. 544–62.

IPCC (2013) *Climate Change 2013: The Physical Science Basis* (Cambridge: Cambridge University Press).

(2014a) *Climate Change 2014: Impacts, Adaptation and Vulnerability* (Cambridge: Cambridge University Press).

(2014b) *Climate Change 2014: Mitigation of Climate Change. Contribution of Working Group III to the Fifth Assessment Report of the Intergovernmental Panel on Climate Change* (Cambridge: Cambridge University Press).

Jackson, Richard, Marie Breen Smyth and Jeroen Gunning eds. (2009) *Critical Terrorism Studies: A New Research Agenda* (London: Routledge).

Jackson, Robert H. (1992) 'Pluralism in International Political Theory', *Review of International Studies*, 18:3, pp. 271–81.

Jacob, Cecilia (2018) 'R2P and the Prevention of Mass Atrocities', *Global Responsibility to Protect*, 10:1–2, pp. 75–96.

Jasparro, Christopher and Jonathan Taylor (2008) 'Climate Change and Regional Vulnerability to Transnational Security Threats', *Geopolitics*, 13:2, pp. 232–56.

Kadlec, Alison and Will Friedman (2007) 'Deliberative Democracy and the Problem of Power', *Journal of Public Deliberation*, 3:1, pp. 1–26.

Kaempf, Sebastian (2018) *Saving Soldiers or Civilians?* (Cambridge: Cambridge University Press).

Kaijser, Anna and Annica Kronsell (2014) 'Climate Change through the Lens of Intersectionality', *Environmental Politics*, 23:3, pp. 417–33.

Kaplan, Robert (1994) 'The Coming Anarchy', *Atlantic Monthly*, 273:2, pp. 44–76.

Kareiva, Peter and Emma Fuller (2016) 'Beyond Resilience: How to Better Prepare for the Profound Disruption of the Anthropocene', *Global Policy*, 7, pp. 107–18.

Katz, David (2011) 'Hydro-Political Hyperbole: Examining Incentives for Over-Emphasizing the Risks of Water Wars', *Global Environmental Politics*, 11:1, pp. 12–35.

Keck, Margaret and Kathryn Sikkink (1998) *Activists Beyond Borders: Advocacy Networks in International Politics* (Ithaca, NY: Cornell University Press).

Kelly, P. and W. Adger (2000) 'Theory and Practice in Assessing Vulnerability to Climate Change and Facilitating Adaptation', *Climate Change*, 47, pp. 325–52.

Klein, Naomi (2015) *This Changes Everything: Capitalism v the Climate* (New York: Simon and Schuster).

Kim, Hyunseop (2019) 'An Extension of Rawls's Theory of Justice for Climate Change', *International Theory*, 11, pp. 160–81.

King, Matt and Peter Carruthers (2012) 'Moral Responsibility and Consciousness', *Journal of Moral Philosophy*, 9:2, pp. 200–28.

Kirk, Jessica (2020) 'From Threat to Risk? Exceptionalism and the Logics of Health Security', *International Studies Quarterly*, 64:2, pp. 266–76.

Klein, Johannes, Sirkku Juhola and Mia Landauer (2017) 'Local Authorities and the Engagement of Private Actors in Climate Change Adaptation', *Environment and Planning C*, 35:6, pp. 1055–74.

Kloprogge, Penny and Jeroen Van Der Slujis (2006) 'The Inclusion of Stakeholder Knowledge and Perspectives in Integrated Assessment of Climate Change', *Climatic Change*, 75:3, pp. 359–89.

Kolk, Ans (1996) *Forests in International Environmental Politics: International Organizations, NGOs and the Brazilian Amazon* (Utrecht: International Books).

Kolodziej, Edward A. (1992) 'Renaissance in Security Studies? Caveat Lector!', *International Studies Quarterly*, 36:4, pp. 421–38.

Krampe, Florian and Malin Mobjork (2018) 'Responding to Climate-Related Security Risks: Reviewing Regional Organizations in Asia and Africa', *Current Climate Change Reports*, 4:4, pp. 330–7.

Krause, Keith and Michael C. Williams (1996) 'Broadening the Agenda of Security Studies: Politics and Methods', *Mershon International Studies Review*, 40:2, pp. 229–54.

Krebs, Ronald and Patrick Jackson (2007) 'Twisting Tongues and Twisting Arms: The Power of Political Rhetoric', *European Journal of International Relations*, 13:1, pp. 35–66.

Krebs, Ronald and Jennifer Lobasz (2007) 'Fixing the Meaning of 9/11: Hegemony, Coercion, and the Road to War in Iraq', *Security Studies*, 16:3, pp. 409–51.

Kriegler, Elmar et al. (2009) 'Imprecise Probability Assessment of Tipping Points in the Climate System', *Proceedings of the National Academy of Sciences of the United States of America*, 106:13, pp. 5041–6.

Kumssa, Asfaw and John Jones (2010) 'Climate Change and Human Security in Africa', *International Journal of Sustainable Development and World Ecology*, 17:6, pp. 453–61.

Lang, Sabine (2013) *NGOs, Civil Society and the Public Sphere* (Cambridge: Cambridge University Press).Latour, Bruno (1999) 'On Recalling Actor Network Theory', *The Sociological Review*, 47:1, pp. 15–25.

Latour, Bruno (2015) 'Fifty Shades of Green', *Entitle Blog*, 27 June. Available at https://entitleblog.org/2015/06/27/fifty-shades-of-green-bruno-latour-on-the-ecomodernist-manifesto/

Le Quere, C. et al. (2015) 'Global Carbon Budget 2014', *Earth System Science Data*, 7:1, pp. 47–85.

Leander, Anna (2011) 'The Promises, Problems and Potentials of a Bourdieu-Inspired Staging of International Relations', *International Political Sociology*, 5, pp. 294–313.

Lenette, Caroline and Natasa Miskovic (2018) '"Some Viewers May Find the Following Images Disturbing": Visual Representations of Refugee Deaths at Border Crossings', *Crime, Media, Culture*, 14:1, pp. 111–20.

Lenton, Timoth and Juan-Carols Ciscar (2013) 'Integrating Tipping Points into Climate Impact Assessments', *Climatic Change*, 117:3, pp. 585–97.

Levy, Marc A. (1995a) 'Is the Environment a National Security Issue?', *International Security*, 20:2, pp. 35–62.

(1995b) 'Time for a Third Wave of Environment and Security Scholarship', *Environmental Change and Security Project Report*, pp. 44–6.

Lewis, Bridget (2018) 'The Rights of Future Generations within the Post-Paris Climate Regime', *Transnational Environmental Law*, 7:1, pp. 69–87.

Lidskog, Rolf, Ingemar Elander and Adam Standring (2020) 'COVID-19, the Climate, and Transformative Change', *Sustainability*, 12, pp. 1–21.

Lieven, Anatol (2020) *Climate Change and the Nation State* (Oxford: Oxford University Press).

Liftin, Karen T. (1999) 'Constructing Environmental Security and Ecological Interdependence', *Global Governance*, 5, pp. 359–77.

Linklater, Andrew (1998) *The Transformation of Political Community* (New York: Columbia: South Carolina).

(2001) 'Citizenship, Humanity and Cosmopolitan Harm Conventions', *International Political Science Review*, 22:3, pp. 261–77.

Linklater, Andrew and Hidemi Suganami (2006) *The English School of International Relations: A Contemporary Reassessment* (Cambridge: Cambridge University Press).

Lomborg, Bjorn (2001) *The Skeptical Environmentalist* (Cambridge: Cambridge University Press).

Lonergan, Stephen and Barb Kavanagh (1991) 'Climate Change, Water Resources and Security in the Middle East', *Global Environmental Change*, 1:4, pp. 272–90.

Lövbrand, Eva et al. (2015) 'Who Speaks for the Future of the Earth? How Critical Social Science Can Extend the Conversation on the Anthropocene', *Global Environmental Change*, 32, pp. 211–18.

Lövbrand, Eva, Mattias Hjerpe and Bjorn-Ola Linner (2019) 'Making Climate Governance Global: How UN Climate Summitry Comes to Matter in a Complex Climate Regime', *Environmental Politics*, 26:4, pp. 580–99.

Lovelock, James (2000) *Gaia: A New Look at Life on Earth*, 3rd ed. (Oxford: Oxford University Press)

Luke, Timothy (2013) 'The Anthropocene and Freedom: Terrestrial time as political mystification', *Platypus Review*, October. http://platypus1917.org/2013/10/01/anthropocene-and-freedom/

Lynas, Mark (2011) *The God Species* (Washington, DC: National Geographic).

Lyotard, Jean-Francois (1984) *The Postmodern Condition* (Minneapolis: University of Minnesota Press).

Maertens, Lucile (2018) 'Depoliticisation as a Securitizing Move: The Case of the United Nations Environment Programme', *European Journal of International Security*, 3:3, pp. 344–63.

(2021) 'Climatizing the UN Security Council', *International Politics*. Online before print: https://doi.org/10.1057/s41311-021-00281-9

Malm, Andreas and Alf Hornborg (2014) 'The Geology of Mankind? A Critique of the Anthropocene Narrative', *The Anthropocene Review*, 1:1, pp. 62–9.

Mann, Michael E. and Tom Toles (2016) *The Madhouse Effect* (New York: Columbia University Press).

Mann, Geoff and Joel Wainwright (2017) *Climate Leviathan* (London: Verso).

Marzec, Robert P. (2015) *Militarizing the Environment: Climate Change and the Security State* (Minneapolis: University of Minnesota Press).

Maslin, Mark and Patrick Austin (2012) 'Climate Models at Their Limit?', *Nature*, 486, pp. 183–4.

Mathews, Jessica (1989) 'Redefining Security', *Foreign Affairs*, 68:2, pp. 162–77.

Mattern, Janice (2001) 'The Power Politics of Identity', *European Journal of International Relations*, 7:3, pp. 349–97.

Matthew, Richard A. and Bishnu Upreti (2010) 'Environmental Change and Human Security in Nepal', in Matthew et al. eds. *Global Environmental Change and Human Security* (Cambridge, MA: MIT Press), pp. 137–54.

Matthew, Richard A., Jon Barnett, Bryan McDonald and Karen L. O'Brien eds. (2010) *Global Environmental Change and Human Security* (Cambridge, MA: MIT Press)

Matthews, H. Damon et al. (2018) 'Focus on Cumulative Emissions, Global Carbon Budgets and Implications for Climate Emissions Targets', *Environmental Research Letters*, 13, pp. 10–20.

Mazo, Jeffrey (2010) *Climate Conflict* (London: Routledge).McDonald, Matt (2002) 'Human Security and the Construction of Security', *Global Society*, 16:3, pp. 277–95.

McDonald, Matt (2003) 'Environment and Security: Global Eco-politics and Brazilian Deforestation', *Contemporary Security Policy*, 24:2, pp. 69–94.

(2005) 'Fair Weather Friend? Ethics and Australia's Approach to Global Climate Change', *Australian Journal of Politics and History*, 51:2, pp. 216–34.

(2008) 'Securitisation and the Construction of Security', *European Journal of International Relations*, 14:4, pp. 563–87.

(2009) 'Emancipation and Critical Terrorism Studies', in Jackson, Smyth and Gunning eds., *Critical Terrorism Studies: A New Research Agenda* (London: Routledge).

(2011) 'Deliberation and Resecuritization: Australia, Asylum-Seekers and the Normative Limits of the Copenhagen School', *Australian Journal of Political Science*, 46:2, pp. 281–95.

(2012) *Security, the Environment and Emancipation: Contestation over Environmental Change* (London: Routledge).

(2013a) 'Discourses of Climate Security', *Political Geography*, 33, pp. 43–51.

(2013b) 'Climate Security and Economic Security: The Limits to Climate Change Action in Australia?', *International Politics*, 52:4, pp. 484–501.

(2015) 'The "Climate Games" Aren't Just Activist Stunts – They're Politics beyond the UN', *The Conversation*, 10 December. Available at https://theconversation.com/the-climate-games-arent-just-activist-stunts-theyre-politics-beyond-the-un-51872

(2016) 'Bourdieu, Environmental NGOs and Australian Climate Politics', *Environmental Politics*, 25:6, pp. 1058–78.

(2017) 'What Keeps Global Security Academics Awake at Night?' *The Interpreter, Lowy Institute*, 9 March. Available at www.lowyinstitute.org/the-interpreter/what-keeps-global-security-academics-awake-night

(2018) 'Climate Change and Security: Towards an Ecological Security Discourse?', *International Theory*, 10:2, pp. 153–80.

(2021) 'After the Fires: Climate Change and Security in Australia', *Australian Journal of Political Science*, 56:1, pp. 1–18.

McDonald, Matt and Matt Merefield (2010) (with Matt Merefield), 'How Was Howard's War Possible? Winning the War of Position over Iraq, *Australian Journal of International Affairs*, 64:2, pp. 186–204.

McLaren, Duncan (2016) 'Mitigation Deterrence and the "Moral Hazard" of Solar Radiation Management', *Earth's Future* 4:12, pp. 596–602.

McLaren, Duncan and Olaf Corry (2021) 'Clash of Geofutures and the Remaking of Planetary Order', *Global Policy*. Early view: doi: 10.1111/1758-5899.12863

McLeman, Robert (2011) *Climate Change, Migration and Critical International Security Considerations* (Geneva: IOM).

McMaster, Don (2002) 'Asylum-Seekers and the Insecurity of a Nation', *Australian Journal of International Affairs*, 56:2, pp. 279–90.

McShane, Katie (2014) 'Ecocentrism', in Carl Death ed., *Critical Environmental Politics* (London: Routledge), pp. 83–90.

McSweeney, Bill (1999) *Security, Identity and Interests* (Cambridge: Cambridge University Press).

Mearsheimer, John (1995) 'The False Promise of International Institutions', *International Security*, 19:3, pp. 5–49.

Merchant, Carolyn (1980) *li* (San Francisco: Harpo).

Methmann, Chris and Angela Oels (2015) 'From Fearing to Empowering Climate Refugees', *Security Dialogue*, 46:1, pp. 51–68.

Methmann, Chris and Delf Rothe (2012) 'Politics for the Day after Tomorrow', *Security Dialogue*, 43:3, pp. 323–44.

Mikler, John and Neil Harrison (2013) 'Climate Innovation: Australian Corporate Perspectives on the Role of Government', *Australian Journal of Politics and History*, 59:3, pp. 414–28.

Miller, Kathleen A. (2000) 'Pacific Salmon Fisheries', *Climatic Change*, 45:1, p. 37061.

Milliken, Jennifer (1999) 'The Study of Discourse in International Relations: A Critique of Research and Methods', *European Journal of International Relations*, 5:2, pp. 225–54.

Ministry of Defence (MoD), France (2015) *The Implications of Climate Change for Defence* (Paris: Ministry of Defence).

Mische, Patricia M. (1989) 'Ecological Security and the Need to Reconceptualize Sovereignty', *Alternatives*, 14:4, pp. 389–427.

(1994) 'Peace and Ecological Security', *Peace Review*, 6:3, pp. 275–84.

Mitchell, Audra (2014) 'Only Human? A Worldly Approach to Security', *Security Dialogue*, 45:1, pp. 5–21.

(2017) 'Posthuman Security', in Clara Eroukhmanoff and Matt Harker eds., *Reflections on the Posthuman in International Relations* (Bristol: E-International Relations).

Molloy, Sean (2018) 'Morgenthau and the Ethics of Realism', in Brent J. Steele and Eric A. Heinze eds., *Routledge Handbook of Ethics and International Relations* (London: Routledge), pp. 182–95.

Moncel, Remi and Harro van Assalt (2012) 'All Hands on Deck! Mobilizing Climate Change Action beyond the UNFCCC', *Review of European, Comparative and International Environmental Law*, 21:3, pp. 163–76.

Moon, Ban Ki (2007a) 'A Climate Culprit in Darfur', *Washington Post*, 16 June, p. 15.

Moon, Jeremy (2007b) 'The Contribution of Corporate Social Responsibility to Sustainable Development', *Sustainable Development*, 15:5, pp. 296–306.

Moore, Margaret (2010) 'Defending Community: Nationalism, Patriotism and Culture', in Duncan Bell ed., *Ethics and World Politics* (Oxford: Oxford University Press), pp. 130–45.

Morgan, Jennifer and David Waskow (2013) 'A New Look at Climate Equity in the UNFCCC', *Climate Policy*, 14:1, pp. 17–22.

Morgan, Wes (2018) 'Climate Change: At the Frontlines', *The Interpreter*, 20 September. Available at www.lowyinstitute.org/the-interpreter/climate-change-frontlines

Morgenthau, Hans (1952) *In Defense of the National Interest* (London: Methuen).

Moser, Susanne (2012) 'Adaptation, Mitigation and Their Disharmonious Discontents', *Climatic Change*, 111:2, pp. 165–75.

(2014) 'Communicating adaptation to climate change', *WIREs Climate Change*, 5, pp. 337–58.

Muuls, Mirabelle et al. (2016) 'Evaluating the EU Emissions Trading System: Take It or Leave It? An Assessment of the Data after Ten Years'. *Grantham Institute Briefing paper* No 21. October. Available at www.imperial.ac.uk/media/imperial-college/grantham-institute/public/publications/briefing-papers/Evaluating-the-EU-emissions-trading-system_Grantham-BP-21_web.pdf

Myers, Norman (1989) 'Environment and Security', *Foreign Policy*, 74, pp. 23–41.

(1993) *Ultimate Security: The Environmental Basis of Political Stability* (New York: WW Norton).

Myers, Norman and Jennifer Kent (1995) *Environmental Exodus: An Emergent Crisis in the Global Arena* (Washington, DC: Climate Institute).

Najam, Adil (2005) 'Developing Countries and Global Environmental Governance: From Contestation to Participation to Engagement', *International Environmental Agreements*, 5:3, pp. 303–21.

Nansen Initiative (2015) *Fleeing Floods, Earthquakes, Droughts & Rising Sea Levels* (Baden: Lars Muller Publishers).

Neocleous, Mark (2008) *Critique of Security* (Edinburgh: Edinburgh University Press).

Newell, Peter (2008) 'Civil Society, Corporate Accountability and the Politics of Climate Change', *Global Environmental Politics*, 8:3, pp. 122–53.

(2020) *Global Green Politics* (Cambridge: Cambridge University Press).

Newell, Peter and Mathew Paterson (2010) *Climate Capitalism* (Cambridge: Cambridge University Press).

et al. (2015) 'Governance Traps in Climate Change Politics', *WIREs Climate Change*, 6, pp. 535–40.

Niemeyer, Simon (2011) 'The Emancipatory Effect of Deliberation: Empirical Lessons from Mini-publics', *Politics and Society*, 39:1, pp. 103–40.

(2013) 'Democracy and Climate Change: What Can Deliberative Democracy Contribute?', *Australian Journal of Politics and History*, 59:3, pp. 429–48.

Nolt, John, (2011) 'Nonanthropocentric Climate Ethics', *Wiley Interdisciplinary Review: Climate Change*, 2:5, pp. 701–11.

North, Peter (2011) 'The Politics of Climate Activism in the UK: A Social Movement Analysis', *Environment and Planning A*, 43:7, pp. 1581–98.

Nsiah-Gyabaah, Kwasi (2010) 'Human Security as a Prerequisite for Development', in Richard Matthew et al. eds., *Global Environmental Change and Human Security* (Cambridge, MA: MIT Press), pp. 237–60.

O'Brien, Karen (2006) 'Are We Missing the Point? Global Environmental Change as an Issue of Human Security', *Global Environmental Change*, 16:1, pp. 1–3.

et al. (2007) 'Why Different Interpretations of Vulnerability Matter in Climate Change Discourses', *Climate Policy*, 7:1, pp. 73–88.

O'Callaghan-Gordo, Cristina and Josepf Anto (2020) 'COVID-19: The Disease of the Anthropocene', *Environmental Research*, 187, pp. 1–2.

O'Driscoll, Cian (2008) *Renegotiation of the Just War Tradition and the Right to War in the Twenty-First Century* (London: Palgrave).

(2018) 'The Irony of Just War?' *Ethics and International Affairs*, 32:2, pp. 227–36.

Oels, Angela (2012) 'From "Securitization" of Climate Change to "Climatization" of the Security Field: Comparing Three Theoretical Perspectives', in Jurgen Scheffran et al. eds., *Climate Change, Human Security and Violent Conflict* (Berlin: Springer), pp. 185–204.

(2015) 'Resisting the Climate Security Discourse', in Shannon O'Lear and Simon Dalby eds., *Reframing Climate Change* (London: Routledge), pp. 188–202.

Okereke, Chukwumerije (2010) 'Climate Justice and the International Regime', *WIRES Climate Change*, 1:3, pp. 462–74.

Okereke, Chukwumerije, Harriet Bulkeley and Heike Schroeder (2009) 'Conceptualizing Climate Governance Beyond the International Regime', *Global Environmental Politics*, 9:1, pp. 58–78.

O'Neill, Robert V. (2001) 'Is It Time to Bury the Ecosystem Concept?' *Ecology*, 82:12, pp. 3275–84.

Osborne, Natalie (2015) 'Intersectionality and Kyriarchy: A Framework for Approaching Power and Social Justice in Planning and Climate Change Adaptation', *Planning Theory*, 14:2, pp. 130–51.

Page, Edward A. (2006) *Climate Change, Justice and Future Generations* (Cheltenham: Edward Elgar).

Page, Edward and Michael Redclift eds. (2002) *Human Security and the Environment* (Cheltenham: Edward Elgar).

Palmer, Clare (2011) Does Nature Matter? The Place of the Non-human in the Ethics of Climate Change', in Denis Arnold ed., *The Ethics of*

*Global Climate Change* (Cambridge: Cambridge University Press), pp. 272–91.

Parenti, Christian (2011) *Tropic of Chaos* (New York: Nation Books)

Parfit, Derek (1987) *Reasons and Persons* (Oxford: Clarendon Press).

  (2011) *On What Matters* (Oxford: Oxford University Press).

Paris, Roland (2001) 'Human Security: Paradigm Shift or Hot Air?', *International Security*, 26:2, pp. 87–102.

Park, Susan (2005) 'How Transnational Environmental Advocacy Networks Socialize International Financial Institutions', *Global Environmental Politics*, 5:4, pp. 95–119.

Paterson, Matthew (1996) *Global Warming and Global Politics* (London: Routledge).

  (2001) 'Principles of Justice in the Context of Global Climate Change', in U. Luterbacher and D. Sprinz eds., *International Relations and Global Climate Change* (Cambridge, MA: Cambridge University Press), pp. 119–26.

Peet, Richard, Paul Robbins and Michael Watts eds. (2010) *Global Political Ecology* (London: Routledge).

Petheram, Lisa et al. (2010) '"Strange Changes": Indigenous Perspectives of Climate Change and Adaptation in NE Arnham Land (Australia)', *Global Environmental Change*, 20:4, pp. 681–92.

Pickering, Jonathan (2019) 'Ecological Reflexivity: Characterising an Elusive Virtue for Governance in the Anthropocene', *Environmental Politics*, 28:7, pp. 1145–66.

Pirages, Dennis (1997) 'Demographic Change and Ecological Security', *Environmental Change and Security Project Report*, Spring (Washington, DC: Woodrow Wilson Center).

  (2005) 'From Resource Scarcity to Ecological Security', in Dennis Pirages and Ken Cousins eds., *From Resource Scarcity to Ecological Security* (Cambridge, MA: MIT Press), pp. 1–20.

Plesch, Dan (2018) 'Nuclear Disarmament Is Crucial for Global Security', *The Conversation*, 21 July. Available at https://theconversation.com/nuclear-disarmament-is-crucial-for-global-security-it-shouldnt-have-to-wait-99550

Plumwood, Val (1993) *Feminism and the Mastery of Nature* (London: Routledge).

  (2002) *Environmental Culture: The Ecological Crisis of Reason* (London: Routledge).

Podesta, John and Peter Ogden (2007–8) 'The Security Implications of Climate Change', *The Washington Quarterly*, 31:1, pp. 115–38.

Pogge, Thomas (2008) *World Poverty and Human Rights*, 2nd ed. (Cambridge: Polity).

Pojman, Louis ed. (2005) *Environmental Ethics: Readings in Theory and Application*, 4th ed. (Belmont, CA: Wadsworth).

Pouliot, Vincent (2010) *International Security in Practice* (Cambridge: Cambridge University Press).

Preston, Christopher J. ed. (2016) *Climate Justice and Geoengineering* (London: Rowman and Littlefield).

Purvis, Nigel and Joshua Busby (2004) 'The Security Implications of Climate Change for the UN System', *Environmental Change and Security Project Report*, 10, pp. 67–73.

Rajamani, Lavanya (2012) 'The Changing Fortunes of Differential Treatment in the Evolution of International Environmental Law', *International Affairs*, 88:3, pp. 605–23.

Ralph, Jason (2018) 'Pragmatic Constructivist Ethics and the Responsibility to Protect', *International Organization*, 72:1, pp. 173–203.

Rawls, John (1999) *The Law of Peoples* (Cambridge: Harvard University Press).

Rayner, Steve and Elizabeth Malone (1998) 'Introduction', in Rayner and Malone eds., *Human Choice and Climate Change* (Columbus, OH: Battelle Press), pp. xiii–xlii.

Rayner, Steve et al. (2013) 'The Oxford Principles', *Climatic Change*, 121:3, pp. 499–512.

Renner, Michael (1996) *Fighting for Survival: Environmental Decline, Social Conflict and the New Age of Insecurity* (New York: WW Norton).

Riley, Tess (2017) 'Just 100 Companies Responsible for 71% of Global Emissions, Study Says', *The Guardian*, 10 July. Available at www .theguardian.com/sustainable-business/2017/jul/10/100-fossil-fuel-com panies-investors-responsible-71-global-emissions-cdp-study-climate-change

Robbins, Paul (2012) *Political Ecology: A Critical Introduction*, 2nd ed. (London: John Wiley and Sons).

Roe, Paul (2008) 'Actor, Audience(s) and Emergency Measures', *Security Dialogue*, 39:6, pp. 615–35.

Rogers, Katrina (1997) 'Ecological Security and Multinational Corporations', *Environmental Change and Security Project Report 3*.

Ronnfeldt, Carsten (1997) 'Three Generations of Environment and Security Research', *Journal of Peace Research*, 34:4, pp. 473–82.

Rothe, Delf (2015) *Securitizing Global Warming: A Climate of Complexity* (London: Routledge).

Rothschild, Emma (1995) 'What Is Security?' *Daedalus*, 124:3, pp. 53–99.

Ruth, Matthias (2005) 'Future Socioeconomic and Political Challenges of Global Climate Change', in Denis Pirages and Ken Cousins eds., *From*

*Resource Scarcity to Ecological Security: Exploring New Limits to Growth* (Cambridge, MA: MIT Press), pp. 145–64.

Ruttinger, Lukas et al. (2015) *A New Climate for Peace* (Paris: EU Institute for Security Studies).

Salehyan, Idean (2008) 'From Climate Change to Conflict? No Consensus Yet', *Journal of Peace Research*, 45:3, pp. 315–26.

Sanders, Lynn (1997) 'Against Deliberation', *Political Theory*, 25:3, pp. 347–76.

Sandin, Per et al. (2002) 'Five Charges against the Precautionary Principle', *Journal of Risk Research*, 5:4, pp. 287–99.

Saran, Shyam (2015) 'Developed Countries Must Do More Than Reduce Their Emissions', *The Guardian*, 23 November. Available at www .theguardian.com/environment/2015/nov/23/paris-climate-talks-developed-countries-must-do-more-than-reduce-emissions

Sardo, Michael (2020) 'Responsibility for Climate Justice', *European Journal of Political Theory*, online first. https://doi.org/10.1177/1474885120955148

Sayes, Edwin (2014) 'Actor-Network Theory and Methodology: Just What Does It Mean to Say That Nonhumans Have Agency', *Social Studies of Science*, 44:1, pp. 134–49.

Schäfer, Mike, Jurgen Scheffran and Logan Penniket (2016) 'Securitization of Media Reporting on Climate Change', *Security Dialogue*, 47:1, pp. 76–96.

Scheffler, Samuel (1988) *Consequentialism and Its Critics* (Oxford: Oxford University Press).

Scherer, Glenn (2012) 'How the IPCC Underestimated Climate Change', *Scientific American*, 6 December. Available at www.scientificamerican .com/article/how-the-ipcc-underestimated-climate-change/

Schick, Kate (2011) 'Acting Out and Working Through: Trauma and (In) security', *Review of International Studies*, 37:4, pp. 1837–55.

Schlosberg, David (2013) 'Political Challenges of the Climate-Changed Society', *PS Symposium*, January, pp. 13–17.

Schmidt, Brian C. and Michael C. Williams (2008) 'The Bush Doctrine and the Iraq War: Neoconservatives versus Realists', *Security Studies*, 17:2, pp. 191–220.

Schmink, Marianne and Charles Wood (1992) *Contested Frontiers in Amazonia* (New York: Columbia University Press).

Scholz, Imme (2005) 'Environmental Policy Cooperation among Organised Civil Society, National Public Actors in the Brazilian Amazon', *The European Journal of Development Research*, 117:4, pp. 681–705.

Schwartz, Peter and Doug Randall (2003) *An Abrupt Climate Change Scenario and its Implications for United States National Security*. Available at www.edf.org/documents/3566_AbruptClimateChange.pdf

Scott, Shirley (2015) 'Implications of Climate Change for the UN Security Council: Mapping the Range of Potential Policy Responses', *International Affairs*, 91:5, pp. 1317–33.

Scott, Shirley and Charlotte Ku (2018) 'The UN Security Council and Global Action on Climate Change', in Scott and Ku eds., *Climate Change and the UN Security Council* (Cheltenham: Edward Elgar), pp. 1–24.

Seck, Sara L. (2018) 'Climate Change, Corporate Social Responsibility, and the Extractive Industries', *Journal of Environmental Law and Practice*, 31:1, pp. 271–89.

Selby, Jan and Clemens Hoffman eds. (2017) *Rethinking Climate Change, Conflict and Security* (London: Routledge).

Selby, Jan et al. (2017) 'Climate Change and the Syrian Civil War Revisited', *Political Geography*, 60 (September), pp. 232–44.

Shapcott, Richard (2008) 'Anti-cosmopolitanism, Pluralism and the Cosmopolitan Harm Principle', *Review of International Studies*, 34:2, pp. 185–205.

Sharma, Serena and Jennifer Welsh eds. (2015) *The Responsibility to Prevent* (Oxford: Oxford University Press).

Shearman, David and Joseph Smith (2007) *The Climate Change Challenge and the Failure of Democracy* (Westport, CT: Praeger Publishers).

Shue, Henry (1993) 'Subsistence Emissions and Luxury Emissions', *Law and Policy*, 15:1, pp. 39–60.

(1999) 'Global Environment and International Inequality', *International Affairs*, 75:3, pp. 531–45.

(2014) *Climate Justice: Vulnerability and Protection* (Oxford: Oxford University Press).

(2015) 'Historical Responsibility, Harm Prohibition, and Preservation Requirement', *Moral Philosophy and Politics*, 2:1, pp. 7–31.

(2017) 'Responsible for What? Carbon Producer $CO_2$ Contributions and the Energy Transition', *Climatic Change*, 144:4, pp. 591–6.

Sikor, Thomas ed. (2013) *The Justices and Injustices of Ecosystem Services* (London: Routledge).

Singer, Peter (1975) *Animal Liberation* (New York: Harper Collins).

(2002) *One World: The Ethics of Globalization* (New Haven, CT: Yale University Press).Skjærseth, Jon Birger and Tora Skodvin (2009) *Climate Change and the Oil Industry* (Manchester: Manchester University Press).

Slezak, Michael (2017) 'Queensland Tree Clearing Wipes Out Federal Emissions Gains', *The Guardian*, 6 October. Available at www .theguardian.com/environment/2017/oct/06/queensland-tree-clearing-wipes-out-federal-emissions-gains

Smit, Barry and Johanna Wandel (2006) 'Adaptation, Adaptive Capacity and Vulnerability', *Global Environmental Change*, 16:3, pp. 282–92.

Smith, Dan and Janani Vivekananda (2007) *A Climate of Conflict: The Links between Climate Change, Peace and War* (London: International Alert).

Smith, Steve (1999) 'The Increasing Insecurity of Security Studies', *Contemporary Security Policy*, 20:3, pp. 72–101.

Soper, Kate (1995) *What Is Nature? Culture, Politics and the Non-Human* (Oxford: Blackwell Publishers Ltd).

Starr, Joyce (1991) 'Water Wars', *Foreign Policy*, 82, pp. 17–36.

Steffan, Will et al. (2004) *Global Change and the Earth System: A Planet under Pressure* (Heidelberg: Springer).

Steffan, Will, Paul Crutzen and John McNeill (2007) 'The Anthropocene: Are Humans Now Overwhelming the Great Forces of Nature?', *Ambio*, 36:8, pp. 614–21.

    et al. (2018) 'Trajectories of the Earth System in the Anthropocene', *Proceedings of the National Academy of Sciences of the United States of America*, Published ahead of print. https://doi.org/10.1073/pnas .1810141115

Stengel, Frank (2019) 'Securitization a Discursive (Re)Articulation: Explaining the Relative Effectiveness of Threat Construction', *New Political Science*, 41:2, pp. 294–312.

Stritzel, Holger (2011) 'Security, the Translation', *Security Dialogue*, 42:4–5, pp. 343–55.

Sturrock, Robert and Peter Ferguson (2015) *The Longest Conflict: Australia's Climate Security Challenge* (Sydney: CPD).

Sunstein, Cass R. (2003) 'Beyond the Precautionary Principle', *University of Pennsylvania Law Review*, 151:3, pp. 1003–58.

    (2005) 'Introduction', in Sunstein and Martha C. Nussbaum eds., *Animal Rights: Current Debates and New Trends* (Oxford: Oxford University Press), pp. 1–18.

Sunstein, Cass R. and Martha C. Nussbaum eds. (2004) *Animal Rights: Current Debates and New Trends* (Oxford: Oxford University Press).

Sutter, John D. (2017) 'Sixth Mass Extinction: The Era of Biological Annihilation', CNN, 11 July. Available at https://edition.cnn.com/ 2017/07/11/world/sutter-mass-extinction-ceballos-study/index.html

Svarstad, Hanne and Tor Benhaminsen (2020) 'Reading Racial Environmental Justice through a Political Ecology Lens', *Geoforum*, 108, pp. 1–11.

Symons, Jonathan (2018) 'Geoengineering Justice: Who Gets to Decide Whether to Hack the Climate?', *The Breakthrough Institute*, 1 March.

(2019a) *Ecomodernism: Technology, Politics and the Climate Crisis* (Cambridge: Polity).

(2019b) 'Realist Climate Ethics', *Review of International Studies*, 45:1, pp. 141–60.

Symons, Janathan and Rasmus Karlsson (2015) 'Green Political Theory in a Climate-Changed World: Between Innovation and Restraint', *Environmental Politics*, 24:2, pp. 173–92.

Sze, Julie et al. (2009) 'Best in Show? Climate and Environmental Justice Policy in California', *Environmental Justice*, 2:4, pp. 179–84.

Szerszynski, Bronislaw et al. (2013) 'Why Solar Radiation Management Geoengineering and Democracy Won't Mix', *Environment and Planning A*, 45:12, pp. 2809–16.

Thomas, Caroline (2000) *Global Governance, Development and Human Security* (London: Pluto).

Thomas, Chris D. (2017a) *Inheritors of the Earth: How Nature Is Thriving in an Age of Extinction* (New York: Public Affairs).

Thomas, Michael (2017b) *The Securitization of Climate Change* (Berlin: Springer).

Thomas, Nicholas and William T. Tow (2002) 'Gaining Security by Trashing the State? A Reply to Bellamy and McDonald', *Security Dialogue*, 33:3, pp. 379–82.

Thompson, Dennis (2010) 'Representing Future Generations: Political Presentism and Democratic Trusteeship', *Critical Review of International Social and Political Philosophy*, 13:1, pp. 17–37.

Thrall, Trevor (2007) 'A Bear in the Woods? Threat Framing and the Marketplace of Values', *Security Studies*, 16:3, pp. 452–88.

Tobin, Paul (2017) 'Leaders and Laggards: Climate Policy Ambition in Developed States', *Global Environmental Politics*, 17:4, pp. 28–47.

Tomlinson, Luke (2015) *Procedural Justice in the United Nations Framework Convention on Climate Change* (New York: Springer).

Ullman, Richard (1983) 'Redefining Security', *International Security*, 18:1, pp. 129–53.

UNDP (1994) *New Dimensions of Human Security* (New York: Oxford University Press).

(2007) *Fighting Climate Change: Human Solidarity in a Divided World* (New York: Palgrave).

UNEP (2007) *Sudan: Post-Conflict Environmental Assessment* (Nairobi: UNEP).

UN General Assembly (UNGA) (2009a) 'Climate Change and its Possible Security Implications: Report of the Secretary-General', A64/350, 11 September. Available at https://digitallibrary.un.org/record/667264

(2009b) 'General Assembly, Expressing Deep Concern, Invites Major United Nations Organs to Intensify Efforts in Addressing Security Implications of Climate Change', A63/GA/10830, 3 June. Available at https://www.un.org/press/en/2009/ga10830.doc.htm

UNSC (2007). 5663rd Meeting. S/PV.5663 and S/PV.5663 Resumption 1. 17 April. Available at http://repository.un.org/bitstream/handle/11176/9273/S_PV.5663%28Resumption1%29-EN.pdf?sequence=3&isAllowed=y

(2011a) 6587th Meeting. S/PV.6587 and S/PV.6587 Resumption 1. 20 July. Available at http://repository.un.org/bitstream/handle/11176/15697/S_PV.6587%28Resumption1%29-EN.pdf?sequence=3&isAllowed=y

(2011b) S/PRST/2011/15, 20 July. Available at www.securitycouncilreport.org/atf/cf/%7B65BFCF9B-6D27-4E9C-8CD3-CF6E4FF96FF9%7D/CC%20SPRST%202011%205.pdf

Urban, Mark (2015) 'Accelerating Extinction Risk from Climate Change', *Science*, 384:6234, pp. 571–3.

Uvin, Robert (1996) 'Tragedy in Rwanda: The Political Ecology of Conflict', *Environment*, 18:1, pp. 7–15; 26.

Vanderheiden, Steven (2015) 'Justice and Climate Finance', *The International Spectator*, 50:1, pp. 31–45.

Vogel, Brennan and Daniel Henstra (2015) 'Studying Local Climate Adaptation', *Global Environmental Change*, 31, pp. 110–20.

Voigt, Christina and Felipe Ferreira (2016) 'Differentiation in the Paris Agreement', *Climate Law*, 6, pp. 58–74.

Von Lucke, Franziskus, Zehra Wellman and Thomas Diez (2014) 'What's at Stake in Securitizing Climate Change?', *Geopolitics*, 19:4, pp. 857–84.

Wæver, Ole (1995) 'Securitization and Desecuritization', in Ronnie D. Lipschutz ed., *On Security* (New York: Columbia University Press), pp. 46–86.

(2000) 'The EU as a Security Actor', in M. Kelstrup and M. C. Williams eds., *International Relations Theory and the Politics of European Integration* (London: Routledge), pp. 250–94.

(2002) Security: A Conceptual History for International Relations. Paper presented at the *British International Studies Association Conference*, London, 16–18 December.

(2011) 'Politics, Security, Theory', *Security Dialogue*, 42:4–5, pp. 465–80.

Wakefield, Stephanie, Kevin Grove and David Chandler (2020) 'Introduction', in D. Chandler, K. Grove and S. Wakefield eds., *Resilience in the Anthropocene* (London: Routledge), pp. 1–19.

Walt, Stephen (1991) 'Renaissance of Security Studies', *International Studies Quarterly*, 35:2, pp. 211–39.

Walzer, Michael (1977) *Just and Unjust Wars* (New York: Basic Books).
    (1983) *Spheres of Justice: A Defense of Pluralism and Equality* (New York: Basic Books).
Wapner, Paul (1995) 'Politics beyond the State: Environmental Activism and World Civic Politics', *World Politics*, 47, pp. 311–40.
Warner, Jeroen and Ingrid Boas (2019) 'Securitization of Climate Change: How Invoking Global Dangers for Instrumental Ends Can Backfire', *Environment and Planning C*, 37:8, pp. 1471–88.
Wiener, Antje (2014) *A Theory of Contestation* (Berlin: Springer).
Weijers, Dan, David Eng and Roman Das (2010) 'Sharing the Responsibility of Dealing with Climate Change: Interpreting the Principle of Common but Differentiated Responsibilities', in Jonathan Boston, Andrew Bradstock and David Eng eds., *Public Policy: Why Ethics Matters* (Canberra: ANU Press), pp. 141–58.
Weldes, Jutta (1996) 'Constructing the National Interest', *European Journal of International Relations*, 2:3, pp. 275–318.
Welzer, Harald (2012) *Climate Wars* (Cambridge: Polity).
Wendt, Alexander (1992) 'Anarchy Is What States Make of It', *International Organization*, 46:2, pp. 391–425.
Werrell, C. et al. (2017) 'A Responsibility to Prepare', *Briefer 38, Center for Climate and Security*, 7 August (Washington, DC: CCS).
Werrell, C. and F. Femia (2016) 'EU to Focus on Climate Diplomacy, Security, Stability, Migration Links', *Climate & Security*, 23 February.
Western, Jon (2005) 'The War over Iraq: Selling War to the American Public', *Security Studies*, 14:1, pp. 106–39.
WGBU (2007) *World in Transition – Climate Change as a Security Risk* (London: Earthscan). Available at www.wbgu.de/wbgu_jg2007_engl.pdf
Wheeler, Nicholas J. (2000) *Saving Strangers: Humanitarian Intervention in International Society* (Oxford: Oxford University Press).
Wheeler, Nicholas J. and Tim Dunne (1996) 'Hedley Bull's Pluralism of the Intellect and Solidarism of the Will', *International Affairs*, 72:1, pp. 91–107.
White, Gregory (2011) *Climate Change and Migration* (Oxford: Oxford University Press).
Wienhues, Anna (2020) *Ecological Justice and the Extinction Crisis* (Bristol: Bristol University Press).
Wigley, T. M. L. (2006) 'A Combined Mitigation/Geoengineering Approach to Climate Stabilization', *Science*, 314:5798, pp. 542–4.
Williams, John (2005) 'Pluralism, Solidarism and the Emergence of World Society in English School Theory', *International Relations*, 19:1, pp. 19–38.

Williams, Michael (1998) 'Identity and the Politics of Security', *European Journal of International Relations*, 11:3, pp. 307–37.

(2006) *Culture and Security: Symbolic Power and the Politics of International Security* (London: Routledge).

Williams, Paul (2004) 'Critical Security Studies', in Alex J. Bellamy ed., *International Society and Its Critics* (Oxford: Oxford University Press), pp. 135–50.

Wissenberg, Marcel and David Schlosberg eds. (2014) *Political Animals and Animal Politics* (New York: Palgrave).

Wolff, Aaron T. (1998) 'Conflict and Cooperation along International Waterways', *Water Policy*, 1:2, pp. 251–65.

Wolfers, Arnold (1952) '"National Security" as an Ambiguous Symbol', *Political Science Quarterly*, 67:4, pp. 481–502.

Wong, Poh Poh (2011) 'Small Island Developing States', *WIRES Climate Change*, 2:1, pp. 1–6.

Woocher, Lawrence (2012) 'The Responsibility to Prevent: Towards a Strategy', in W. Andy Knight and Frazer Egerton eds., *The Routledge Handbook of the Responsibility to Protect* (London: Routledge), pp. 22–35.

Wyn Jones, Richard (1999) *Security, Strategy and Critical Theory* (Boulder, CO: Lynne Rienner).

Youatt, Rafi (2014) 'Interspecies Relations, International Relations: Rethinking Anthropocentric Politics', *Millennium: Journal of International Studies*, 43:1, pp. 207–23.

(2017) 'Personhood and the Rights of Nature', *International Political Sociology*, 11:1, pp. 39–54.

Young, Iris Marion (2000) *Inclusion and Democracy* (New York: Oxford University Press).

Yusoff, Kathryn (2013) 'Geologic Life: Prehistory, Climate, Futures in the Anthropocene', *Environment and Planning D*, 31, pp. 779–95.

Zebrowski, Chris (2013) 'The Nature of Resilience', *Resilience*, 1:3, pp. 159–73.

Zhou, Jiayi (2017) 'National Climate-Related Security Policies of the Permanent Members of the UN Security Council', *SIPRI Working Paper*, December (Stockholm: SIPRI). Available at www.sipri.org/publications/2017/working-paper/national-climate-related-security-policies-permanent-member-states-united-nations-security-council

Zielinski, Sarah (2015) 'Climate Change Will Accelerate Earth's Sixth Mass Extinction', *Smithsonian Magazine*, 30 April. Available at www.smithsonianmag.com/science-nature/climate-change-will-accelerate-earths-sixth-mass-extinction-180955138/

# Index

Milton Keynes UK
Ingram Content Group UK Ltd.
UKHW022225090923
428399UK00021B/133